P9-AOU-117

Gender, Class, Race, and Reform in the Progressive Era

Gender, Class, Race, and Reform in the Progressive Era

NORALEE FRANKEL
NANCY S. DYE
Editors

THE UNIVERSITY PRESS OF KENTUCKY

Scholarly publisher for the Commonwealth,
serving Bellarmine College, Berea College, Centre
College of Kentucky, Eastern Kentucky University,
The Filson Club, Georgetown College, Kentucky
Historical Society, Kentucky State University,
Morehead State University, Murray State University,
Northern Kentucky University, Transylvania University,
University of Kentucky, University of Louisville,
and Western Kentucky University.

Editorial and Sales Offices: Lexington, Kentucky 40508-4008

Library of Congress Cataloging-in-Publication Data

Gender, class, race, and reform in the progressive era / Noralee
Frankel, Nancy S. Dye, editors.

p. cm.

"The essays in this volume were originally delivered as papers at the Conference on Women in the Progressive Era held March 10-12, 1988 at the National Museum of American History, Smithsonian Institution, Washington, D.C."—Preface.

Includes bibliographical references and index.

1. Women—United States—History—19th century—Congresses. 2. Women—United States—History—20th century—Congresses. 3. Progressivism (United States politics)—Congresses. 4. Women social reformers—United States—History—19th century—Congresses. 5. Women social reformers—United States—History—20th century—Congresses. I. Frankel, Noralee, 1950- . II. Dye, Nancy Schrom, 1947- . III. Conference on Women in the Progressive Era (1988 : National Museum of American History)

HQ1419.G46 1991 91-16843

This book is printed on acid-free paper meeting
the requirements of the American National Standard
for Permanence of Paper for Printed Library Materials.

∞

Contents

Preface

The essays in this volume were originally delivered as papers at the Conference on Women in the Progressive Era held March 10-12, 1988, at the National Museum of American History, Smithsonian Institution, Washington, D.C.

This conference was sponsored by the American Historical Association and the National Museum of American History, with financial assistance from the Division of Research Programs of the National Endowment for the Humanities, the Rockefeller Foundation, the Quaker Hill Foundation, and the Smithsonian Institution's Office of Fellowships and Grants.

William Chafe, Nancy S. Dye, Noralee Frankel, Alice Kessler-Harris, Susan Tank Lesser, Edith P. Mayo, Karen Offen, and Rosalyn Terborg-Penn served as members of the conference's program committee. Roger Kennedy, director, and the staff of the National Museum of American History generously shared the museum's facilities. Edith P. Mayo and Mary Grassick capably coordinated the conference arrangements at the Museum of American History. Rosemary Wozniak and Debbie Wozniak provided invaluable assistance in preparing this manuscript, and Maureen Vincent-Morgan edited the manuscript.

1

Introduction

NANCY S. DYE

The movement called progressivism flourished in the years between the depression of 1893 and the United States' entry into World War I, as Americans struggled to come to terms with the profound dislocations wrought by massive industrialization, the rise of the corporation, and rapid urban growth. A complex, sometimes contradictory amalgam of social ctiticism, popular protest, political restructuring, economic regulation, and social welfare legislation, progressive reform embodied a vast array of responses to the changes taking place in American society at the turn of the twentieth century.

Women filled the progressive landscape. Throughout the 1890s, when progressivism consisted in good measure of widespread popular outcry against new corporate order, many women joined in boycotts against local traction company and utilities magnates and in protesting corporate arrogance and political corruption. In towns and cities throughout the nation, women formed their own civic clubs and municipal improvement associations. Pointing to their communities' needs for "municipal housekeeping" and invoking their maternal duties to protect children and care for the poor, women organized around local issues: the improvement of working conditions, especially for women and child wage earners; maternal and child welfare; clean water; pure food and milk; adequate sanitation; the creation of playgrounds, recreation centers, and parks; and improved housing and schools.[1] "Since men are more or less closely absorbed in business," one clubwoman declared, "it has come to pass that the initiative in civic matters has developed largely upon women. It is more than a coincidence that the civic awakening that is stirring in our cities . . . has come with the civic activities of women's clubs. I have yet to hear of a town that is experiencing a civic awakening that has not had an active women's club."[2] Through their clubs and civic organizations, middle-class women explored local social and economic conditions and compiled extensive documentation of the dimensions of poverty in the United States and the specific impact of industralization on American communities.

Women also entered politics. Although largely disfranchised except in school elections, women played active and highly visible roles in municipal and state politics. They claimed credit for a variety of progressive victories: electing women to local school boards; winning appointments for women as sanitation, health, and factory inspectors; marshalling votes for new city charters and for bond issues to fund municipal improvements; helping to oust corrupt officials; and organizing to win the passage of housing, labor, corrections, and health legislation. That settlement houses flourished in American cities in the decades around the turn of the century was also the result of women's initiative and organization. In these women's communities, residents explored new alternatives for meaningful work and social service and pioneered new approaches to understanding the causes and ameliorating the conditions of poverty. Women's grass-roots activisim and their vision of a new civic consciousness lay at the heart of early progressive reform.

By the twentieth century's second decade, the initial local emphasis of progressivism had given way to a national focus. Women's clubs, settlement leaders, and women's organizations such as the Consumer's League and Women's Trade Union League forged a national political network and a coherent legislative agenda. After 1910, women turned increasingly to the government, especially at the federal level, to implement their reforms. In doing so, women envisioned a new, humane state, identified with the values of the home rather than those of the marketplace, with expanded powers to protect its powerless and dependent constituencies. This national women's network was instrumental in creating and supporting the federal Children's Bureau in the United States' Department of Labor and in enacting an array of social legislation. Most of the laws that comprised women's legislative agenda were measures intended to improve the lives of women and children: minimum wage and maximum hours statutes, mother's pensions, juvenile justice codes, the prohibition of child labor and industrial homework, and compulsory school attendance. The body of state and federal legislation for which women progressive reformers worked provided much of the foundation for American welfare legislation for the remainder of the twentieth century.

What prompted American middle-class women to become such active proponents of social reform? In good measure, protests over such issues as clean food and pure milk, maternal and infant welfare, industrial pollution, inadequate and highly politicized school systems, and the like were rooted in the realities of middle-class domesticity and motherhood. Never the haven of tranquillity depicted in nineteenth-century domestic literature, the American middle-class household by the latter decades of the century was often the seat of anxiety and uncertainty. Central to the anxiety that women experienced were the contradictions inherent in the ideology of separate spheres that was so pervasive in American culture: women were enjoined to protect their households and their children, but in the new industrial order, the well-being of households and the safety of children seemed increasingly out of individual women's control. Danger seemed everywhere at hand in the modern industrial city: in the streets, where trolley cars often ran over children; in the markets, where foodstuffs were often adulterated; in the dairies, where milk was liable to be contaminated with the bacillus of tuberculosis or diphtheria. Even the most affluent and knowledgeable of mothers often felt inadequate in confronting the difficulties of modern urban life and powerless to influence the distant, faceless "interests" that had become so powerful.

Early in the Progressive Era, women's domestic experience served as one justification for their entry into politics and social reform. Increasingly, middle-class women came to the realization that in modern industrial society, the doctrine of separate spheres no longer held: the home and the community were inextricably bound together, and those concerns once defined as the private responsibility of individual housewives and mothers were in actuality public and political. Women argued that their domestic duties compelled their interest in municipal politics. "It is an eminently proper thing for women to interest themselves in the care and destination of garbage, the cleanliness of the streets, the proper killing and handling of meats, the hygienic and sanitary condition of the public schools, the suppression of stable nuisances, the abolishing of the vile practice of expectorating in public conveyances and buildings, the care of milk and Croton water, the public exposure of foods, and in fact everything which constitutes the city's housekeeping," the New York Ladies' Health Protective Association declared in its first annual report. "It is the right of women to undertake these matters as they are brought into constant contact with the results of this housekeeping and will therefore be able to judge how it should properly be carried out."[3]

Over the course of the Progressive Era, women reformers constructed a historical interpretation of domestic life that stressed the erosion of female control over the middle-class household. In the not-too-distant past, this interpretation ran, the home had been the hub of economic production. With industrialization, however, women exchanged the role of producer for the less powerful role of consumer. With this shift, they lost control of their households and, as isolated individuals, were left to the mercy of organized capital: the beef and dairy trusts that charged exorbitant prices and the manufacturers and middlemen concerned with profit rather than with human need. As muckraker Louise Eberle concluded succinctly in her 1910 exposé of the food industry. "In these days . . . food is made to sell and not to eat."[4]

When we view reform through women's eyes, redefining the relationship between the home and the community—the private sphere and the public—emerges as central to progressivism. The traditional doctrine of spheres posited a clear separation between the home and the public worlds of the workplace, the market, and the polity—a separation that women reformers realized existed no longer. Many of women's reform efforts were directed at exploring and documenting the connections between the private world of the household and the political and economic institutions of the larger society. By entering politics, women tempted to gain some control over the economic forces that affected their lives and the lives of their children and to protect what they saw as the integrity of the home from the forces of the market. In the early years of progressive reform, women's efforts centered on improving the quality of life in American towns and cities through providing better city services and more municipal oversight of business practices that affected the health and well-being of individual households. In the later years of the movement, particularly after 1910, women's attempts at social protection increasingly involved legislative proposals to regulate the labor of women and children.

The involvement of women in progressive reform marks the high-water point of women's engagement in American politics. But despite the visibility and vitality of women on the progressive scene, we have only just begun to explore the centrality of women to progressivism. Women's role in shaping the progressive agenda has given rise to many questions. How did women reformers envision American society and women's role within it? What beliefs about gender, race, class, and ethnicity informed women's political culture and their reform agenda? How did black, immigrant, and working-class women contribute to and experience progressive reform? What was the relationship between progressivism and feminism? What legacy did progressivism leave for succeeding generations of American women? It is these questions that the essays in *Gender, Class, Race, and Reform in the Progressive Era* address. Taken together, they help us construct a new scaffolding for progressivism that illuminates women's reform efforts and the impact of reform on women of all classes. Then, too, the historical work on women in the Progressive Era gives us new insights into the phenomenon of progressivism itself.

These essays take as their starting point questions about the meaning of gender in turn-of-the-century America. Gender consciousness suffused progressive women's thinking about themselves and American society and shaped their conception of reform. Consciousness of gender difference, rooted in middle-class women's belief in the universality of domesticity and maternity as female experiences, initially impelled and justified women's entry into social reform and politics, gave women reformers a powerful sense of collective identity, and provided the basis for a female critique of modern American social values. Progressive women's sense of collective female identity and difference enabled them to see the extent of poverty in the United States, particularly the poverty of women and children. It also enabled them to criticize the indifference of American political institutions to social needs. And, as Barbara Sicherman argues in her essay on the career of Alice Hamilton, women's exclusion from the traditions of American individualism may well have enabled them to envision "collective solutions to the problems of urban and industrial life" more readily than did male reformers.

But even as gender consciousness enabled middle-class women to cast a critical eye on the institutions and values of their own society and to insist upon recognizing the needs of families, women, and children, it limited them as well. Much of the work in this collection documents the ways in which the experiences of American women varied across racial, class, and ethnic lines and explores the frequent inability of middle-class reformers to overcome the barriers of race and class in their attempts to restructure the relationship between the home and the community at large. These essays also document the ways in which women reformers' belief in gender difference mirrored social attitudes concerning women's "place" in American society generally at the turn of the twentieth century. By failing to challenge prevailing stereotypes, women reformers helped codify a limited public domain for women, particularly in the workplace.

Women's understanding of the relationship between family and community and between home and work varied as a function of the social realities they experienced. The work of Eileen Boris, Nancy Hewitt, Ardis Cameron, Sharon Harley, and Jacqueline Rouse illuminates these differences. Unlike white, middle-class women, whose norms for domesticity encompassed nuclear households, economic self-sufficiency, and a clear separation between home and work, black women and white working-class women did not experience domesticity within isolated, nuclear households. Instead, they relied upon collective networks and strategies in their struggle to, in the words of a Lawrence, Massachusetts, millworker, "piece together a livelihood." Living in collective households, sharing household goods and resources, relying on friends and relatives for child care were all common strategies relied upon by many American women in the early twentieth century—strategies that were largely invisible or incomprehensible to white, middle-class reformers. Nor were the worlds of home and work separate in the lives of immigrant working-class or black women. As Ardis Cameron reveals in her study of New England textile operatives, work merged with home, neighborhood, and community. Writes Cameron, "Mutual dependence and cooperative assistance bound women together in a latticework of reciprocity." In these respects, the lives of working-class and black women differed dramatically from those of white, middle-class reformers.

These differences in domestic realities affected the impact of progressive reform on women's lives. Two major goals of women progressives were to eliminate child labor and to abolish industrial homework. To their minds, both were unquestionably inhumane practices that should be outlawed. But as Eileen Boris, Ardis Cameron, and Molly Ladd-Taylor reveal, working-class mothers did not always view the prohibition of child labor in the same light. Given the precarious finances of working-class families and the necessity of pooling the wages of as many family members as possible in order to make ends meet, immigrant, working-class families viewed the passage and enforcement of stringment child labor statutes as a personal economic disaster and made strenuous efforts to circumvent child labor laws. Reformers rarely understood this resistance in terms of the desperate economic situation of working-class families. Instead, most middle-class female reformers interpreted working-class resistance as evidence of poor parenting. The point here is not that child labor was more a social good than the terribly exploitative practice that reformers understood it to be. Rather, the point is that women reformers' understanding of child labor and their legislative solutions for ending it were limited in that they did not take account of the economic needs of working-class families. As a result, as Molly Ladd-Taylor reveals in her work on the Children's Bureau, child labor legislation pitted women of different classes against one another instead of enabling them to create cross-class alliances to work to eradicate the economic conditions that led to sending children into the workplace.

Different social realities also influenced women's definitions of reform and the ways in which women envisioned the relationship between domesticity and politics. Nancy Hewitt's work on progressivism in one city is especially illuminating on the ways in which class, race, and ethnicity mediated reform. In early twentieth-century Tampa, black, working-class Latin, and middle-class Anglo women shared the broad progressive goals of "civic improvement, community order, and social justice," but they differed in their definitions of meaningful and beneficial social change. Anglo women entered politics in the belief that the public sphere desperately needed an infusion of domestic values. Latin women, whose experiences with domesticity were rooted in communal housekeeping and who were often caught up in labor struggles in the city's cigar industry, came to define domestic politics in more militant, socialist ways.

Black women's definitions of civic improvement and social justice centered on racial consciousness and were shaped by the Progressive Era realities of segregation and disenfranchisement. Rosalyn Terborg-Penn documents black women's centrality to the anti-lynching movement. It was black women who first spoke out on the horrors of lynching and who persistently campaigned to bring it to an end. Lynching was one of the primary concerns of the black women's club movement that began in the 1890s and was often the issue around which black women initially organized. Black women's reform associations also took up many of the same issues that white women's clubs addressed: maternal and child health, child care, improved schools, recreation, and public services. Jacqueline Rouse, in her work on black women's fight against segregation in early twentieth-century Atlanta, traces efforts to compel the segregated city to allocate adequate resources for black schools and neighborhoods. Cut off from the sources of support white women reformers could turn to—leading businessmen, professional associations, reform-minded politicians—black women could not build the reform coalitions that so often accounted for white women's successes. Nor could Atlanta's black women count upon like-minded white women for assistance. The black Women's Civic and Social Improvement Committee received no support from Atlanta white women in its efforts to improve the deplorable conditions in the city's segregated black schools. Black women learned to use what limited political leverage they had in local and special elections to win concessions from the white city government.

Progressive women's sense of female difference, then, often could not overcome the boundaries of race and class. Did women reformers' gender consciousness enable them to understand and restructure women's relationship to the new industrial order? The evidence is mixed. As Barbara Sicherman argues in her essay, the "gender consciousness of progressive reformers helped them chart their way into new and daring political paths and life choices, but as the ERA debate reveals, it also marked out limits beyond which they would not go." Sicherman's division between personal choice and social change is useful. As she argues, many middle- and upper-class women, were personally empowered by their conviction that women had a special role to play in American public life at the turn of the twentieth century. That conviction enabled them to explore new alternatives for meaningful work and social relationships and to envision American society in new ways. But as the work of Alice Kessler-Harris makes clear, women reformers' efforts to protect women through measures such as the minimum wage reflected, and ultimately reified rather than challenged, dominant societal beliefs in gender difference.

Women progressives' views on gender difference and their conceptions of the relationship between the home and the polity not only helped shape their perspectives on social and political reform, but also served to define early twentieth-century feminism. Indeed, many of the essays in this volume provide new evidence that progressivism and feminism were intertwined as social movements. To a very significant extent, the concept of a distinctive female political culture grounded in deeply held beliefs about separate private and public sphere has helped historians recognize the ideological and strategic overlap between the two. Historical research on women's political culture has generally stressed the continuity between nineteenth-century female reform activities and ideology and those of women progressives in the early years of the twentieth century. But as Ellen DuBois points out in her essay, historians' stress on the continuity of women's political culture may well be misleading. DuBois makes a strong case for the existence of two distinct generations of women progressives—an earlier generation, born in the 1850s and 1860s, who saw their reform activities as growing out of deeply rooted cultural conceptions of maternity, and a second generation of reformers, born in the 1870s and 1880s, who centered their understanding of women on the emerging role of the woman worker. As DuBois writes, "If the mother was the symbolic center of the first generation's understanding of womanhood, the woman worker was the emblem of the second. Paid labor, not social mothering, represented their route to women's emancipation, as well as the organizational basis for their reform efforts." Underlying this "shift from woman-as-mother to woman-as-worker" lay profound changes in American women's conceptions of their relationship to the public life and politic—changes that helped shape both the history of feminism and the development of modern American political and social institutions in the Progressive Era.

Progressivism emerges in these pages as a movement more complex and multifaceted than traditional interpretations suggest. Focusing upon women enables us to see both how central women reformers were to progressivism and how important issues concerning gender, family, and the relationship between private and public spheres were in shaping this reform movement. Women's attempts to redefine the relationship of the home to the workplace, the market, and the state in modern industrial society and to create ways for women to play meaningful and influential roles in the public sphere have had a lasting impact on American concepts of social justice, American public policy, and the role of women in the United States.

For generations of historians, progressivism has exuded powerful fascination. The reasons for continuing historical interest are clear: the Progressive Era marks the beginning of contemporary America, and within it we can trace the roots of institutions, policies, and values that still define the United States as a nation nearly a century later. Each succeeding generation of historians has brought current social and political concerns to the continuing riddle of progressivism's nature: was progressivism radical or conservative, a democratic movement of popular political protest or a movement dominated by a few large businessmen and industrialists bent upon creating a centralized liberal state? Did progressive reformers work toward a genuinely pluralistic society, or were their efforts with the immigrant poor largely rooted in the desire to control the working class and homogenize American culture? The essays in this volume—and the excitement generated by the 1988 Smithsonian conference at which they were first delivered—suggest that the Progressive Era holds compelling interest for a new generation of historians who find within that reform movement new questions and answers about the meaning of gender and the meaning of pluralism in twentieth-century America.

Notes

1. The best source for gaining a sense of women's varied reform activities on the local level remains Mary Beard, *Woman's Work in Municipalities* (New York: Appleton, 1915).
2. Imogen Oakley, "The Women's Club Movement," *American City* 6(June 1912): 805.
3. *Report of the Ladies' Health Protective Association, 1894-96*, New York, 1897: 17.
4. Louise Eberle, "The Faking of Food," reprinted in Harvey Swados, ed., *Years of Conscience*, (Cleveland: World, 1965), 268-69.

2

Atlanta's African-American Women's Attack on Segregation, 1900-1920

JACQUELINE A. ROUSE

By the turn of the twentieth century, Atlanta was the most segregated city in Georgia. As early as 1890, Atlanta had instituted Jim Crow laws that separated the city into distinctive African-American and white areas. These discriminatory laws reinforced white supremacy by excluding African-Americans from public accommodations, establishing residential ordinances that restricted the living patterns of African-Americans and contributed directly to Atlanta's neglect of blighted areas, exposing African-American customers to shabby treatment when they entered downtown stores, and excluding African-Americans from political participation and denying them due process of law.[1]

Segregation worked in Atlanta as long as African-Americans obeyed these laws and as long as African-Americans were kept subordinate. Segregation was legal; opposition meant breaking the law, and violence was considered acceptable when necessary to maintain the status quo, as in Atlanta's race riot of 1906.[2]

In 1900, Atlanta's political leadership instituted the white primary "on the grounds that Black participation corrupted local politics." Atlanta, a bulwark of democratic rule, feared the return of the African-American voter to the polls. In the past, disgruntled whites had used African-American voters to decide conflicts between two or more white candidates during the general elections. Eligible African-American voters were bribed, rounded up, and wagoned to the polls for the Democratic ticket. Though unscrupulous politicians used alcohol and money to purchase votes, it was the African-American voters exclusively who were judged corruptible. So in 1908, under the tutelage of Hoke Smith, Georgia adopted disfranchisement laws.

Although the number of African-American voters was dramatically reduced, disfranchisement laws and the white primary did not apply to general, open, or special elections. Furthermore, some liberal white and African-American leaders organized an interracial committee to promote racial harmony. Nonetheless, race relations in Atlanta during the Progressive Era reached an all-time low, the "nadir."[3]

By 1900, Atlanta's African-American community numbered sixty-three thousand living in varied pockets throughout the city. The Fourth Ward and Auburn Avenue had for some time housed the older African-American Atlantans who made up the city's African-American aristocracy. Mainly of mulatto ancestry, this upper class consisted of entrepreneurs and businesspeople whose clientele was predominantly white. By 1900, a new group of African-Americans, mostly migrants to Atlanta, belonged to this professional and business class. This new group of professionals never accounted for more than 4 percent of the population, for the majority of African-American Atlantians were poor, living in slum areas with dilapidated houses and schools. African-American men were mainly unskilled or semiskilled laborers, while the women worked in domestic and personal services. The men were frequently jobless because urban employers usually hired African-American men only for the duration of a particular construction project or contract. As Jacqueline Jones noted, "These sporadic wage-earning opportunities guaranteed low wages and long periods of enforced idleness." African-American women therefore became the breadwinners for their families, working in white households as laundresses and washerwomen, and in the marketplace as sellers of vegetables, fruits, and flowers. Women of the upper and middle class were generally seamstresses and schoolteachers. The latter became the promoters of racial consciousness and the organizers of women's clubs.[4]

African-American Atlantans had previously had a notable artisan class that dominated brickmasonry, carpentry, and barbering, but by 1900 these skilled laborers had lost their positions and patronage to white laborers. Throughout the South, labor unions began using African-Americans as strikebreakers to destroy the union movement. White employers who hired African-Americans, even in menial capacities, were forced by white employees to fire all the African-Americans and replace them with whites. White workers even went on strike to maintain white supremacy.[5]

The twentieth century also ushered in the Progressive Era, with its championship of social justice and municipal reforms. While sexual and racial equalities were agenda items in some parts of Progressive America, progressivism in Georgia was conservative, racist, and elitist. Throughout the state, African-Americans were routinely denied basic city services, whether the municipal government was corrupt or honest, reformist or reactionary. In Atlanta, progressivism was for whites only; African-Americans were either excluded or attacked outright. White Atlantans, arguing that African-Americans corrupted the political process, endorsed African-American disfranchisement as a method of cleaning up the government. Progressives in Atlanta campaigned for Prohibition so that liquor would be unavailable as a means of buying votes in "wet" areas. They called for the end of the convict-lease system in Georgia, using as examples the 10 percent of convicts who were white to solicit public support, even though 90 percent of the victims were African-Americans. Progressives argued for the chain gang as a humanitarian substitute. Because too many educated African-Americans would threaten white supremacy, white progressives campaigned for compulsory education bills in Atlanta in order to force white children to attend school. Southern suffragists supported the Nineteenth Amendment only if it guaranteed that African-American women would be disfranchised; this amendment therefore did not benefit African-American Georgians. The progressive movement, which could have united all reformers, instead became a major component in promoting white supremacy and solidarity and in maintaining African-American subordination and intimidation. African-American Atlantans therefore turned inward, using their organizations, churches, businesses, fraternal lodges, literary groups, women's clubs, and colleges to meet social, economic, medical, educational, recreational, and civic needs.[6]

Racial-conscious organizing by some of Atlanta's African-American females commenced during the early years of the twentieth century with their participation in the Conference on Negro Problems, directed by W.E.B. Du Bois and inaugurated at Atlanta University. The 1898 conference addressed "The Welfare of the Negro Child." Planned by Atlanta University's kindergarten training school teacher, Gertrude Ware, this conference began with a discussion on the care of the children whose mothers had to work and who were left daily either in locked homes or wandering unattended in the streets. Some of the mothers in attendance decided to establish free kindergartens so that those who had to work could have facilities at which to leave their preschoolers for at least half of each school day. Following the conference, Ola Perry, whom Ware had trained, began the first school in her home. Together with Ida Wynn, Ware decided to ask several women to help them finance the effort. From the responses emerged the Gate City Free Kindergarten Association. Among the people asked to contribute was Alonzo Herndon, founder of the

Atlanta Life Insurance Company. Impressed with the association's goals and accomplishments, Herndon purchased a large old stone building in White's Alley and gave it to the association to be used as a school and playground for the children. For several years he also paid for a teacher and daily milk delivery. With the additional space, the kindergarten was expanded into a day-care center. Soon four more kindergartens were opened throughout the city, supported with money raised from annual Thanksgiving dinners.[7]

The core of the association's members lived in the West Fair area surrounding Spelman and Atlanta Baptist Colleges (the latter became Morehouse College in 1913). The area was enclosed by a slum that stank and smoked and was surrounded by streets and alleys that were unpaved, full of holes, and without water mains. Activities in these areas terrified the neighborhood children. Lugenia Burns Hope, a member of the association, conducted a survey among the working mothers of the vicinity. The mothers interviewed wanted full day-care centers and safe recreational lots where their children could play. Hope carried this information back to her kindergarten committee, emphasizing that kindergartens could be but one of many services rendered by the centers. She suggested that four day-care centers be opened throughout the city of Atlanta and that the work be expanded to include all areas of the city. The committee did not adopt her suggestion. The kindergarten association continued merely to operate day nurseries, now under the name of Gate City Day Nursery Association.[8]

As a result of surveying the working mothers, Hope and her followers learned of the lack of adequate play space for children. They discovered that there was not a single municipal park or playground for African-American children. Influenced by Hope, the administration of Atlanta Baptist College allowed the committeewomen to use part of the campus as a playground. These women supervised the children and hosted fund-raisers to purchase needed equipment. Subsequently, this same nucleus of women began to inspect the community for other problems needing attention, laying the foundation for the Neighborhood Union, the Atlanta Branch of the Southeastern Federation of Colored Women's Clubs, and the Women's Civic and Social Improvement Committee, which focused on improving the "colored public schools."[9]

The most noted African-American female organization of Atlanta was created during the Progressive Era. The specific incident that led to its development was the death of a young woman in the community of West Fair. The young woman, who lived with two male relatives, always sat alone on her porch watching the community, but she rarely spoke. When she became ill, no one knew it, though they realized they had not seen her on the porch. Upon learning of her death, Hope saw the opportunity to organize the community. Believing no one had known about the death because of the absense of neighborly feelings, Hope brought together most of the women of her community. The result was the creation in 1908 of the Neighborhood Union.

Aided by the students of Atlanta Baptist College, the union conducted house-to-house surveys to introduce the organization to the community. Union members canvassed one hundred families living around the college, informing the residents that the union's purpose was to provide for children, in an effort to "raise the standard of living in the community and to make the West Side of Atlanta a better place to rear our children."[10]

After developing a very thorough, complex structure, the union provided most of the basic needs of African-American Atlantans, especially the preschoolers, addressing moral, physical, educational, recreational, health, civic, cultural, and social concerns. By 1914, branches of the union had been established in all parts of the city. The union's community building and settlement work would become role models for similar national and international programs. These African-American Atlantans emerged as challengers to racism as they promoted interracial work, established a African-American branch of the YWCA in Atlanta, and confronted the discriminatory policies of the city council and the board of education.

The Women's Civic and Social Improvement Committee, a subcommittee of the Neighborhood Union, demanded equal facilities and appropriations for the city's African-American schools during the early decades of the twentieth century. From its inception, the Women's Committee agreed that its mission would be to investigate the city's African-American schools. Chaired by Lugenia Burns Hope, the committee was determined to "investigate conditions with a view of remedying the evils" that plagued the system. For several years these women were besieged with reports from parents and teachers that exposed inequalities between African-American and white schools. For example, in 1910, African-American teachers learned that the board of education was considering raising the salaries of the city's white teachers but not those of African-Americans. They decided to petition the board for a raise, pointing out that African-American pay had been reduced by five dollars a month since 1906 to make possible the white teachers' raises. Humbly and respectfully, they reminded the board that African-American teachers had long taught double sessions, without complaining, and that they were now willing to accept additional work that the white teachers openly refused. The petitioning African-American teachers did not ask for parity: instead, they asked the board to "make the highest Black salary $60.00 a month which would be at least equal to the lowest paid white salary."[11]

The teachers' petition was accompanied by another from a group of African-American parents who requested additional classrooms for their children. In a spirit of deference and humbleness, the parents also reminded the board that forty-five hundred African-American children were without seating in the schools; many of the children refused even to apply, knowing that seating was limited. As a result, these children, some the children of the whites' servants, were left without discipline and therefore reduced to a state of crime and immorality.[12]

Both petitions were passed on to the city council with favorable recommendations from the board of education. Impressed by the tone of both petitions, the council voted to increase the salary of the teachers but dismissed the request for additional classrooms. The teachers then asked the Women's Civic and Social Improvement Committee to intervene.

In 1913, the committee began to investigate the double sessions. The committee received from all the school principals the names and addresses of absentees from their schools each month. Members also secured a list of responsible parents who testified that their children's health was impaired by crowded conditions in the public schools. Physicians gave estimates of the extent of ill health among teachers because of overwork and poor conditions in the schools. Churches provided estimates of the number of children who could not enter school because of the limited seating capacity.[13]

For six months the committee investigated and inspected the twelve schools in Atlanta. Overall conditions were found to be deplorable. The school environment was unhealthy: lighting and ventilation were usually poor, causing many children to suffer eyestrain and sickness; classrooms were crowded; and there were double sessions with the same teachers for both sessions. For the 1913-1914 school year, there was a seating capacity in the African-American schools of 4,102 but an enrollment of 6,163, making the number of pupils served by each double session 3,081.[14]

The committee contacted every influential white woman in the city, including members of the Board of Lady Visitors of the Board of Education, soliciting their support. Some of these white women visited the schools and saw firsthand the conditions. The committee also interviewed each member of the city council, the mayor, the members of the board of education, African-American ministers, members of African-American women's clubs, and members of other African-American organizations. They solicited help from influential African-American men, some of whom they were married to. Committee members spoke before African-American congregations, explaining the nature of their project and urging parents to pay their personal taxes and to have their children vaccinated. The committee reached other members of the community by asking insurance agents to inform their clients of the committee's work as they made their collections. Using newspapers and mass meetings, the committee publicized the deplorable conditions they had discovered, publishing pictures of the schools in local newspapers.

The women were given permission by the board of education to have a committee of six at each African-American school on the first day to collect the names and addresses of those children who had not been vaccinated. Members then visited the children's parents and made sure that the children were vaccinated and returned to school the following day. The women kept a running campaign for better conditions by posting placards and giving illustrated lectures to show the problems. They drew up a petition to attack the inadequacies of the schools and forwarded it to the board of education:

Gentlemen:—

We, a committee of women representing residents and tax-payers of the City of Atlanta, upon visiting and making a careful inspection of the public schools for Negroes, find most of them in very unsanitary condition. The lighting capacity in many instances is insufficient, the playgrounds small as compared to the seating capacity of the buildings. For a number of years the overcrowded condition of the schools in the four or five lower grades has resulted in double sessions in those grades, in lieu of additional buildings, and the continuous increase of the population has resulted in the use of annexes that fall far below the conditions necessary for effectual work by the teachers, and by the pupils.

In view of these conditions, we hereby respectfully beg leave to present, in the interest of the civic and social welfare of our Negro boys and girls of Atlanta, this petition, asking that your honorable body at the earliest time practical effect changes relative to the following:

First, Sanitary Conditions. We find unhealthful conditions existing in all of our public schools except in Yonge Street School, and in Gray Street School. We wish to call especial attention to the schools mentioned below: Houston, Mitchell, Pittsburg, and L&N. At the Houston Street School the condition of the toilets is such to impair the health of all concerned. We believe that this condition is due to the fact that the toilets are too small to accommodate the large number of children.

At Pittsburg and at Mitchell Street Schools the toilet arrangements are indecent and tend to immorality, in that only a wooden partition separates that section . . . used by the boys from that section used by the girls. In many schools, especially in the Summerhill and L&N Schools, the walls are in a deplorable condition. The basement room in daily use for the first and second grade(s) at Roach Street School necessitates artificial light on dark days, and is so damp as to injure the health of the children.

Second, a School in South Atlanta. South Atlanta, with its hundreds of children who are of school age, and whose parents are taxpayers is without a school.

Third, Feeble-minded children. We beg that special provisions be made for the feeble-minded and the defective children.

Fourth, Double Sessions. We urge the Board's prayerful consideration of abolishing the system of double sessions. We find that under the existing system three hours and a half are devoted to a set of children for work outlined for a five hour schedule. This, we maintain, is conducive to poor scholarship in grammar school subjects. We believe that the double sessions enforce idleness, and thereby promote shiftlessness in our children. Employers can not use help in the morning during one month, and in the afternoon during the next month. The majority of the parents are in service and their children being unemployed are on the streets out of school hours. We hold that children who attended the afternoon session do so at a great disadvantage. A teacher who has taught from forty to sixty children in the morning can not properly teach another set of children in the afternoon. Another evil of the system of double sessions is evidenced in the impaired health of teachers.

It is for this, then, that we beg of you: better sanitary conditions in our public schools; a school for South Atlanta; provisions for the feeble-minded and for the defective children; and the abolition of the system of double sessions. We earnestly trust that your honorable body will grant our petition the ultimate aim of which is to reduce crime, and to make of our children good citizens. Atlanta, Georgia

Signed: August 19, 1913

Mrs. L.B. Hope, Chairman in behalf of the Women's Civic and Social Improvement Committee.[15]

The board of education discussed possible remedies to the reported conditions: bonds, a special tax, and new allocations from existing city funds. All proposals met with varying degrees of disapproval. Board member James L. Key reacted by stating that he believed the conditions had been exaggerated and that "this agitation is going to do the schools more harm than good." He had formerly made it known to the committee members that the teachers—"the girls"—were not compelled to teach double sessions but wanted to, and he thought "it better to have poor schools than have the children out of school."[16]

The clerk of the council reported that the city had authorized the purchase of a lot in East Atlanta on which to build a modern school to relieve congestion at the Inman Park, Faith, East Atlanta, and Grant Park schools, which were all white. In connection with this, the council had also authorized five thousand dollars of the bond money left over from the Fourth Ward Negro School fund for the erection of a building on the lot donated to the city by Clark University for a Negro school in South Atlanta.[17]

The board of education reacted by appointing a special committee to make recommendations. By November, this committee recommended to the council and the board that the literary course in African-American schools end with the sixth grade and that the work of the sixth grade include industrial work that would be redistributed over a period of eight years. This was not the first time the board had considered revising the curriculum in the African-American schools. In 1905, the Board of Lady Visitors had urged the board of education to abandon all grades above the fourth, arguing that education for African-Americans beyond the primary grades was a waste of time and money. If the board concentrated on primary education, they argued, then more African-American students would be served.[18] When the issue resurfaced in 1913, the Women's Civic and Social Improvement Committee fired off a protest to the *Atlanta Constitution,* objecting to the "type of education suggested" and declaring such actions to be "fundamentally undemocratic and unjust." The committee pointed out that African-American children had to be transferred from one school to another in order to enter the seventh and eighth grades; this could be corrected by building more schools for them. They opposed the suggested limiting of the literary course for eight grades and a high school at the public's expense: "To open opportunities for industrial courses is a step . . . desired, but it is to be hoped that the facilities for seventh and eighth grade(s) work will in no way be curtailed . . . for the Negro youth. In this matter, we are sure that we expressed the sentiments of the great majority of Negro citizens . . . The public schools are supported by the taxes of all people and to confine the Negro population to a peculiar type of education against its will"[19] would mean open discrimination.

The immediate results were unsettling for the committee. A small school was built in South Atlanta on the lot donated by Clark University, and the African-American teachers' salaries were raised, but the board of education failed to address other major concerns uncovered by the women. African-American schools still suffered with severe overcrowding, double sessions, inadequate and unsafe recreational facilities, and extreme understaffing.

The efforts of the committee were strengthened in 1917 by such Atlantans as Benjamin Davis, John Hope, Peter James Bryant, William Penn, and A.D. Williams (grandfather of Martin Luther King, Jr.). Appearing before the board as members of Atlanta's chapter of the NAACP, these men, "demanded concessions in behalf of black schools." They recounted the previous attempts of Atlanta's African-Americans to seek a redress of grievances. These efforts only produced humiliation and frustration because of the insensitivity and racism of the board of education. The board was about to reconsider (for the third time) the abolition of the seventh grade in African-American schools and the provision of vocational training centers as replacements. In an air of open defiance, the committee reminded the board that it was the servant of all the citizens of Atlanta. The committee demanded: "Not only, do not take out the seventh grade of the Negro department, but that you provide facilities and teachers in order that Negro children may be able to do the eight years work in seven years as the white children are able to do, by eliminating double sessions from the Negro department. . . . We are entitled to the seventh grade and the vocational idea, in common with your children."[20] African-Americans informed the board that they wanted for their children ample school classrooms and both a classical and a technical school. They added: "We submit that you provide ample industrial features, including the vocational ideas for the Negro schools, providing them with practical workshops: We mean practical industries. We do not mean simply making baskets, toys, paper boxes and needle work. We mean the allied trades that our boys may become shoemakers, carpenters, bricklayers . . ." Determined, the African-American delegates warned: "We are going to dwell on your tracks and continue to pursue you until these betterments are realized."[21]

Between 1900 and 1930, African-American Atlantans realized the emptiness of the promises made to them by the board and the council. It became apparent that concessions from both agencies would materialize only through political pressure at the polls. This became clearer to the African-American community after the city began to float bonds in general elections to raise funds for public improvements. Bond issues could pass only if two-thirds of the registered voters supported them. African-Americans could insure the defeat of the bonds merely by staying at home, so their votes become their leverage for demanding equal educational opportunities for their children.

Beginning in 1903, the city council used the bond issues during elections. In 1903 and 1909, African-Americans were persuaded to support the bonds because of the equal appropriations that they would receive for their children; in both elections, they were disappointed. In 1909, for example, African-American schools received only $35,000, while the white schools were awarded $550,000. African-Americans considered this division "outrageous since their children made up about one-third of the school age population,"[22] yet African-Americans had to support the bonds to receive even these meager appropriations.

When the city attempted to propose a bond in 1914, the Women's Civic and Social Improvement Committee organized opposition because African-American schools were only promised $37,000 out of a total of $1.5 million. The committee was able to convince Benjamin Davis, editor of the African-American newspaper, the *Atlanta Independent,* to oppose the bond in his columns, for in reality the proposal would serve only white schools. Sensing defeat, the city council pulled the bond issue from the ballot.[23] When the city proposed to raise taxes and issue bonds in 1919, the African-American community again appeared before the board of education, demanding parity. Frustrated, the board told African-Americans that they would not be included in the appropriations and that they were powerless to "do anything about it." They subsequently defeated the bond.

By 1917, key white Atlantans had acquired increased respect for the African-American vote. African-American voters were approached by unscrupulous city officials, who tried to trade dilapidated buildings for African-American classrooms in return for their ballots. Others, including the mayor, decided to approach the African-American leadership, including the Women's Civic and Social Improvement Committee. The whites promised that three of the four million dollars in the proposed bond would be used to renovate existing African-American schools and to build new ones, including a high school. The committee, the Neighborhood Union, and other community groups worked zealously throughout Atlanta to turn out the African-American voters, for one-third of the white voting public opposed the bond. On election day, African-American and white poll-watchers were stationed at the voting booths. The bond passed.

The bond brought only 1.25 millon of the promised three million dollars to the African-American schools. Modern schools were constructed and new equipment was purchased, but accommodations were still inadequate for students. Each of the new buildings was supposed to be large enough to house the enrollments of two of the old schools, but the twelve thousand new African-American students who entered the system during the 1920s "wrought havoc on these calculations." Although the new African-American schools contained rooms for libraries, cafeterias, and manual training shops, the lack of seating necessitated using these specialty rooms as regular classrooms.[24] In September 1923, the committee sent a new survey of African-American schools to the city council. It reported:

> The city has 17,750 Negro children, 34% of the school population. For the instruction of these children, there are twelve public school buildings. These have a total seating capacity of 4,877. The total enrollment is 11,469. Therefore, the seating capacity is only 42% of the total enrollment. The children are on triple sessions, and many children are on 2½ hour school sessions. Including the half-day teachers, there are 159 teachers for these 11,469 pupils, or an average of 72 children for each teacher employed. Only 203 pupils in the entire system are getting adequate school work, or less than 2% of the total.[25]

By the mid-twenties, the board of education became more overt in its discrimination toward African-American schools and students. Needing funds to complete projects in white schools, the board began to use funds that had been earmarked for African-American schools; some board members believed that no new funds should go to African-American schools until all of the white children were cared for. They argued that African-Americans did not need junior or senior high schools or even the night schools. African-American education, they asserted, should be limited to the primary grades. The board failed to provide sanitary facilities inside and outside of the schools. Roads leading to many of the African-American schools were washed out during heavy rains. Furthermore, the board failed to stand up to white pressure groups who challenged its attempts to improve African-American schools. African-American schools were closed, and the students were assigned to other schools miles from their homes. Funds that were supposed to be used in building new African-American schools were transferred to renovate white facilities.

With the NAACP, the Women's Civic and Social Improvement Committee organized several mass protest meetings, but the board continued to ignore their complaints. In 1927, the board cut back the number of African-American night schools because of a financial exigency and in response to several board members who wanted African-American night schools eliminated completely. By 1930, however, the protest from the African-American community had restored the night schools.[26]

Though the Women's Civil and Social Improvement Committee did not solve the complex problems of inadequate school facilities for African-American children in Atlanta, it was one of the first organized efforts to investigate and confront the blatant racism of the city council and the board of education. The committee constantly challenged the segregation and discrimination present in Atlanta's public school system. The efforts of these women were germane to the eventual opening of the city's first African-American high school, Booker T. Washington, in 1924. Ironically, the struggles of the Women's Civic and Social Improvement Committee in demanding parity in the educational opportunities for African-American children in Atlanta marked a continuum in the history of African-American female organizing. From the days of Maria Stewart and Ellen Frances Watkins Harper, to those of Ida Wells Barnett, Mary McLeod Bethune, and Lugenia Burns Hope, to those of Marion W. Edelman and Marva Collins, African-American females have always given high priority to the education of their youth. Determined African-American women focused their energies on producing literate, committed, and responsible students who would "rise up" and become the next generation's leadership. To fulfill their objectives, they organized elementary and secondary schools; Sunday schools; youth meetings; mothers' meetings; classes in cooking, arts and crafts, and sewing; citizenship schools with primers they penned; normal training schools; and even female institutions of higher learning. These women became responsible for the creation and maintenance of day-care centers, kindergartens, and nurseries. They also produced facilities to promote culture, recreation, medical assistance, and social and civic affairs. They became the architects and guardians of community building and organizing. Thus the Atlanta women's frontal attack on the racism of the board of education and the elected officials of the city represents one of numerous examples of what has been the ancestral mission of many African-American women.

Notes

This article appeared in somewhat different form in the biography *Lugenia Burns Hope: Black Southern Reformer* (Athens: Univ. of Georgia Press, 1989).

1. John Dittmer, *Black Georgia in the Progressive Era* (Urbana: Univ. of Illinois Press, 1977), 12-22.

2. See Mary F. Berry, "Repression of Blacks in the South, 1890-1945: Enforcing the System of Segregation," in Robert Haws, ed., *The Age of Segregation: Race Relations in the South, 1890-1945* (Jackson: Univ. Press of Mississippi, 1978), 28-32.

3. Dittmer, *Black Georgia,* 95-97; Clarence A. Bacote, "The Negro in Atlanta Politics" *Phylon* 16 (Fourth Quarter, 1955): 339-43.

4. Jacqueline Jones, *Labor of Love, Labor of Sorrow: Black Women, Work, and the Family from Slavery to the Present* (New York: Basic, 1985), 111.

5. Dolores Janiewski, "Sisters under Their Skins: Southern Working Women, 1880-1950," in Joanne V. Hawks and Sheila L. Skemp, eds., *Sex, Race, and the Role of Women in the South* (Jackson: Univ. Press of Mississippi, 1983), 20-35.

6. Michael L. Porter, "Black Atlanta: An Interdisciplinary Study of Blacks on the East Side of Atlanta, 1890-1930" (Ph.D. diss., Emory University, 1974), 90, 108.

7. Personal notes of Lugenia Burns Hope, Biographical Folder, John and Lugenia Burns Hope Papers, Atlanta University Center, Woodruff Library, Atlanta, Georgia.

8. "Biographical Statement of Mrs. John Hope," Neighborhood Union Collection (hereafter cited as NUC), Atlanta University Center, Woodruff Library, Atlanta, Georgia.

9. Ibid.

10. Minutes of Meeting, July 8, 1908. NUC.

11. Philip N. Racine, "Atlanta Schools: A History of the Public School System, 1869-1955" (Ph.D. diss., Emory University, 1969), 116-17; see also the Petition of Black Teachers to the Board of Education, June 7, 1910; Aug. 1, 1910; and the Proceedings of the Atlanta City Council, Dec. 9, 1911, NUC.

12. Racine, "Atlanta Schools," 117-18.

13. Louie D. Shivery, "The History of Organized Social Work among Negroes in Atlanta, 1890-1935" (M.A. thesis, Atlanta University, 1936), 131, 53.

14. Annual Report of the Neighborhood Union, 1913-1914, NUC.

15. Survey of Colored Public Schools (1913-1914) and the Petition of the Women's Civic and Social Improvement Committee, Aug. 19, 1913, NUC.

16. Tenth Annual Report of the Women's Civic and Social Improvement Committee, 1913, NUC.

17. Ibid.

18. Racine, "Atlanta Schools," 118-20.

19. Shivery, "History of Organized Social Work," 101-2.

20. *Atlanta Independent,* Dec. 26, 1914, 2; *Atlanta Independent,* Jan. 7, 1915, 2; see also Racine, "Atlanta Schools," 179-80.

21. Racine, "Atlanta Schools," 182.

22. Ibid., 121. See Walter White, *A Man Called White* (New York: Macmillian, 1948).

23. *Atlanta Independent,* Dec. 26, 1914, 94.

24. The Petition to the Mayor, City Council, and the Board of Education, 1923, Women's Civic and Social Improvement Committee, NUC.

25. Shivery, "History of Organized Social Work," 219-20.

26. See Proceedings of the City Council, Nov. 21, 1927 and Dec. 5, 1927, and Minutes of the Board of Education, Feb. 8 and 22, 1927, July 8, 1930, Sept. 9, 1930, and Apr. 12, 1932, NUC. See also Helen G. Holland, "The Development of the Night School Program for Negroes in Atlanta, Georgia for the Period 1915-1946" (M.A. thesis, Atlanta University, 1947).

3

Politicizing Domesticity: Anglo, Black, and Latin Women in Tampa's Progressive Movements

NANCY A. HEWITT

"As society grows more complicated it is necessary that woman shall extend her sense of responsibility to many things outside her own home if she would continue to preserve the home in its entirety. . . . [I]f woman would keep on with her old business of caring for her house and rearing her children she will have to have some conscience in regard to public affairs lying quite outside of her immediate household."[1] Thus did Hull House founder Jane Addams articulate the relationship between domesticity and female activism. This "social housekeeping" rhetoric pervaded women's reform activities at every level; it cut across region and religion, if not always class and race. Kate V. Jackson, for example, a prominent Catholic activist in Tampa, Florida, echoed the sentiments of her more well-known northern counterpart. In a speech to the female graduates of the Academy of the Holy Names, she proclaimed, "If the women of this City would only become convinced of how much the City's Progress depends upon them—of how much they can do to make the City more sanitary—and more beautiful, I feel sure the City would advance by leaps and bounds."[2]

Jackson may have literally echoed Addams since it was on a trip to Chicago in 1910 that she became inspired by the potential of women's club work, leading her to establish the all-female Tampa Civic Association on her return. This transplantation of northern programs was not unique to the Civic Association. Founders of the local Women's Christian Temperance Union, Suffrage League, Children's Home, and Woman's Club were also either Florida residents influenced by visits north or northern residents "wintering" in Florida.

Tampa's cosmopolitanism was shaped by more than its elite tourists, however. Cigars created a thriving urban center out of a sleepy, swampy military outpost. Cigars brought the railroads, steamships, and hotels that also attracted tourists to the Gulf Coast, and they fostered the urbanization, industrialization, and immigration that made northern social housekeeping rhetoric resonate in the ears of Tampa ladies.

In the 1880s and 1890s, hundreds of Spaniards and thousands of Cubans flooded into the cigar centers on Tampa's periphery. There they joined native-born blacks, resident in the area since slavery days, and opened the way for an influx of Italians by the turn of the century. This heterogeneous population spawned dozens of organizations, institutions, and movements in the city. Black and Latin as well as Anglo women advocated progressive goals in Tampa, but more often in tension than in tandem with each other, as they drew on divergent perceptions of the proper relationship between domesticity and activism.

This essay will analyze the relations between the distinctive patterns of domestic life among Tampa's three major racial-ethnic groups and each group's particular forms of political action. Through such a community study, we can trace both the universal dimensions of the domestication of politics and the multiple forms in which different domesticities became politicized.[3]

The extent and timing of progressivism in Tampa was directly related to the variety and constancy of disorders that prevailed there. From a quiet village of some eight hundred residents in 1885, Tampa exploded into a city of over fifteen thousand by 1900, when roughly 30 percent of local inhabitants were foreign-born and another 25 percent Afro-American. The population boom reflected, as well as reinforced, a leap in industrial activity, expansion of the city's boundaries, and increased demands for social services. The disorder created by these changes in the city's size and complexion was exacerbated by a series of medical, political, economic, and social crises. A yellow fever epidemic in 1887 gave birth to voluntary (female) and official (male) relief efforts and to the male-formed Hillsborough County Medical Society and the female-managed Emergency Hospital. Beginning in the early 1890s, Cuban emigrés began organizing revolutionary clubs to support demands for independence in their homeland, leading to sporadic clashes with some Spanish factory owners. Other Spaniards and a small circle of Italians, inspired by anarchist and socialist doctrines, joined Cubans in May Day demonstrations and wildcat strikes.

When the struggle for *Cuba Libre* erupted into war in 1895, emigré activity in the cigar centers increased, as did crime and violence in the city at large. The *Ocala Mail and Express* proclaimed: "Tampa is establishing a reputation for being a very wicked city. She has surpassed all records for brutal fights, desperate deeds, ugly murders. . . ."[4] These records were broken in 1898 when Tampa was selected as the disembarkation point for U.S. troops entering the Cuban-Spanish conflict.

With the arrival of thousands of soldiers, including Theodore Roosevelt and his Rough Riders, the city experienced a burst of cross-class and interethnic cooperation, especially among women, and a simultaneous collapse of public services, moral standards, and race relations. A rush of refugees from the war-torn island added to the needs of women and children left behind by emigré men serving in Cuba as soldiers. At the same time, U.S. troops created an insatiable demand for food, housing, health services, and entertainment. Visiting local brothels and gambling dens, baiting local black residents (including Afro-Cubans joining insurgent ranks), carousing throughout the town, or just attempting to survive in the hot and humid climate of Gulf Coast Florida, American soldiers tested the limits of local provisions for social services and social control. Adding to the upheaval, white troops clashed regularly with black units, culminating in a race riot in early June 1898, involving soldiers and civilians of both races.[5]

At the war's end, a continued influx of war refugees combined with a revitalized labor movement to keep the immigrant enclaves of Ybor City and West Tampa in constant turmoil. Major strikes in 1899 and 1901 threatened the city's financial future and led to outbreaks of vigilante violence organized by Anglo elites. Vigilantism was also visited on the black community, including the shooting of a vocal black editor in 1899, the harassment of a black woman by white police the same year, and the castration of one black man accused of rape and the lynching of another in 1903.[6]

Though blacks benefited little from this era of upheaval, for Anglos and Latinos, it allowed, even encouraged, a fluidity of boundaries between private and public domains, immigrant and native-born neighborhoods, and men's and women's spheres.[7] Female professionals and entrepreneurs were welcomed to the city, and women's political activity in civic clubs, social welfare associations, revolutionary organizations, and mutual aid societies was approved by city fathers. The transformation of domestic skills and resources into vehicles for social and political change was not only accepted but applauded. For a time, differences in the form, substance, and purpose of these transformations were obscured, ignored, and misperceived, but after 1900 they crystallized quickly. Racial tensions and class strife in the new century illuminated not only differences in the daily lives of blacks, Latins, and Anglos, but also the conflicts generated as each group pursued its own version of civic improvement, community order, and social justice.

For Anglos, the fear of contagion, medical and social, and of chaos, political and economic, turned even humanitarian activists toward social control. The events that fostered the emergence of progressivism in Tampa also nurtured class- and race-specific, often class- and race-antagonistic, solutions. This reflected in part the success of working-class, especially immigrant, Tampans in organizing on their own behalf, creating greater potential for conflict as groups fought to define the meaning and form of social change.

Since progressivism was, in very important ways, locally oriented and organized, the timing of its emergence was closely tied to local developments. In Tampa, the cataclysmic events just recounted compelled city residents to become pioneer progressives.[8] As in other parts of the country, many of Tampa's earliest reform organizations were composed of the wives and daughters of the city's Anglo founders.[9] These women, the female kin of cattle barons, professionals, and entrepreneurs, established a range of civic improvement and social welfare associations comparable to that in many northern cities.

Officers of these organizations and managers of the institutions they founded were more often single or widowed than were women in the city as a whole. Those who were married had grown children or hired domestics from Tampa's ex-slave population. Of all Tampa residents, these women were the likeliest to live in nuclear families, reside in privately owned houses, and accept the ideology of separate sexual spheres. They, like their counterparts across the nation, assumed that home and city were two distinct entities and that the latter could be improved by an infusion of values from the former. From this perspective, the best ways to improve society and simultaneously support women's familial obligations were to provide services and training for less privileged citizens, to investigate exploitative conditions and devise protective legislation accordingly, and to fight for prohibition and women's suffrage, which would place in women's own hands greater control over private relations and public policy.

The first and most influential reform organization in the city was the Women's Christian Temperance Union, founded only a few months after Cubans first arrived in Port Tampa. In its first year of operation, the association established a public reading room, a temperance Saturday school, and an auxiliary branch in Ybor City. Members also appointed a superintendent of "colored work,"[10] petitioned legislators for laws punishing "crimes against women and children,"[11] and launched a campaign for countywide prohibition. The WCTU gradually expanded through neighborhood and juvenile auxiliaries and spawned the Door of Hope Rescue Home, Working Woman's Mission, Woman's Home and Hospital, and the local kindergarten and public library movements.

In addition to establishing moral order, affluent Anglo women labored for civic improvement, including the creation of a Court House Square by the Ladies' Improvement Society, the construction of an emergency hospital by the Ladies' Relief Society, and the care of local cemeteries by the Ladies' Memorial Society. The Wolff Mission School for Cuban immigrants, the Old Ladies' Home, and the Day Nursery Association, along with a number of female religious societies, were also in place by 1900.[12]

If these endeavors replicated those further north, they nonetheless retained certain distinctive features reminiscent of more personal and less scientific efforts of the antebellum era. Tampa's pioneer activists adapted to frontier conditions, such as shortages of housing and supplies, much as northern ladies had done a half-century earlier. In one case, the house of Mrs. E.A. Clarke—daughter of the county's first judge, sister of a Ladies' Improvement Society charter member, and widow of a pioneer merchant—became headquarters for the Children's Home. Mrs. John M. Long—widow of the Tampa Ice Company founder, treasurer of the Emergency Hospital, and charter member of Tampa Woman's Club—donated her house and one year's insurance to the Old Ladies' Home. Institutional "families" were supplied with clothing, bedding, and other items from the cupboards of female reformers, who still relied on such old-fashioned forms of benevolence as begging trips into the surrounding countryside for furniture, wood, and foodstuffs.[13]

Matrons of various institutions, always widowed or single, resided at their respective facilities: Carrie Hammerly (until her marriage to Dr. John Giddens) at the Children's Home, Elizabeth Davis at the Woman's Home and Hospital, and Mrs. Mary Cull at the Working Woman's Mission, among others. In a boomtown community, such conflations of domesticity and reform were especially necessary and were also convenient for respectable single women pursuing careers in public services.

Religion, as much as domesticity, proved a central resource for female activism in Tampa. Religious missions served as the foundation for day nurseries, kindergartens, and settlement houses. The Children's Home, for example, began as a project of the local Methodist Women's Home

Missionary Society. The founders of the Door of Hope Rescue Home procured the old Episcopal Church mission to house its "fallen angels." When the home fell into debt, the founders transferred the facility to the Methodist Board of Ladies, who in turn transferred it to the Men's Board, at which point the Rescue Home became a day nursery. Some of the earliest educational facilities for immigrants, adults as well as children, also were opened by Methodist, Congregationalist, Catholic, and Baptist missionaries. Two, funded and managed by the Methodist Woman's Home Missionary Society, evolved into settlement houses during the 1910s.[14]

The only other early woman's organization to reach directly into ethnic neighborhoods was the WCTU. Not until the early 1900s, in the aftermath of the Spanish-American War, would Anglo women make deeper incursions into immigrant enclaves. Then, following upon cooperative Anglo-Cuban ventures during the war and braced by the interventionist rhetoric that accompanied the war, Tampa's women reformers extended their search for order.[15] In 1901, Tampa women joined the American presence in Cuba, opening a WCTU reading room in Havana. Closer to home, the American Mother's League opened its first day nursery in Ybor City, assuring its supporters that "it is work of this kind which is necessary if the foreigners who come to our shores are ever to understand American ideals."[16]

After 1900, the Wolff Mission in Ybor City and what was to become the Rosa Valdes Settlement House in West Tampa expanded their religious and educational projects. These centers now sought to train immigrant girls in sewing and lace making, reflecting Anglo women's sense of proper roles for women in both home and workplace. That such pursuits were undertaken in facilities where every breeze carried the aroma of tobacco leaves and cigar smoke through the open windows suggests the degree to which Anglo women's mission was at odds with the material conditions of Cuban girls' lives. Such contradictions went largely unrecognized, at least by Anglos, and by the 1920s, a full-blown Americanization program, replete with lessons for preparing deviled eggs, would emerge through such organizations as the West Tampa Americanization and Charity League, a member of the Hillsborough County Federation of Women's Clubs (HCFWC).[17]

By the second decade of the twentieth century, the domestic and vocational skills that Anglo women attempted to teach their Latin charges deviated considerably from those most useful to them. Increasingly, Anglos defined working-class (and specifically immigrant) home life as a problem, one to be solved by retraining the second generation and regulating familial and sexual activities. Campaigns by the HCFWC for child labor laws, a higher age of sexual and marital consent, the removal of "salacious magazines"[18] from public sale, mother's pensions, and similar legislation, though often well-intentioned, assumed that immigrant, working-class families were incapable of regulating their own lives and that such incapacity warranted the intervention not only of Anglo reformers but of the state.

If Latins rejected Anglos' negative characterizations of their home life, they nonetheless agreed that their version of domesticity was not only different from but frequently at odds with that of their more affluent neighbors. Author and Tampa resident Jose Yglesias captured one aspect of this difference in *The Truth about Them,* in which he described an exchange with his Americanized Uncle Candido: "He did not say Old Folks Home with the sad, pitying accent of Latins who believed only Americans are so callous as to rid themselves of the old. That worried me."[19]

Still, the initial contacts between Cuban and Anglo women did not portend these future antagonisms. In the mid-1890s, Cubans and sympathetic Spaniards had initiated organizational efforts to cope with war orphans, widows, and refugees. They established the *Sociedad de Beneficencias* in 1896, modeled on self-help associations in their native isle. This society formed the basis for the Central Relief Committee, the interethnic organization established two years later at the initiative of Latins. This Anglicized committee did adopt more benevolent values as women like Children's Home president Mrs. William B. Henderson joined the effort, but such influences did not flow in only one direction. In the same year that Henderson contributed to refugee relief efforts, "representatives of the various cigar factories"[20] donated funds for much-needed repairs on the Children's Home.

It is unclear whether women like Henderson understood the cross-class and biracial composition of Latin relief agencies or whether they took such elite members as Mrs. Vicente Ybor, wife of the cigar industry's founder, as representative of the real power behind such efforts. Whatever Anglo women's perceptions, the capacity for Cuban emigrés to support themselves, a war in Cuba, and refugees at home, while also contributing to the Children's Home, was rooted in the activities of the community as a whole—women and men, workers and owners, Afro-Cubans and white Cubans. These organizational efforts emerged from both factories and families in a company town that was constructed to attract both.

Vicente Martinez Ybor constructed two hundred houses along with his first factory. They were one-story duplexes, the two halves being separated by a long open-air hallway on which the front doors faced, or wooden double-deckers with both porches and balconies. Beginning with the first fifty cigar workers, who arrived in the spring of 1886 with families in tow, Ybor rented homes at reasonable rates, with part of the rent being applied to any future purchase.

In these houses, the boundaries between family and neighbor, family and community, and family and factory were blurred and fluid. Extensive kin groups might share a duplex, or residents of the same Cuban community might forge familylike bonds across the shared porch. In any duplex or double-decker, one might find tobacco leaves and the tools of the trade: a wooden board, a sharp blade, and a little paste. These could be used to craft a few smokes for the male inhabitants; train wives and children in the art of stemming, bunching or rolling; supply a small workshop or *chinchale*, as a means of gaining economic independence; or provide all of these in different combinations depending on circumstances.[21]

The family also intruded into the factory. Many factories were family enterprises, managed by fathers and sons, brothers and brothers-in-law, even a daughter or widow now and then. Employees, though paid individually, were often hired in family groups; into the 1920s, kinship connections were a primary means of finding jobs. Latin daughters were expected to turn the bulk of their pay over to parents, sharing in the family's general poverty or prosperity. Moreover, by working in the same factories, fathers, brothers, aunts, or uncles could serve as chaperones for young girls amid strange men.[22]

During the 1890s, these dense family-factory networks were mobilized in support of *Cuba Libre.*[23] Cuban men, women, and children formed dozens of revolutionary clubs to support the independence struggle. Women employed their household skills in a variety of ways to raise funds and care for victims of war. When men offered their support to the *Partido Revolucionario Cubano* (PRC), that too placed demands on women to stretch domestic resources. In 1895, for instance, Francisco Delgado, in a moment of revolutionary passion, announced to his fellow cigar makers: "I am the father of a family, [and] what I earn is hardly enough to provide them with the necessities for supper but when it is a question of the needs of my native country, I do not hesitate in lending it my poor though decided cooperation; for my part, I offer one day of work for my homeland."[24] This commitment of a day's wage to the PRC, standard for Cuban cigar workers by the mid-1890s, clearly increased the pressure on housewives seeking "the necessities for supper."

Throughout the war, domestic goods were auctioned for the cause, and homes were used to store bandages, uniforms, medicine, even munitions, and to shelter the homeless. Even with the financial support offered by Anglo sympathizers in the late 1890s, it was Latin women who shouldered the major burden of housing, feeding, and clothing the needy. The number of needy increased when the fighting worsened and when cigar workers went on strike as the war ground to an end.

If the war fostered the politicization of immigrant households and illuminated class differences, it also stirred racial conflicts. The massing of federal troops not only revealed and exacerbated the inadequacy of Tampa's sanitation and health services and focused attention on brothels and gambling dens hiding behind factory walls, it also led to the eruption of racial violence. Black soldiers refused to submit "to the discriminatory treatment accorded black civilians."[25] They used their numbers and their arms to gain fair treatment and to rescue comrades who fell into the hands of white police and sheriffs.

Tensions flared into a riot on June 10, 1898, when white soldiers grabbed a two-year-old black boy from his mother and used him as a target to demonstrate their marksmanship. Rampages followed in Ybor City and elsewhere in Tampa, and conflicts between the black soldiers and the white troops sent in to quell the riot resulted in extensive damage and dozens of injuries. Other conflicts also surfaced, though less violently. Before the war ended, differences between affluent and working-class Latins were sharpened, as strikes flared throughout the cigar city. The class character of the cigar centers crystallized as wealthier emigrés returned to Cuba in the immediate postwar period. They and their counterparts who made Tampa their permanent home committed themselves to the goals and programs first outlined by Anglo social housekeepers. For example, Maria Luisa Sánchez, a revolutionary orator as a teenager in Tampa and the daughter of a rebel general, married an Italian radical after the war and resettled in Havana. In 1923, as a well-to-do matron, she appeared at the first Federation of Cuban Women conference to urge her sisters to join civic beautification projects. Her countrywomen who remained in Tampa—the wives and daughters of cigar factory owners and professionals—also entered mainstream progressive movements, joining the boards of the Children's Home, WCTU, Ladies' Memorial Society, Methodist missionary societies, and even the Tampa Women's Club.[26]

Still, such women did not cut their ties to the Latin community. Rather, they simultaneously joined associations of elite Anglo women and, with their husbands, the mutual aid societies and social clubs formed within the cigar neighborhoods. Working-class women remembered the mutual aid societies mainly as sources of youthful entertainment and medical care. More affluent members, beginning with women from the most elite ethnic club, *Centro Español,* formed auxiliaries to raise funds, beautify club buildings and grounds, and improve medical facilities.[27]

The presence of immigrants and their continued ethnic solidarity was a source of concern and contention among Anglos, yet it also seemed to provide Tampa elites with an excuse for ignoring the plight of resident Afro-Americans. Even members of the Methodist Woman's Home Mission, who took hesitant steps toward interracial cooperation elsewhere in the South, devoted themselves almost solely to religious and educational efforts among immigrants in Tampa. In part, this may be explained by the fact that while blacks, like Latins, lived in segregated and isolated neighborhoods in Tampa, they, unlike Latins, did not provide essential labor for the city's primary industry.

Most local blacks lived in an area known as "the Scrub" or in other segregated sections of town. Extended families shared neighborhoods, if not always homes, many houses being too small for large numbers of residents. Women outnumbered men in the prime age groups from 20 to 50. Married, single, or widowed, women served in Anglo households or worked in public laundries. Latins generally displaced African-Americans in such traditional male trades as carpentry, barbering, bootblacking, and truck farming, putting more pressure on black women to contribute to family support. By 1920, over 53 percent of all of Tampa's native-born black females were in the paid labor force.[28]

Black churches provided some relief in periods of crisis (epidemics, economic panics, racial conflicts), but little is known of the more permanent associations they fostered. They may have also served as the organizational bases for such annual celebrations as Emancipation Day, when local blacks staged parades, concerts, and speeches at which they advocated such reform measures as temperance.[29] Still, blacks remained largely disfranchised after 1885, excluded from public institutions constructed by Anglo women and without the financial resources to support Latin-style mutual aid societies. Blacks therefore depended more heavily on informal familial and communal support networks to sustain themselves.[30]

One of the few documented social-welfare institutions founded by local blacks before 1920 suggests that this was indeed the case. In 1908, a black woman who required surgery could find no hospital to take her. A local black nurse, Clara Frye, suggested that an improvised operating room be set up in her cottage. Soon she had transformed her home into a temporary hospital, and, after several years' struggle to gather supplies and funds, she opened a permanent institution. She personally ran Clara Frye Hospital for two decades. Though local physicians and even the Urban League complained about the inadequate care provided there, a public facility was not established until New Deal agencies provided the necessary funds.[31]

Blacks, though involved in a stevedores' association and a short-lived Laundresses' Union, were never able to match the complex network of labor organizations developed by Latins. Cubans in particular, both women and men, sought to establish their version of industrial order through participation in and support of a variety of trade associations. It was the persistent battle for a reordering of the economic and social system sustained by these organizations that revealed the real chasm between Anglo and Latin, elite and working-class, progressive agendas.

In 1901, on the heels of cooperative wartime ventures, cigar workers waged their longest strike to date. Closing down the industry for five months, Cubans sought union recognition, higher wages, and a veto power over manufacterers' right to open competing factories elsewhere. An industrial union, *La Resistencia,* embraced two or three thousand male and female workers in a wide range of occupations in and outside the cigar factories. The association rooted itself in the community as much as in the workplace, organizing its members in neighborhood rather than factory units. The support attracted by *La Resistencia* in 1901 was so extensive and cohesive that cigar workers never walked the picket line.

The union provided benefits through nine soup kitchens. Community women also took in evicted neighbors, stretched family budgets, redistributed household goods, and refused strike rations when possible so that all needy workers could be supported.[32] In the face of vigilante attacks, these women circulated a letter to their Anglo "sisters," asking them to intervene to stop illegal abductions, and as wives and mothers, petitioned the governor to see that justice was done. The arrests of male strikers for vagrancy several months into the strike led to a women's march on the mayor's office, where pleas for intervention were again based on both justice and family needs.[33] Yet these Latin women only called on elite Anglo women and the state as auxiliary strategies. More often, and more successfully, they sought support in the Cuban communities of Tampa, Key West, and Havana.

What is critical for the analysis of the relations between domesticity and activism is that Latin women did not challenge their traditional domestic roles as they became labor militants. Rather, they employed domestic skills to help wage earners defeat employers. Housekeeping was not only social, it was socialist, a logical extension of its normally communal and contentious character in Latin working-class neighborhoods.

For native-born blacks, with fewer economic resources and without a heritage of revolutionary ideology, communal housekeeping was also a critical resource, but it lacked the specifically socialist dimension developed among Latins. In addition, the plight of most local blacks was not bound to a new industrial order. Domestic service remained the primary employment for black women, and attempts to improve conditions in this occupation did not always originate with workers. Blanche Armwood, a prominent local graduate of Spelman Seminary, convinced the Tampa Gas Company to fund a School of Household Arts for black women in 1915. This effort continued under Armwood's direction with the support of the Colored Women's Clubs of Tampa, one of the few citywide federations of black women's clubs in the nation. In the 1920s, the HCFWC followed Armwood's example and began opening model kitchens to demonstrate the utility of electrical appliances to both housewives and domestics.[34]

Other women from Tampa's small black middle class—teachers in black schools; hairdressers, clerks, or cooks in black establishments; wives of black businessmen—formed at least four clubs in the 1910s, among them one devoted to business and professional women, one to mothers, and one to public service. The women who formed the leadership of these organizations came from *relatively* wealthy and small families, which were somewhat isolated from the rest of the black community as well as excluded from parallel Anglo organizations. For several years in the mid-1920s, the two top offices of three major black women's organizations were filled by the same two women, and all three organizations shared a single address.

Such clubs were linked into citywide and national federations, however. In 1923, Hallie Q. Brown, president of the National Association of Colored Women, spoke at St. Paul's African Methodist Episcopal Zion Church in Tampa, and two years later one local club renamed itself the Mary B. Talbert Club in honor of the recently deceased national club leader.[35] Aware of movements afoot elsewhere, clubwomen voiced concern about the "forces among our own people and outside of the Black community who tended to humiliate and destroy"[36] black womanhood. Other organizations shared the clubwomen's concern with securing the autonomy and dignity of their people. Among these was the Lily White Security Benefits Association, whose male and female members provided pallbearers for funerals and raised funds for church events.

In addition, black women joined a variety of lodges and auxiliaries, some of which provided sick and burial benefits. They also sought to establish a "colored branch" of the YWCA, though the plan was apparently blocked by unsympathetic leaders of the white local.[37] It was only with the Urban League's growth in the mid-1920s, and its 1927 report on race relations and conditions in segregated neighborhoods, that Tampa's black community began to forge unity across class lines and to use that solidarity for leverage with city politicians and reformers.[38]

Throughout the Progressive Period, blacks remained largely dependent on their own resources to fund day nurseries, a sanatorium, church schools, and an orphanage. They certainly could not depend on the leaders of Anglo women's organizations for assistance. Though the YWCA was considered a "Monument to [the] City's Progress Spirit" by local white journalists, its leaders asserted that African-Americans and Latins were uninterested in their programs, an assertion they supported by pointing to both groups' lack of involvement in Y activities. Other organizations, including the HCFWC, offered small sums on a monthly basis to one or two woefully underfunded black child-care and health-care facilities.[39]

As black women struggled to establish and sustain self-help organizations out of informal modes of familial and communal support, Latin working women extended their socialist housekeeping into patterned means of pressuring employers, city fathers, and, more rarely, their male peers. Strikes in 1910, 1916, 1919, and 1920-21 sharpened their skills and assured that resources and lessons learned in an earlier era would be passed on to the next generation. In the process, they moved ever further from cooperation with Anglos and elite Latins to open conflict with the former and chronic tension with the latter.

By 1910, for example, Cuban women no longer appealed to Anglo city mothers for assistance, instead pleading with Latin (including Italian) coworkers to establish women's "premier place"[40] in class struggle. In 1910 and 1911, they sought cooperation from the "sweethearts, wives, and daughters of union men,"[41] as cigar makers attempted to establish a Woman's Union Label League in the city. In 1916, female cigar workers staged their own wildcat strike, offering their skirts to mock male comrades who refused to join the walkout, thereby asserting their autonomy within the Latin community.[42] Latin women had now established themselves as critical to and potentially independent within the activist movements of Ybor City and West Tampa.

The year 1920 was important for Tampa women. Only a minority acquired the ballot that year, since most immigrant and black women were ineligible to vote or were disfranchised. The more significant event was a cigar strike, which revealed in particularly stark terms the distinctions between working-class Latin and affluent Anglo women's activism and the relations of each to home and state. The mutual support between revolutionary emigrés and Children's Home leaders displayed in 1898 had turned to mutual suspicion by 1920 as the two proceeded further down divergent paths to civic improvement, community order, and social justice.

In June 1920, with workers already on strike, Mayor D.B. McKay, at the behest of Anglo women leaders, offered the Children's Home as a refuge for children of strikers. This offer "was met with a firm refusal," much to the consternation of Robert Lovett, Anglo secretary of Florida's State Federation of Labor. Yet a month later, when McKay had taken over leadership of the fight against cigar workers and utilized a variety of vigilante tactics, Lovett reported to the *Tampa Citizen*: "One can only admire the foresight of those starving Latin families. I would regret to leave my children to the tender mercy of men, who will try to squeeze the lifeblood out of me while living."[43]

Starving families were responding not only to the fear of temporarily leaving their children to the mercy of Home leaders, but to a wider perception that employers, politicians, and reformers, male and female, Anglo and Latin, had formed a united front, the purpose of which was to "squeeze the lifeblood" out of the entire working community. In 1920, the Children's Home had wives of cigar magnates on its board of managers and owners themselves on its board of trustees. The home, after a devastating fire earlier in the year, had relocated to a refurbished factory, donated by the A.J. Mugge Cigar Co. The ties between Anglo women progressives and cigar manufacturers were close and dense.

In addition, Anglo women's clubs were urging the state to intrude ever more directly into immigrant lives at the same time that leading Anglo men were organizing vigilante actions against strikers.[44] Compulsory education laws were advocated as a means of reinforcing lax implementation of child labor laws. Protective labor (including maximum-hour) legislation, social purity laws, and the construction of a juvenile detention home were also on the HCFWC agenda. These issues received a far more sympathetic hearing in the state capital than did pleas by strikers for protection against abductions and beatings of labor radicals.

Even before Tampa's female progressives gained the vote, they had run a woman for the school board in Ybor City's district. As soon as women got the ballot, they used it to support adoption of a city-commission form of government and at-large elections that would further restrict input from minority communities. In these and other ways, Anglo women and their elite Latin allies appeared to be simply the female branch of those local and state forces seeking to deprive workers and their families of a decent living, a reasonable privacy, and increased representation in local government. Indeed, black and Latin working-class women activists may have had a better perception than their more affluent counterparts of the ways that women's domesticated political culture could be co-opted by male officeholders with somewhat different progressive goals.

The version of civic improvement, community order, and social justice promoted by elite Anglos and Latins left little room for working-class Latins or blacks to assert their own progressive claims. When such claims were voiced, it was not through domesticated politics. Indeed, in Tampa, where vigilante actions against strikers and radicals went unpunished and racial violence formed a chronic refrain in the police blotter, the notion that the state was becoming more domesticated would have seemed entirely ludicrous.

It was to assert an alternate vision, against what were viewed as repressive political and institutional regimes, that Latin and African-American women employed domestic resources and skills as instruments of class and racial struggle. They founded unions as well as mutual aid societies, clubs, and social welfare institutions as means through which to channel these domestic weapons. What was more important for them than the domestication of politics was the politicization of domesticity. In utilizing woman-controlled and home-based resources, their communities brought the fullest range of weapons to bear in the battle for an acceptable standard of living, a voice in social and political policies, and a society committed to economic, ethnic, and racial justice—the critical elements on their progressive agenda.

Notes

The author wishes to thank Judith Bennett, Cynthia Herrup, Steven Lawson, and participants in the Women's History Seminar at the Institute for Historical Studies, London, and in the Progressive Era Conference for their insights and encouragement and Peggy Cornett for her detective skills.

1. Jane Addams, "Why Should Women Vote (1910)," reprinted in Emily Cooper Johnson, ed., *Jane Addams: A Centennial Reader* (New York: Macmillan, 1960), 104, 105.

2. Quoted in Lula Joughin Dovi, "I Remember Aunt Kate," *Sunland Tribune*, Nov. 1978, v. 5, p. 13.

3. Paula Baker, "The Domestication of Politics: Women and American Political Society, 1780-1920," *American Historical Review* 89:3 (June 1984): 620-47, provides an excellent summary of literature on women and progressivism and offers an important new interpretation, but she focuses only on middle- and upper-class white women.

4. Quoted in Gary R. Mormino and George Pozzetta, *The Immigrant World of Ybor City: Italians and Their Latin Neighbors in Tampa, 1885-1985* (Urbana: Univ. of Illinois Press, 1987), 57.

5. On the Tampa riot of 1898, see Willard B. Gatewood, Jr., "Negro Troops in Florida, 1898," *Florida Historical Quarterly* 49 (July 1970): 1-15.

6. See Robert P. Ingalls, "Strikes and Vigilante Violence in Tampa's Cigar Industry," *Tampa Bay History* 7 (Fall/Winter 1985): 117-34, and Mormino and Pozzetta, *Immigrant World*, 56-58.

7. In general, such fluidity did not characterize race relations, except within the Cuban community.

8. It is also possible that these events had larger implications. Theodore Roosevelt was stationed in Tampa with his Rough Riders during the months of social chaos and political turmoil that preceded U.S. entry into the Spanish-American War. If concern about the possibility of revolution and race suicide (the belief that African-Americans and immigrants would soon outnumber old stock white Americans) in the United States did influence Roosevelt's demand for and definition of reform programs, then Tampa may well be viewed as the southern seedbed of his brand of progressive reform.

9. The collective portrait of this and other circles of activist women is derived from a variety of sources, incluing newspapers, city directories, census data, organizational records, *Tampa Blue Books* of 1912-13 and 1914, and local histories, all located at the Tampa Public Library or Special Collections, University of South Florida, Tampa.

10. *Tampa Journal*, January 1887 [specific date illegible].

11. *Tampa Journal*, April 1887 [specific date illegible].

12. The range of local women's efforts is catalogued in Milly St. Julien, "'We Are Our Neighbors' Keepers': The Role of Women in Tampa's Benevolent Organizations, 1895-1915," unpublished paper in the author's possession.

13. See St. Julien, "Neighbors' Keepers," and Hillsborough County Federation of Women's Clubs (hereafter HCFWC), Scrapbook, 1920-31, Special Collections, University of South Florida, Tampa.

14. See the *Annual Report of the Woman's Home Mission Society of the Methodist Episcopal Church, South,* 1898-1915, published annually by the Methodist Episcopal Church, South Publishing House in Nashville, Tennessee.

15. For commonalities between progressive programs and interventionist foreign policy, see John Whiteclay Chambers II, *The Tyranny of Change: America in the Progressive Era, 1900-1917* (New York: St. Martin's 1980).

16. *Tampa Morning Tribune*, Sept. 5, 1901; see also Nov. 23, 1902 and Dec. 6, 1903. If the ideas mentioned were democracy, independence, and justice, apparently they were

already understood by Cubans who had offered their support and their lives to the cause of *Cuba Libre.*

17. See *Annual Report of the Woman's Home Mission Society of the Methodist Episcopal Church, South,* 1898-1915; HCFWC, Scrapbook, 1920-1931; and Mrs. Dolores Rio, interview with author, Tampa, Sept. 4, 1985.

18. HCFWC Records, Minutes, 1920-1931, Special Collections, University of South Florida, Tampa.

19. Jose Yglesias, *The Truth about Them* (New York: World Publishing, 1971), 80. Yglesias's account is drawn from his childhood in Ybor City.

20. Children's Home, Scrapbooks, vol. 1, 1892-1902, Children's Home Papers, Special Collections, University of South Florida, Tampa. See also Joan Marie Steffey, "The Cuban Immigrants of Tampa, Florida, 1886-1898" (M.A. thesis, University of South Florida, 1975), 120-25; and St. Julien, "Neighbors' Keepers."

21. On housing, see José Muñiz, *The Ybor City Story* (Tampa: Tampa Tribune Press, 1969), 93-101, 131.

22. Mrs. Dolores Rio, interview with author, Tampa, Sept. 4, 1985; Mrs. Rose B. Anello, interview with author, Tampa, Aug. 23, 1985; and Mrs. Angie V. Garcia, interview with author, Tampa, Dec. 18, 1984.

23. See Steffey, "Cuban Immigrants," and Nancy Hewitt, "Cuban Women and Work: Tampa, Florida, 1886-1901" (paper presented at the Annual Meeting of the American Historical Association, Washington, D.C., Dec. 1987).

24. "Gonzalo de Quesada—Su Visita a los Talleres," *Patria* (New York City), Feb. 18, 1895, p. 3, reporting on factory visit of PRC leaders in Tampa (translated from Spanish by the author).

25. Gatewood, "Negro Troops," 4.

26. See "Un Primer Congress de Federacion Mujeres Cubanas," *Bimestre Cubana* 18:2 (1923), on Maria Luisa Sanchez Ferrera; Tampa city directories; Children's Home and HCFWC Papers, Special Collections, University of South Florida, Tampa; and *Tampa Blue Book, 1912-13* (Tampa: Tribune Publishing, 1913).

27. See *History of Centro Español de Tampa, 1891-1941* (Tampa: Tribune Press, n.d.), 98-99; and *Centro Asturiano: Album de Recuerdos, 1902-1985* (Tampa: Centro Asturiano, 1985). See also Nancy A. Hewitt, "Mutual Aid or Charity: Two Approaches to Philanthropy in a Latin Community," in Kathleen D. McCarthy, ed., *Ladies Bountiful: Women and Philanthropy* (New Brunswick, N.J.: Rutgers Univ. Press, 1990)

28. *Abstract of the Fourteenth Census of the United States, 1920* (Washington, D.C.: GPO, 1923), 114, 130, 524.

29. The earliest evidence of a local celebration appears in the *Tampa Journal,* May 26, 1887.

30. Information on black Tampans is derived from city directories, census data, newspapers, and Otis R. Anthony and Marilyn T. Wade, comps., *A Collection of Historical Facts about Black Tampa* (Tampa: Tampa Electric Company, 1974).

31. Paul Diggs, "Clara Frye Memorial Hospital," 1938, WPA Files, Special Collections Department, University of South Florida, Tampa.

32. See Durward Long, "*La Resistencia:* Tampa's Immigrant Labor Union," *Labor History* 6 (1965): 193-213.

33. See *Tampa Morning Tribune,* Aug. 29, 1901 and Oct. 5, 1901; Long, "*La Resistencia,*" 210; and Petitions, 1901 William Sherman Jennings Papers, Florida State

Archives, Tallahassee, Fla. Of the 715 signers of the 1901 petition, at least 145, or 20 percent, were female.

34. See John Durham, "Blanche Armwood: The Early Years, 1890-1922" (M.A. thesis, University of South Florida, 1988), 32-38; HCFWC, Scrapbooks, 1920-31; and *Tampa Morning Tribune*, Jan. 14, 1912.

35. See city directories, 1921, 1925, and 1928; Anthony and Wade, *Historical Facts;* Mary Claire Crake, "In Unity There Is Strength: The Influence of Women's Clubs on Tampa, 1900-1940" (M.A. thesis, University of South Florida, 1988).

36. Quoted from an article on "Womanhood," written for the *Afro-American Monthly* in 1915, published by the Afro-American Civic League. It is not known if women were members of this association. The article is cited in Anthony and Wade, *Historical Facts*, 15.

37. See Local Files, Reel 169: Florida and Georgia, Papers of the Young Women's Christian Association, National Board of the YWCA Archives, New York, N.Y. As late as 1936, the national board was concerned that local Tampa leaders were members of the Ku Klux Klan. See Eleanor Coperhaven, Report of Interview with Miss Gladys Taber (General Secretary, Tampa YWCA), Oct. 10, 1936.

38. Information for the black community in the 1910s and 1920s comes from city directories, the Raper Report published by the Urban League in 1927, and Anthony and Wade, *Historical Facts*.

39. Newsclipping, 1922, Local Files, Reel 169: Florida and Georgia, Papers of the YWCA; see also HCFWC, Minutes, 1920-1931.

40. "A Los Trabajadores de Tampa," 1910, Labor Union Manifestos, Microfilm of *El Internacional* and related papers, Reel 1: University of South Florida, Tampa.

41. *Tampa Morning Tribune*, Nov. 11, 1916.

42. *El Internacional*, Dec. 30, 1910, Feb. 24, 1911, and Dec. 1, 1916. For a more detailed analysis of gender relations within the Latin community, see Nancy Hewitt, "'The Voice of Virile Labor': Labor Militancy and Gender Identity in Tampa's Cigar Cities," in Ava Baron, ed., *Work Engendered* (Ithaca, N.Y.: Cornell University Press, 1991).

43. Robert Lovett to L.P. Dickie, editor, July 20, 1920, published in the *Tampa Citizen*, July 30, 1920.

44. On vigilante actions against Latin workers throughout Tampa's history, see Robert P. Ingalls, *Urban Vigilantes in the New South: Tampa, 1882-1936* (Knoxville: Univ. of Tennessee Press, 1988).

4

When Your Work Is Not Who You Are: The Development of a Working-Class Consciousness among Afro-American Women

SHARON HARLEY

May Anna Madison, a middle-aged former domestic quoted in John Langston Gwaltney's *Drylongso: A Self-Portrait of Black America,* declared: "One very important difference between white people and black people is that white people think that you *are* your work. . . . Now, a black person has more sense than that because he knows that what I am doing doesn't have anything to do with what I want to do or what I do when I am doing for myself. Now, black people think that my work is just what I have to do to get what I want."[1]

To the extent that attitudes toward wage work and occupational status are a reflection of racial and gender differences, Madison, a contemporary black female domestic, offers an accurate description of the traditional difference between how blacks and whites, women and men perceive the meaning of paid work in their lives—a perceptual difference that was present during the Progressive Era. As a consequence of both low status in the occupational structure and a desire to abide by conventional notions of women's proper role, the majority of black wage-earning women, especially mothers and wives, usually did not believe that their presence or their position in the labor force was an accurate reflection of who they were or of how they should be viewed by members of the black community. For most black women, opportunities for social status existed outside the labor market—in their family, neighborhood, and organizational and church lives.[2] Likewise, the development of a working-class consciousness among black women during the Progressive Era was affected by their domestic roles and occupational status, which differed somewhat from those of their white counterparts.

The operational definition of working-class consciousness as it is applied to black working women during the Progressive Era or in this paper is the expression of shared interests and the articulation of work-related concerns. Because of the racially exclusive practices of labor unions in the opening decades of the twentieth century, a working-class consciousness in the trade-unionist vein should not be expected of most black women and men of the period. Indeed, as sociologist Cynthia Costello indicates in a recent study of contemporary female clerical workers in a Wisconsin insurance company, the women who took collective action against their employer rarely identified with the concerns of the male-dominated trade union. They identified with the concerns of other working women. The seemingly contradictory nature of the working-class consciousness that characterized the women in Costello's study was even more apparent among black women, who were almost universally excluded from the major Progressive Era trade unions.[3]

Few would deny that the overwhelming majority of Progressive Era blacks were working-class in terms of their objective position in the class structure and their lack of control over the means of production. Undoubtedly, the social isolation and the work schedule of the majority of black working women, whether farmhands on southern plantations or domestics in private homes in the city, and their exclusion from trade unions impeded the development of a working-class identity and consciousness and the ability to act consistently on this consciousness during the early decades of the Progressive Era. Yet, individually and in organized groups, black women acted to improve their working conditions.

To what extent did black women identify themselves as wage-earners and express shared interests with other workers? How did black female wage earners express their working-class concerns and consciousness? What impact did black women's self-perceptions and the black community's attitudes toward wage-earning women have on their labor activism?

The large representation of the black female population in the paid labor force reveals the importance of women's paid work to the economic survival of black families and households in the United States. During the period from 1880 to 1920, loosely defined as the Progressive Era, the black female wage-earning population rose steadily. The percentage of black women (ten years and older) in the paid labor market averaged 57 percent in the District of Columbia over the five decades of the Progressive Era. During the same period, the average proportion of employed black women in most large urban communities of similar size was approximately one-half that of the District.

Despite the large presence of black women in the labor market, a higher percentage of the black male population worked for wages in the United States. In 1910, 87 percent of the black male population in the United States was listed as gainfully employed, compared to only 55 percent of the female population. In the District of Columbia more black men (81 percent) worked than black women (60 percent) in 1910. Similarly, in Mississippi 90 percent of the black male population worked for wages, compared to only 68 percent of the black female population.[4]

Even in the poorest black families, husbands and fathers, not wives and mothers, were considered the primary breadwinners, regardless of the duration of their employment. Although seasonally unemployed, black men usually earned higher wages than black women. Since a married woman's proper place, even in the black community, was considered to be in the home caring for her children and her husband, black men were more likely to engage in wage work than women. When black fathers and husbands could not earn enough to make ends meet (which was often), black women, regardless of marital status, age, or the presence of children, joined the labor force. Of course, many never left.[5]

According to some blacks and whites, the presence of black mothers in the labor market was one of the most blatant examples of the lack of family stability and racial progress among the largely uneducated, rural black migrant class, regardless of the economic pressures on black households. Indicative of black male attitudes toward wage-earning wives and mothers were the views expressed by Giles B. Jackson and D. Webster Davis, authors of *The Industrial History of the Negro Race,* published in 1911. They argued: "The race needs wives who stay at home, being supported by their husbands, and then they can spend time in the training of their children."[6] In light of the precarious financial condition of most black households, this call for black mothers and wives to remain at home and be cared for by their husbands was an unrealistic expectation at best.

The racial barriers that black male wage-earners faced in the employment market forced a larger percentage of the married black female population to seek gainful employment. In 1890, approximately 23 percent of married black women in the United States participated in the labor force, compared to only 3 percent of the married white female population. The District of Columbia, with 43 percent of the married black female population in the labor force in 1890, had one of the largest work forces of this group, as well as a significantly higher percentage of married white women. By 1920, slightly more than 50 percent of the married black female population in the nation's capital was gainfully employed, compared to less than one-fourth of the married white female population. Similar ratios existed between black and white women in cities and towns throughout the United States during this period.[7]

Poverty, not a black cultural ethos favoring married women's wage labor, was the most significant explanatory factor for married black women's larger presence in the labor force. The difference in the level of employment of married black and white women reveals the degree to which racial identity affected an individual's economic condition. Greater economic pressures on black households, largely resulting from the low wages and seasonal employment of many black men, forced a larger number of married black women to work for wages. The financial survival of most black families and households (and not a small number of white households) prevented them from fully abiding by middle-class norms against married women in the paid labor market, especially in jobs outside the home.

Consequently, it would be incorrect to assume that a strong positive correlation existed between the large presence of married black women in the labor market and black male support for it. Black male response to working wives and mothers reveals a range of often contradictory emotions. Some black husbands forbade their wives to work for wages while others offered verbal support for such employment. Black male responses, though varied, can be characterized generally as reluctant acceptance rather than outright support. Despite a history of black female labor, total acceptance from black men was not forthcoming. Black women had often worked alongside their men in the antebellum and postbellum South. In addition, a religious and cultural tradition favorable to work existed in the black community, and black women's financial contributions to their households were important to their family's economic survival.

Although members of the black community knew the history of black women's work and, indeed, knew why married black women had to work for wages, they did not wholeheartedly support this activity. A married woman, especially if she had young children, who did not work for wages was a positive reflection of her husband's ability to provide for his family. Wives who worked, especially outside the home, only served to reinforce publicly the inability of black men to care for their families. Tensions increased within some black households as blacks became more aware of and affected by middle-class notions of women's and men's proper roles in society, as articulated by Jackson, Davis, and middle-class blacks.[8]

Black men were generally more "supportive" of their wives' employment than were men in other ethnic and racial groups, as fewer black men could make ends without their wives' financial assistance. A more important influence on married black women's labor, however, was the cultural ethos in the black community, which emphasized cooperation, sacrificing for kin, and "principled survival."[9] Members of the black community believed strongly that parents and adult relatives should sacrifice their own needs and wants for the advancement of their children and kin. The limited opportunities available to blacks for economic and social advancement without the benefit of a formal education and the importance that blacks generally attached to educating their youth contributed to the decision of black mothers to join the labor force in lieu of sending their children to work.[10]

Regardless of the noble purposes for married women's wage work, notions of acceptable behavior, especially among middle-class blacks and those aspiring to middle-class respectability and status, resulted in both public and private criticism of married women's employment. Negative responses came from diverse quarters: from middle-class, prominent black men like Jackson and Davis and from far less formally and professionally trained black men like Zora Neale Hurston's father. In her autobiography, *Dust Tracks on the Road* (1942), Hurston recounted that her father loved to boast to his male friends that "he had never let his wife hit a lick of work for anybody in her life."[11] The caveat was that Zora's mother had so many children (a fact about which her father also boasted) that it was virtually impossible for her to work for wages outside her home.

Male attitudes toward wage-earning married women reveal the dichotomy between the ideal and the real in the black community. The reality was that black women, irrespective of marital status, frequently had to work for wages, but this did not preclude members of the black community from articulating what they believed was the ideal role for married black women or from opposing married women's paid employment.[12]

Clearly, blacks were no more immune to middle-class white expectations about the roles of women than were many non-middle-class whites and members of various immigrant groups. Regardless of how many black mothers and wives worked and how much they needed to work for their family's economic survival, their presence in the labor force was not the ideal. Even among the poorest blacks, whose own standards of respectability were largely determined by the church and by the community in which they lived, their domestic ideology was not always diametrically opposed to middle-class norms of behavior.

Opposition to married women's wage work in the black community was generally strongest toward families who needed the income of a wage-earning wife or mother the most. Fewer professional black married women encountered such sentiments in their home, especially when married to professional men, although they likely encountered them in the workplace, especially when they competed with black men for jobs. The dissimilar responses to professional married women, as opposed to other groups of wage-earning women, was based in part on their higher place in the occupational hierarchy. In addition, the presence in the paid labor force of an educated, professional black woman who was married to a professional man was less often viewed as a reflection of her husband's inability to care for his wife and family.[13]

How was it possible for a working-class consciousness to develop among black wage-earning women? The majority were domestic servants and farmhands, and many were married. They occupied low-status, unskilled jobs in the marketplace and, if married, were considered to be in violation of an accepted code of behavior. They tended to view their work as temporary (regardless of their length of employment), and they were grossly discriminated against by most labor organizers as well as by other workers. Although the issue of low status obviously did not affect the consciousness of professional black women toward their employment, these women tended to de-emphasize, at least publicly, the wage-earning aspect of their gainful employment and instead emphasize their reform activities. Irrespective of a particular occupation or its place in the occupational hierarchy, the working-class consciousness of black women throughout the Progressive Era was seldom in the trade unionist vein (which most labor and radical historians traditionally perceived as the only indication of the existence of a working-class consciousness).[14]

That wage-earning women of either race, and black men, for that matter, did not share with trade unionists a certain outlook about their status as workers and about the working class in general should not be surprising. It was difficult for women, regardless of race, and for black men to develop a working-class consciousness along the lines of a white male trade unionist while at the same time being denied membership in a white male-dominated union or, if granted membership, while being discriminated against. Besides, union organizing and strikes were relatively unknown phenomena for many rural southern-born blacks and for women in general. On this point Irene Goins, a black female organizer in the Chicago stockyards in 1918, remarked: "My people . . . know so little about organized labor that they have had a great fear of it, and for that reason the work of organizing has proceeded more slowly than I anticipated."[15]

The gender-based exclusionary practices and policies of Progressive Era trade union and labor organizations were compounded frequently by women's own ambivalence about their roles and status as wage earners. This ambivalence frequently encouraged them to deny, at least publicly, that they were wage-earning women or that their wage work was in any way a reflection of who they were. It was no accident that wage-earning women frequently referred to themselves as everything from "temporary helpmates" to "race uplifters" but less frequently as breadwinners or wage earners.[16]

While the economic motivation for their wage work was often similar to that of male wage earners, wage-earning women tended to view themselves as self-sacrificing mothers, wives, aunts, and sisters or as race uplifters rather than as workers. Their attitude toward their employment was, in part, an effort (not always conscious) to reconcile the domestic ideology about women's expected roles with the reality of their paid work lives and, in the case of domestic service workers, to de-emphasize the importance of their paid work lives to their everyday life and self-perception. Professional black women and their families were often as financially burdened as unskilled working-class families (although not always for the same reasons), but by couching their work roles in primarily racial uplift terms, they frequently sought a safe haven from criticism of their presence in the labor force.

Working women's often public disclaimers about their wage-earning roles should not be interpreted, however, as a lack of working-class consciousness or as a lack of concern about issues involving their lives as wage earners, their work conditions, and their wages. Expressions of working-class attitudes were revealed more often in private correspondence and conversations than in the public arena. Personal recollections of work-related concerns and activism have been divulged in recent personal interviews with black working women and in recent publications by women and labor historians.[17]

The private correspondence of female teachers revealed that, despite their public emphasis on the uplift nature of their wage work, issues concerning wages and occupational mobility were equally as important to them as they were to wage earners in general. In black women's public and private protests against the ban on married women teachers in the District of Columbia's public schools prior to 1918 and other forms of gender-based discrimination, the working-class attitudes and activism of professional black women were quite apparent.

The issues that female teachers emphasized in protest letters and public denunciations of sex discrimination were of an economic nature rather than an uplift nature—specifically, their inability to fulfill certain financial obligations. A female teacher in the District of Columbia public school system, who wished to remain anonymous for "obvious reasons," wrote Mrs. Raymond B. Morgan, a member of the Board of Education for the District of Columbia, to express her support for Morgan's opposition to the motion to reenact the ban against married female teachers. Questioning why women who had made enormous sacrifices for a professional career should be penalized for marrying, the anonymous correspondent declared that professional women's "personal obligations—to relatives, for example—do not cease with their marriage and, therefore, [they] have legitimate reasons for continuing to work." Besides, she warned, "in view of the high cost of living, the proposed motion would lead to secret marriages, fewer families, and fewer vacancies."[18]

The sentiments expressed in this letter reveal common concerns that professional black women shared with all black wage-earning women. Professional women needed to work for wages as much as the masses of uneducated black women and for many of the same reasons: to fulfill personal and familial obligations. The fulfillment of obligations to kin was considered a legitimate, even noble, purpose for women's employment. Attempts to restrict black women's employment and to pay them lower wages were issues that all black wage-earning women encountered, regardless of occupational and marital status.

Throughout the Progressive Era, despite their exclusion from or subordination within the major trade unions of the period, including those comprised of working women such as the International Ladies Garment Workers Union and the National Women's Trade Union League, black women took action to redress work-related grievances either on an individual basis or as members of various associations rather than as members of a trade-unionist group. Impressed by what the union did for women nurses, a black Chicago hospital worker decided to become a nurse. Knowing that she would be excluded from the existing nurses' union because she was black, this woman enrolled in a nurse's training program in anticipation of organizing black nurses at the hospital. Southern black women, not unlike their northern counterparts, also recognized the benefit of labor activism. Black women tobacco workers affiliated with the National Tobacco Workers Union participated in successful strikes in the late nineteenth and early twentieth centuries. In Florence, South Carolina, and Danville, Virginia, black female tobacco stemmers engaged in labor actions in 1898.[19]

Most middle-class black women showed their concern for working women and girls by establishing clubs and homes to assist them rather than by organizing black women workers into labor unions. In 1897, Victoria Earle Matthews, along with other prominent black women in New York City, formed the White Rose Industrial Association and established the White Rose Working Girls' Home. Yet, despite its reformist character, this home and association shared similar ground with trade unions of the period in seeking to prevent working women, largely domestic servants, from being exploited by employment agencies and potential employers.[20]

In addition, these Progressive Era working girls' associations and middle-class black women's clubs that dotted the urban landscape, primarily in the North, provided vocational training for working women and girls and offered day-care and kindergarten programs for the preschool children of working mothers. By offering child care and educational programs, the White Rose Association, the Colored Women's League of Washington, and similar groups were even more progressive than most traditional labor unions in meeting the needs of female membership then and now. The training and educational classes offered by black women's associations and clubs, while grossly underfunded, paralleled the apprenticeship programs that most unions offered its mostly white male members.[21]

Both black and white women were active in the Associations for the Protection of Negro Women, the 1905 brainchild of white philanthropist Frances Kellor. Located in New York City, Philadelphia, Norfolk, Memphis, Baltimore, and Washington, D.C., the association, which offered housing assistance, educational classes, and employment help, combined in 1909 to form the National League for the Protection of Colored Women. Willie Layten, a black woman who had been active in the Philadelphia association, became the new general secretary of the league, succeeding Kellor.[22]

In the spring of 1919, a conference was called in New York City by the National Association of Colored Women's Clubs, the major black women's reform organization, to deal with the plight of working black women. Black club women—particularly Nannie Helen Burroughs, founding president of the National Training School for Women and Girls—were concerned with the problems of working women, which led to the formation of the National Association of Wage-Earners in the 1920s. While reform-oriented, the association was no less radical than most of the trade unions of the period that sought relief for workers within the capitalist system, but this association was quite progressive in its publicly-stated goals on behalf of women. It sought, among other purposes, "to secure a wage that will enable women to live decently" and "to influence just legislation affecting women wage earners."[23]

In the 1920s and 1930s, the closing decades of the Progressive Era, a growing number of black women who had had a long tradition of labor market activity and of individual and community-based protest action began expressing their working-class concerns more and more through traditional trade-unionist organizations. In 1920, at least ten union locals of black domestics in the South affiliated with the Hotel and Restaurant Employees' Union of the American Federation of Labor. Black women joined other labor organizations and formed auxiliaries to male labor unions. When given an opportunity to join with other working men and women to express their shared labor concerns and to engage in labor struggles, black women willingly did so.[24]

In the summer of 1933, black and white women workers at the Sopkin Dress Manufacturing Company in Chicago went on strike for higher wages and for an end to the racially segregated and unsanitary restrooms. Led by the Needle Trades Workers' Industrial Union, the strikers' demands were met: "25 cents of an hour for a forty-four-hour week, equal pay for equal work, and no discriminating between white and colored workers." While still victimized by racism within the unions, black women workers, who played a key role in the Chicago strike and in other strikes throughout the 1930s, were increasingly welcomed as members of the largely white and male-dominated labor unions.[25]

A history of working in exploitative situations and of dealing with racial oppression made it easier for black women to identify with the demands of labor organizations and with the plight of other oppressed workers. Their desire to promote their interests in workers led some black women and men to join the so-called radical wings of the labor movement and the Communist Party in the 1930s and 1940s rather than remain outside the labor movement or seek membership in organizations that did not fully promote their interests.[26]

Black women recognized the poor conditions under which they and black men operated in the labor market. Their many and varied expressions of dissatisfaction with their plight as wage earners reflected their working-class consciousness. The degree to which they did not publicly protest is more an indictment of racism and sexism in the American labor movement and of the social expectations for working women than it is an indicator of a lack of working-class consciousness among black women.

The black female domestic quoted in the opening paragraph was politically astute enough to recognize that there was an economic imbalance in the world, in the same sense that Marxists and socialists spoke of "haves" and "have-nots." Rather than encouraging revolutionary activity, however, she relied instead on her religious beliefs for a solution. She remarked: "If I were the Lord, I just wouldn't let nobody get but so rich and I wouldn't let nobody get but so poor. Life just seemed so unfair to me. It still does look that way to me. I have worked hard and tried to carry myself right, but I don't have very much to show for it. If I was the Lord, I wouldn't let things be like they are now. There wouldn't be any of this some-people-with money and some-people-with-nothing."[27]

With such a clear understanding of the inequities of the world, based on a lifetime of oppression and hard work, most black women and men, and oppressed people in general, needed less consciousness-raising to become part of the vanguard of a labor movement that sought to eradicate injustices against oppressed workers, regardless of color, gender, religion, and ethnic background. For a group of wage earners who had worked so hard all their lives, who daily experienced the sufferings of oppressed workers, and whose cultural and religious ethos embodied a deep respect for work, whether for pay or not, a working-class spirit and consciousness was always present. In order for it to surface more fully, it only needed to be encouraged and harnessed by the trade-unionist movement of the Progressive Era. Maybe if the trade unionists had responded, workers would have been the real victors in the struggle against industrial capitalism in Progressive Era America.

Notes

1. John Langston Gwaltney, *Drylongso: A Self-Portrait of Black America* (New York: Vintage, 1981), 173-74. These narratives offer an excellent insight into the thinking of everyday, ordinary ("drylongso") black women and men on a variety of subjects.

2. According to Gwaltney, "the primary status of a black person is that accorded by the people he or she lives among. It is based upon assessments of that person's fidelity to core black standards." See Gwaltney, *Drylongso,* xxiii, xxx. On the subject of status, sociologist Bonnie Thornton Dill writes that "values in the Black community . . . attribute status to success along personal and family dimensions in addition to the basic ones of occupation, education, and income." See Dill, "The Means To Put My Children Through: Child-Rearing Goals and Strategies among Black Female Domestic Servants," in La Frances Rodgers-Rose, ed., *The Black Woman* (Beverly Hills, Calif.: Sage, 1980), 114.

3. While not having black women as their focus, several recent studies of women's labor market work have added to a general understanding of attitudes and life experiences of working-class women. These works represent an important shift in the scholarship in the field, which has traditionally been preoccupied with male wage-earners and white middle-class, professional women. In addition to Cynthia Costello, "Working Women's Con-

sciousness: Traditional or Oppositional?" in Carol Groneman and Mary Beth Norton, eds., *"To Toil the Livelong Day": America's Women at Work, 1780-1980* (Ithaca, N.Y.: Cornell Univ. Press, 1987), consult the other essays in this anthology and in Ruth Milkman, ed., *Women, Work and Protest: A Century of U.S. Women's Labor History* (Boston: Routledge & Kegan Paul, 1985).

4. For statistical data about the labor force participation of black men and women in the United States during this period, consult, for example, U.S. Department of Interior, Census Office, *Compendium of the Eleventh Census, 1890* (Washington, D.C.), pt. 3; U.S. Department of Commerce and Labor, Bureau of the Census, *Special Reports-Occupations at the Twelfth Census: 1900* (Washington, D.C.); U.S. Department of Commerce, Bureau of the Census, *United States Census of Population: 1910* (Washington, D.C.), vol. 4, *Occupations;* and U.S. Department of Commerce, Bureau of the Census, *Fourteenth Census of the United States, 1920: Population* (Washington, D.C.), vol. 4, *Occupation.* See also Joseph A. Hill, *Women in Gainful Occupations, 1870 to 1920,* Census Monograph IX (Washington, D.C.: GPO, 1929).

5. For wage figures, consult Elizabeth Ross Haynes, "Negroes in Domestic Service in the United States," *Journal of Negro History* 8 (October 1928): 389-421.

6. Giles B. Jackson and D. Webster Davis, *The Industrial History of the Negro Race of the United States* (1911; reprint, New York: Books for Libraries Press, 1971), 133.

7. By contrast, the level of unmarried black and unmarried white female employment was comparable (75 percent and 70 percent, respectively). For statistical information about the married black female population in the labor force, consult U.S. Department of Commerce, Bureau of the Census, *Negroes in the United States, 1920-1932* (Washington, D.C.), 151-52.

8. For a discussion of the cultural basis for differences in black and nonblack (in this case, Italian) perception of married women's employment, see Elizabeth H. Pleck, "A Mother's Wages: Income Earning among Married Italian and Black Women, 1896-1911," in Nancy F. Cott and Elizabeth H. Pleck, eds., *A Heritage of Her Own: Toward a New Social History of American Women* (New York: Simon & Schuster, 1979).

9. See Gwaltney, *Drylongso,* for a discussion of core black cultural values, those shared by "the prudent black American masses." For a discussion of antebellum and postbellum black cultural ethos, consult Lawrence Levine, *Black Culture and Consciousness: Afro-American Folk Thought from Slavery to Freedom* (New York: Oxford Univ. Press, 1977).

10. See Pleck, "Mother's Wages." Black children, especially teenagers, engaged in paid work but not nearly as much as children in immigrant families. The importance of sacrificing for one's children is addressed in Dill, "Means to Put My Children Through." Recognizing the obstacles that blacks were likely to face in the job market did not deter black mothers from sacrificing for their children's education. To black women interviewed for the study, Dill writes: "Education was seen as a means of equipping oneself for whatever breaks might occur in the nation's pattern of racial exclusion" (112).

11. Zora Neale Hurston, *Dust Tracks on a Road* (Philadelphia: Lippincott, 1942), 5.

12. Ambivalent feelings about a number of issues, including wage-earning wives, are prevalent among groups who live in oppressed ethnic and racial communities in which survival dictates one set of behavioral patterns and the "national marketplace of issues and ideas" (where white middle-class values predominate) dictates another. Gwaltney, *Drylongso,* xxvi.

13. Professional women maintained that educating the children of poor blacks was

part of their moral and social obligation as educated women. The latter view is revealed in numerous published writings by professional women of the period. See, for example, Josephine Bruce, "What Has Education Done for Colored Women?" *Voice of the Negro* 1 (July 1904): 277-79, and Rosa D. Bowser, "What Role Is the Educated Negro Woman to Play in the Uplifting of Her Race?" in D.W. Culp, ed., *Twentieth-Century Negro Literature: Or, A Cyclopedia of Thought on the Vital Topics Relating to the American Negro* (Toronto: J.L. Nichols, 1920), 167-85. For an analysis of educated women's perceptions of their work in one urban community, see Sharon Harley, "Beyond the Classroom: The Organizational Lives of Black Female Educators in the District of Columbia, 1890-1930," *Journal of Negro Education* 51 (Summer 1982): 254-65.

14. The work attitudes and behavior of married black women often resembled that of the young white American wage-earners depicted in Leslie Woodcock Tentler, *Wage-Earning Women: Industrial Work and Family Life in the United States, 1900–1930* (New York: Oxford Univ. Press, 1979). Tentler's definition of working-class consciousness conforms to that of scholars who limit it exclusively to trade-unionist actions and collective bargaining. This issue is examined in Alice Kessler-Harris, "Where Are the Organized Women Workers?" *Feminine Studies* 3 (Fall 1975): 92-110. Motivated by a different set of historical and economic circumstances, black women have had a much longer and deeper history of developing survival strategies and protest than most white women. The class-consciousness and activities of wage-earning black women represent an extension of their "private troubles to the arena of public issues," as described in Cheryl Townsend Gilkes, "'Holding Back the Ocean with a Broom': Black Women and Community Work," in Rodgers-Rose, *Black Woman.*

15. William M. Tuttle, Jr., "Labor Conflict and Racial Violence: The Black Worker in Chicago, 1894-1919," in Milton Cantor, ed., *Black Labor in America* (Westport, Conn.: Negro Universities Press, 1969), 98. The slow pace at which blacks joined labor unions can be attributed to a number of factors, including the racial antagonism of union officials and white workers, manipulation by employers, and the availability of nonunion rather than union jobs for black workers. Focusing on black workers in Chicago, William M. Tuttle, Jr., discusses the obstacles to organizing black workers. Despite the barriers to organizing wage-earning women, Alice Kessler-Harris writes that, given the opportunity, women became active and committed union members. Trade unionists' failure, especially that of the American Federation of Labor, to seriously organize women is largely responsible for women's absence from the organized labor movement. See Kessler-Harris, "Where Are the Organized Women Workers?"

16. The idea of "helping out" was often an effort on the part of wage-earning women to lessen the importance of the market work and, if married, to overcome their husband's objections. See Pleck, "Mother's Wages," 386.

17. A rare look at the history of black women's collective actions is revealed in historian Rosalyn Terborg-Penn, "Survival Strategies among Afro-American Women Workers: A Continuing Process," in Ruth Milkman, ed., *Women, Work & Protest: A Century of U.S. Women's Labor History* (Boston: Routledge & Kegan Paul, 1985). The frequently militant attitudes that black domestics express toward their work and work conditions are revealed in two recent studies, based largely on life histories obtained through oral interviews: Dill, "Means to Put My Children Through," and Elizabeth Clark-Lewis, "'This Work Had A End': African-American Domestic Workers in Washington, D.C., 1910-1940," in Groneman and Norton, *To Toil the Livelong Day,* 196-212. See also

Verta Mae (Grosvenor), *Thursdays and Every Other Sunday Off* (New York: Doubleday, 1972). For information about black women's involvement in the American trade-unionist movement during the Progressive Era, consult Philip S. Foner, *Women and the American Labor Movement: From Colonial Times to the Eve of World War I* (New York: Free Press, 1979), and *Women and the American Labor Movement: From World War I to the Present* (New York: Free Press, 1980); Barbara Mayer Wertheimer, *We Were There: The Story of Working Women in America* (New York: Pantheon, 1977); and Jacqueline Jones, *Labor of Love, Labor of Sorrow: Black Women, Work, and the Family from Slavery to the Present* (New York: Basic Books, 1985).

18. "An earnest teacher," letter to Mrs. Raymond B. Morgan, Oct. 23, 1923, Terrell Papers, Box 4, Moorland Spingarn Research Center (hereafter cited as MSRC), Founders Library, Howard University, Washington, D.C. Letters to Mary Church Terrell and other board members reveal the depth of black professional women's concerns about wage and mobility issues in one urban community. See, for example, Fredericka Douglass Sprague to Mary Church Terrell, Nov. 5, 1907, Terrell Papers, Ctr. 4, Library of Congress (LC); and Eva F. Ross to Mary C. Terrell, Jan. 5, 1907, Terrell Papers, Ctr. 4, LC.

19. For a discussion of labor efforts to "include" black women during the war years, see Foner, *Women and the American Labor Movement: From World War I to the Present,* ch. 1. Labor organizing was not a new phenomenon for black women during the Progressive Era. In the 1880s, black working women in such occupations as housekeepers, farmers, chambermaids, and washerwomen comprised fifteen women assemblies affiliated with the Knights of Labor. Assemblies of black domestics could be found in Washington, D.C., Norfolk, Virginia, Wilmington, North Carolina, and Philadelphia. See Foner, *Women and the American Labor Movement: From Colonial Times to the Eve of World War I,* and Jones, *Labor of Love.*

20. For a discussion of the White Rose Industrial Associations and other Associations for the Protection of Negro Women, consult Terborg-Penn, "Survival Strategies," 142-43.

21. See Harley, "Beyond the Classroom."

22. Terborg-Penn, "Survival Strategies," 143.

23. *Opportunity* 2 (Dec. 1924): 383, cited in Evelyn Brooks Barnett (Higginbotham), "Nannie Burroughs and the Education of Black Women," in Sharon Harley and Rosalyn Terborg-Penn, eds., *The Afro-American Woman: Struggles and Images* (Port Washington, N.Y.: Kennikat, 1978), 98-101.

24. Terborg-Penn, "Survival Strategies," 144.

25. Foner, *Women in the American Labor Movement: From World War I to the Present,* 274-75.

26. Ibid.

27. Gwaltney, *Drylongso,* 175-76.

5

Landscapes of Subterfuge: Working-Class Neighborhoods and Immigrant Women

ARDIS CAMERON

Several years ago when I first began collecting oral histories for my dissertation, I interviewed a 90-year-old former textile operative who described herself as not having "worked very much" in her youth, doing only "bits of mill work" and "pieces of this and that." Prodded to describe these "bits and pieces" in more detail, she drew what is now a familiar, if still underanalyzed, portrait of female labor in the Progressive Era:

> It all depended on the season, on the kids, on what ya needed to get by. You see, there was always something to do, you know. In the fall I'd put up [500] quarts of tomatoes, two to three barrels of whole peppers, cucumbers, and winter pears, two or three crocks of eggplant—our neighbor, she was Italian and she did this good, so I learned how too. Then, when times were better, sometimes we'd put up two pigs, that's right, I'd do the sausage . . . oh, and sometimes rabbits, I'd cure them too. Then sometimes there were the boarders, and they had wash and I'd cook for them too. My husband he was often out of work, you know, slack times, so in the summers or spring I'd do a bit of mill work, or if we needed clothes as the winter comes or, you know, something like that. They all knew me. Oh sure, here comes Olga. I could usually get jobs 'cause they knew me and they knew I was a good worker.[1]

As it turned out, this Lithuanian woman worked her "bit" in the mills well into the 1930s as necessity and the seasons dictated.

If Olga's initial description of herself as "not having worked very much" suggests that notions of work have come to be identified with a public arena of paid labor, her more detailed definition of "bits of mill work" calls attention away from the divisions between paid and unpaid labor. Drawing together efforts in the kitchen, the garden, and the laundry with those in the mill, this account of female labor accentuates the complex connections between the supposedly separate worlds of unpaid domestic labor and wage work performed outside the home. As many recent studies of poor and working women have shown, in the real world of proletarian daily life, the task of "piecing together livelihoods" involved women in a complicated set of activities which were seldom understood as distinct from or independent of the home, the neighborhood, or the community.[2] Whether in the streets of antebellum New York City, the barrios of turn-of-the-century Tampa, or the working-class neighborhoods of pre-World War I Lawrence, Massachusetts, poor women juggled wage-force participation with the ever-changing circumstances of their households, their families, and their neighbors.[3] The lives of working-class women, therefore, are best understood at the intersection of production and consumption, as the myriad "bits" of female labor converged in the daily struggle to make ends meet.

Analyzing the working environment of proletarian women means exploring not only geographic space (the neighborhood and the shop floor) but social space as well—what one theorist has described as a "landscape of subterfuge."[4] It also means asking not where consciousness is raised, but how. How did women's position in the sexual division of labor in the home, the workplace, and the community shape common-sense notions of the real world? How did strategies of survival translate into "street smart" concepts of life and labor? How did laboring women come to understand their lives as women? As workers? This essay, then, is concerned less with the form and location of women's work than with its meaning. Specifically, it seeks to understand how immigrant women in one particular New England textile town—Lawrence, Massachusetts—thought about the world and their place in it. Attending to female acts, gestures, and space, it is an attempt to move beyond the more readily available journals and speeches of the "aristocracy of labor"—usually male craftsmen—and unravel the more opaque strands of working-class culture and politics, those developed not in the Union hall but in what Natalie Davis once described as "the dangerous nooks and crannies"[5] of women's lives.

While textile manufacturing was not the largest employer of immigrant women in the years before World War I, the industry played a central role (and still does today) in determining immigrant destinations. Labor intensive, it offered the possibility of work for every member of the family, regardless of age, skill, and sex. Thus, while emigration from southern and eastern Europe typically involved large waves of male migrants acting as "pioneers" for Old World families, textile towns received a more evenly balanced sex ratio of immigrants. In New England, especially in Massachusetts, where cotton and woolen textile manufacturing dominated the industrial landscape, women outnumbered men even among the foreign-born.[6]

In the city of Lawrence, which by 1900 was one of the world's largest manufacturers of woolen and worsted cloth, immigrant women not only outnumbered their male counterparts from southern and eastern Europe but were also more likely to have experience in textile manufacturing prior to emigration. According to a 1909 government study of Lawrence woolen and worsted operatives, almost 50 percent of female operatives who reported their occupation before migration had been employed previously in textile manufacturing.[7] While most men from France, England, and Belgium had also worked as operatives, the overwhelming majority of men from Lithuania, Italy, and Russia, as well as Ireland and French Canada, had worked family farms in the Old Country while daughters, sisters, and, at times, wives entered the local factory. This was true even among operatives from predominantly rural areas where industrialization was slow to develop. For example, factory experience was rare for women in Italy, yet southern Italian immigrant women in Lawrence mills were fourteen times more likely than their husands, fathers, or brothers to have worked in a mill before coming to America.[8]

The process of establishing toeholds in textile towns, therefore, was never an exclusively male responsibility. Wives, sisters, and daughters played critical roles in securing immigrant livelihoods; the economic potential of female skills and experience was carefully considered before financing emigration for family "pioneers." This was especially true among Syrian and Jewish families, in which sisters and wives "not infrequently" preceded brothers and husbands to the New World.[9]

Textile manufacturing enhanced a family's ability to secure cash in the New World and provided women with the means to fulfill traditional female obligations such as child rearing, food preparation, and laundry. A notoriously seasonal industry with periodic layoffs and chronic underemployment, cloth production was adaptable to women's rhythms of reproduction, accommodating both changes in the female life cycle and female obligations to kin when male support was absent. A Portuguese wife explained to a government investigator in 1911 how her employment in textile manufacturing blended with female duties. Entering the mills in August, she worked through the fall and winter "in order to make money to buy winter clothing." During this period, she would work twelve hours a day in the mill before beginning the second portion of her "double day" at home caring for the family. This wife, for example, "baked a considerable proportion of the bread used by the family, sometimes baking at night while employed at the mill."[10] During the mill's slack season, she took in children of working neighbors in the same way that she boarded her three children while in the mill. Like Olga, this anonymous woman continued traditional patterns of supplementing the family purse with whatever "bits" were available.

Lawrence offered immigrant families a way to maximize their earning power and hasten the process of emigration. Once in Lawrence, low wages, escalating prices, and underemployment accentuated women's critical position in the household. Only 18 percent of almost three hundred immigrant homes surveyed in 1911 consisted of households in which a husband alone provided the family's entire income.[11] "In Lawrence," observed the *New York Call,* "all the family must work if the family is to live."[12]

Survival in the immigrant community, however, was seldom strictly a "family affair." As recent historians of immigration have made clear, immigrant families were in a constant process of formation, as Old World ties were broken and only gradually or partially replaced in New World circumstances.[13] In Lawrence, as in other industrial cities before the First World War, village sons and daughters entered new households in a complex assortment of relationships. Migrations typically took place in stages, with new immigrants linking up with cousins, sisters, brothers, fathers, and husbands, as well as entering the New World households as friends, former village neighbors, and friends of friends.

"Bitter about her marriage" and unable to find work in Plymouth, Sara Axelrod left her husband and brother behind when she went to Lawrence. Locating a friend of her brother's best friend, Sara found lodgings in a boarding house of Lithuanians, Poles, and Russian Jews.[14] Similarly, Annie Rogosz, coming to Lawrence as a widow from Syria in 1906, moved into an apartment headed by Josephine Stuka, a Polish operative whose two daughters also worked in the mills. Annie and her two children shared rooms with this family and three other boarders.[15] Preferring to "live as they please," as one government investigator put it, immigrant residents of Lawrence's working-class neighborhoods thus shaped family life in ways that reproduced the emotional and financial functions, if not form, of Old World households. Substituting for absent relatives, neighbors and friends frequently assumed roles as surrogate or fictive kin, so that sharing apartments, rooms, and even beds was taken for granted in immigrant neighborhoods.[16]

Such arrangements disrupted traditional household economies and changed customary patterns of authority. When the father of fifteen-year-old Josephine Lis warned his daughter to stay at home one night, she casually dismissed his wishes. "I just took a notion," she explained when arrested later for disorderly conduct. "I wanted to see what was happening."[17] While loosening parental control, newly created household arrangements also nourished aspirations at odds with customary expectations and practices. "I had been living with my cousin and his married friends in Haverhill," explained one woman, "but he wanted to marry me, to settle down like at home. . . . Oh no, I didn't come all the way to America to get married! So I go. I found rooms with a couple, two boys, a Pole woman, and three Lithuanians . . . and we did what we want."[18]

Denounced by Lawrence reformers as both dangerous and all-too-frequent, collective living arrangements helped immigrants reduce costs while broadening networks of support. Women especially found such arrangements useful in easing the burdens of a double day. Compelled to share cramped and crowded physical surroundngs, women utilized the proximity of neighbors, friends, and kin to mutual advantage, socializing a variety of domestic tasks and customizing Old World principles of mutuality and collectivity. Throughout Lawrence's densely packed immigrant neighborhoods in the "Plains," female collaboration was routine and extensive, and what often began as informal arrangements frequently developed into more systematic patterns of exchange. Even the time-honored custom of swapping household items became formalized as women sought to stretch scarce resources. According to a shocked member of the city's Board of Health, kitchen utensils "regularly hung on neighbors' houses,"[19] clearly situated in such a way as to be of service to more than one household.

Casual methods of child care, in which mothers routinely depended on the watchful eyes of others, were similarly transformed into well-organized practices. Increasingly forced into the mill by the "lash of youthful hunger," mothers placed their children in the apartment of a woman who, because of a recent birth or because she had too many young children herself, could not work in the mill. For a modest fee, or in exchange for food, these children's boarding houses formalized traditions of reciprocity, in the process providing an additional female space where women shared information and collective grievances. "We'd go there early in the morning, where a woman, a neighbor, would take care of us," recalled a former boarder. "She'd send us out to school and back, have our lunch—very common. It would always be a woman that was in the building. You were brought up as if you were her child."[20] At night women returned from work and collected children, but not without making contact with other mothers. Often the day's events were shared, future meetings arranged, and mutual concerns aired.[21]

Female collaborative activities, forged out of necessity, fostered networks that took root and strengthened, as women sought to provide for families and mitigate the harsh realities of industrial life. Mutual dependence and cooperative assistance bound women together in a latticework of reciprocity, as friends, neighbors, and disparate kin sought to train and protect children, care for the sick, feed the hungry, keep house, and provide for families and neighbors.

As primary caretakers of homes and families, women also found themelves involved in complex patterns of exchange that frequently cut across categories of ownership and the barriers of ethnicity. "Shops," recalled one resident, "were all mixed up." Stores on Amesbury included "a barber shop run by Italian men, a cobbler—he was Armenian—and then a big Portuguese store."[22] Shopping on busy Elm Street, Lithuanian, Jewish, and Syrian women, often accompanied by their daughters, bargained with Italian shop owners. On Concord Street, Russian and German women mingled with Irish and Portuguese in Faris Brox's popular Syrian fruit store. "Everyone was there," recalled one former resident of Concord Street, "and the stores stayed open 'til late at night."[23]

While grocery stores provided women with critical contact points, "women's work" provided additional pathways to cooperation and mutual exchange. Growing up close to the heart of the Plains, Antonietta Carpinone recalled the mingling of ethnic customs and cultures that often resulted from the exchange of food and recipes. "A German girl taught me how to make doughnuts. The smells from her house, you see, were—well, you know, you wanted to know what they make inside."[24] Food was also the wedge that overcame Mrs. Rocco's shyness toward her German neighbors. "Our yard had a cherry tree and groups of German women would come to gather the fruits. They taught us good ways to make the fruit."[25] At times, such contacts led to long-lasting and occasionally secret friendships. "My father," explained Anna Marino, "never knew our mother had Syrian friends. They would visit each other in the day and eventually my mother could cook like a Syrian."[26] For at least one former resident, such unambiguous contact shaped forever her understanding of American ethnicity. When asked in 1979 if her Lithuanian home on Brook Street had been in an ethnic ghetto, Amelia Stundza told the interviewer: "Yes, oh yes, Lithuanians lived on the first and second floor, Italians on the third, Jews lived across the street, oh boy, you bettcha, it was."[27]

While such experiences of collaboration and exchange were both ordinary and routine, they played a central role in developing both female self-concepts and a consciousness of kind. Standards of behavior, codes of conduct, notions of right and wrong, concepts of fairness and justice—and of manhood and womanhood—took shape as women exchanged local gossip, compared prices, shared advice, offered aid, nursed kin and neighbors, made friends, and built alliances. On street corners and stoops, in kitchens and markets, at bathhouses and public laundries, and on walks to and from factories, news was dissected, newcomers introduced, local "no-accounts" unmasked, community delinquents railed against, names of cheats circulated, misfortunes shared, and misfeasance tried and judged.

In the process, women sorted the common sense from the commonplace. Identifying "no-accounts," for example, involved women in a ritualized retelling of old scandals in which one neighbor and then another recalled past insults, "black acts," and "dirty"cheats. These were supplemented with vivid descriptions of actual or hoped for revenge, encouragement of others to assess the seriousness of the offense, and collective confirmation or contesting of individual action. Out of such negotiations women continually separated right from wrong, the scoundrel from the hero, the true from the false, the alien from the trusted.

As many recent theorists have demonstrated, such an "ordering of things" is far more than a casual process of differentiation, for it sets out and codifies for groups the "conceptual boundaries through which all social action flows." Establishing a frame of reference, the process authorizes one set of "truths," making others marginal or invisible. From the largely unconscious collective wisdom it extracts the logic that makes certain acts and behaviors understandable to some, while incredible and even inconceivable to others. Such conceptual boundaries, while widely perceived as "natural," are nevertheless in constant formation and reformation and in many ways represent the most contested of all terrains. As Robert Darnton wryly put it, "Pigeon holing is . . . an exercise in power."[28]

In other words, female networks were not merely points of contact for individual women but points of reference through which disparate women viewed the world and invested it with meaning. Converting plebian neighborhoods into "landscapes of subterfuge," these autonomous social spaces allowed women to develop and sustain a world of vision and value relatively independent of husbands, bosses, priests, and teachers. These spaces constituted what Victor Turner labeled *communitas,* a "bond uniting people over and above any formal social bonds." Such *communitas* or "anti-structures," argues Turner, are characteristic of a community in a liminal state—that is, "in a middle stage between one set of structural relationships and another—and operate not only in addition to, but on some occasions in opposition to, the usual components of 'social structure.'"[29]

Viewed in this way, female networks take on importance not only as a system of female exchange and reciprocity but as active components in the process of definition, what has also been called the construction of meaning or the struggle over the real. Anna Marino's friendship with her Syrian neighbor was thus both possible and appropriate to Anna, while alien and suspect to her husband. If at times the cause of domestic disputes, such anti-structures, like the female networks that laced through immigrant neighborhoods, were also capable of setting into motion larger struggles, which, as in the case of the Lawrence strike of 1912, called into question fundamental social and economic structures.[30]

Rooted in the sexual division of labor, female networks also allowed women to develop sharp and exacting notions of both female duty and female rights, what some historians have defined as a female consciousness. Honed as women performed domestic labors and strained to provide a decent life for themselves and their families, female consciousness spoke to women's traditional role as "breadgivers and sustainers of life."[31] Female consciousness, a product of female collective efforts, also accentuated the collective or "public" nature of individual misfortunes. Participation in daily rituals of reciprocity strengthened ties between women and called attention to the interconnectedness of individual lives.

Immigrant women, mutually dependent on each other and equally vulnerable to the "vicissitudes of fortune," shared the burdens of economic hardship and understood that loss of income, economic deterioration, and poverty were seldom the results of personal failure. Sensitive to fluctuations in the cost of food, rent, and fuel, women also understood that "changes in the cost of living felt by one would be felt by all."[32] Thus, Lawrence newspapers were filled with brief but telling accounts of neighborhood skirmishes between "knots" of women and various merchants, city officials, and landlords. Typically such disturbances began when neighbors came to the aid or defense of friends and kin, yet even newcomers could at times count on communal pressures to redress grievances.

If female reciprocity helped women understand the public nature of private tragedies and failures, it was the pursuit of female rights and duties that enhanced women's concepts of material rights. Whether coming to the aid of a friend and neighbor or protesting food increases, collective action led women to an expanded awareness of the world around them and encouraged further efforts to negotiate and agitate for rights. Daily events and disasters, including illness, poor food, high prices, rent hikes, unemployment, and wage reductions, could be placed in a larger context when women found their roles as primary caretakers of the home and family undercut by the public world of prices and wages, of alien law and market forces.

Female consciousness developed in response to a sexually segregated world, but it did not emerge in opposition to men. Unlike middle-class women, who tended to define themselves through a set of contrasting characteristics—morality versus corruption, frailty versus strength, virtue versus vice—which one scholar called an "ontology of sex,"[33] proletarian women developed self-concepts relationally, that is, in connection with other women and not necessarily in reference to men.

Sexual difference, therefore, had less meaning as an arbiter of status and power in the working-class community than as a signifier of complementary strategies to make ends meet. In part, this was the result of ongoing disruptions in traditional household economies, as the exigencies of both migration and textile manufacturing transformed gender systems. In neighborhoods like the Plains, where household survival was increasingly dependent on a woman's ability to make a shrewd bargain, to stretch one meal into three, and to move easily in and out of the wage labor force, sexual hierarchies underwent continual realignment and negotiation. As mill hands and machine tenders, of course, neither men nor women had more than limited control over the productive process, but skill and knowledge were seldom monopolized by fathers and sons. This was especially true in textile centers, where the process of de-skilling had seriously eroded exclusionary practices and traditions of a skilled aristocracy of labor. While male artisans and craftsmen could claim a degree of superiority based on their ability to teach household members the details of their craft, textile skills were widely dispersed throughout households. Mothers and wives, as well as fathers and husbands, shared a common position as "learners" passing on information to children and greenhorns with a rough equality of position.

The balance of authority in Lawrence's neighborhoods also provided a constant and dramatic contrast to shop-floor relations, which systematically sought to subordinate the work force in general and women in particular. Hierarchically structured to teach all workers the rudiments of industrial time, work, and discipline, shop-floor authority was also patriarchically constructed, infusing the workplace with notions of female submission, passivity, and frailty. While all workers were denied control over the productive process to varying degrees, women were specifically and continually denied a claim to knowledge or skill, often lending credence to the ideology of gender built on female marginality, subordination, and inferiority. Subsequently, even skilled work performed by women was seen by management as semi-skilled or unskilled labor. In other words, at the point of production, women confronted a world that promoted what one historian has called a "specific psychology of female subordination,"[34] which enhanced men's ability to define their womanhood and control female labor power.

As seasonal household heads, primary distributors and negotiators of scarce resources, and essential contributors to the family budgets, poor and laboring women were situated in a position to experience the contradictions between the observed reality of female economic importance and shop-floor policies that emphasized female marginality, subordination, and dependence. Female mill hands were typically labeled by employers and census takers as operatives, though they varied a great deal in skill, and both families and neighbors recognized and appreciated the differences. Female menders were especially highly regarded, comprising their own aristocracy of labor; like their male counterparts, they often switched from one mill to another, following the highest wages. One mender, Annie Weisenback, who rose to some national prominence as the only female member of the general strike committee in 1912, had earned a reputation as one of the most skilled and highly paid operatives in the city of Lawrence. During the strike itself, husbands, wives, daughters, and parents usually supported each other's efforts, yet where disagreement was strong enough to warrant public notice, wives and daughters typically ignored husbands and fathers, calmly continuing their strike activities. The mother of Amelia Stundza, for example, stayed on the picket line even after she got "hit in the head by a club" and "pleaded with"[35] by her husband. Participation in the strike, explained one female activist, "is but our duty."[36]

Identifying themselves in terms of female rights and duties, proletarian women developed criteria for female behavior that clashed with middle-class codes of femininity and respectability. While middle-class reformers at the City Mission were outraged by the many "schemes" of "unruly" and "saucy" women, who according to one city official went "to extreme means to outwit our [welfare] officers," working-class women defended their actions in the belief of a womanhood denied. "You bet I marched down there with the others," explained one Italian woman when describing a particularly "hungry" afternoon. "Them with all that money and a family goin' hungry. They don't own the earth. We gave that guy hell 'til we got milk for that family. I spit, I was so mad."[37]

City officials were not the only ones to bemoan the aggressive "scheming" and unruly behavior of the town's "female elements." Priests were often horrified to find their female parishioners entering the local YWCA for the sole purpose of securing "free lunches and hot showers." One cleric was especially well-remembered for his notorious "peeping" through the windows in order to catch wayward Catholic girls, whom he would publicly expose as "agents of the devil." Despite threats, neighborhood women continued to send their daughters to the YWCA, for as one woman put it: "Why not? They have the food and we have the hunger."[38] Convinced that women were deliberately exaggerating their plight, and increasingly upset by the hostility of claimants who bullied town officers, city fathers moved both the City Mission and the Board of Health from the neighborhood and into city hall. They hoped that the move would allow application for aid to take place in an orderly fashion, by individual petition rather than by collective negotiation with neighbors and kin.

If reformers sought to make private the mechanisms of public relief, they also hoped to domesticate its recipients. "Just as soon as women disregard constituted authority," wrote one community leader, "why, then you have the foundation for all that follows."[39] Far more than a public nuisance, unruly women increasingly represented to an anxious bourgeoisie the unraveling of the basic fabric of the social order. Images of female rum holes and kitchen bars, of saucy girls and hoydenish women, and of treating (by which, announced a shocked city missionary, "friendships among women are renewed and cemented by strong drink")[40] filled city documents and buttressed the progressive agenda. Linking women's participation in the public sphere with promiscuity and gender deviance, Lawrence reformers pushed for new codes that required widows intending to operate their husbands' businesses to submit written statements of respectability. All wives seeking to do business on their own were also required to obtain a special license. Similarly, peddling, a popular occupation for women, especially among Syrians, was increasingly curtailed by high fees and stiff fines.

Regulating women's public activity coincided with national efforts to recast the private lives of the urban poor. Women especially were targets for such campaigns, although reformers were "doubly anxious" over "children and defective girls," the "potential mothers in our midst,"[41] as one city official put it. In settlement houses, youth clubs, evening classes, and mothers' clubs, as well as in pageants and parades, immigrant women confronted the "respectable" world of domesticity and American home-making, constructed "on a particular middle-class configuration of possessions and housekeeping practices and a particular structure of family relations."[42] Distrustful of autonomous women and girls who overstepped the boundaries of such a world, reformers were especially distressed by the "neglectful" mother who conspired to keep children out of schools and in the mills. Speaking to the Andover Women's Club, a gathering place for the Lawrence elite, Florence Kelley, organizer of the newly created National Child Labor Committee and general secretary of the National Consumer's League, advocated the adoption of stricter guidelines for identifying children in Lawrence's mills. Kelley argued that weight, height, age, and literacy should be taken into account and that identification papers should have physical descriptions to prevent falsification of working papers.[43]

The notions that public relief was a private affair, that individual efforts to peddle and hawk were public concerns, and that personal decisions over children's obligation were the stuff of courts and jails did not fit easily into the context of immigrant life. Immigrants responded to the resulting policies with not only puzzlement and fear, but a hardening and politicizing of familiar practices.

Keenly aware of the burdens that such public acts placed on immigrant households, neighborhood women routinely organized to outwit impossible laws, what one woman called "the deeds of *guzitaekmanas*," or "men in brass buttons."[44] Complained one city father: "Papers are usually of a relative, a neighbor, or an older brother or sister, working in some other mill or out of town or perhaps at home ill!" Social workers agreed: "How little value can be placed upon the mother's oath in this respect is notorious."[45] For women in the Plains, the discovery of an underaged worker was a time of uncertainty and crisis, for it threatened to sever the precarious threads women had spun to sustain life. Describing the emotional turmoil that surrounded her removal from the mill, a former twister remembered the experience as "a kind of disaster" and "a terrible blow." News of the calamity spread rapidly; by nightfall, "all the women came to my mother and told her not to worry. Everyone was angry and in a few days I got a new name, new papers, a new job."[46]

Participation in collective schemes and sporadic skirmishes with city officials, clerics, store owners, and landlords further cemented communal notions of justice, what one former militant called her "just dues" and that workers referred to as a "square deal." Removing city agencies from the neighborhood did not stop women in the Plains from pressuring governmental agents for material rights. Situated in a position to experience the intersection of the public with the private, working women were encouraged to define a wide range of so-called personal issues as publicly relevant. Determined to feed families, women railed against and bullied city officials for aid they deemed not charity but their right. When pleading and bargaining failed, women utilized whatever resources were on hand to fulfill female duties and reclaim lost rights. While the action varied with each crisis, women's belief in the collective or public nature of private, individual misfortune consistently informed group response and helped women mold grievances into specific targets of protest. Violators of the common good were identified and, depending on the nature of the offense, became subjects of derision, public ridicule, and, in extreme cases, violence. The various victims of female abuse reflected the extent to which women held more than one employer or city official accountable for their situation. In strikes, riots, and public disturbances, violence was directed not only at scabs and police, but at notorious overchargers, including a doctor and several grocers, unpopular city officials, and the Board of Health, which was painted red during the strike of 1912.[47]

Because poor and laboring women were in a social position at the intersection of the home and workplace, they did not see themselves as limited to one sphere of activity, for it was precisely their ability to monitor, regulate, and manipulate the public world of rents, prices, wages, and alien laws that allowed working-class women to fulfill female roles and obligations. Securing the bare necessities for their family brought women into the public arena not only as consumers of commodities, but as negotiators for scarce resources and advocates for familial and community needs. Whether haggling at the market, falsifying papers, or outmaneuvering landlords, women acted in ways that assumed an inherent unity between the home and the marketplace, the domestic and the commercial, and they perceived themselves as intimately involved in the comings and goings of each.

Just as in the Lawrence strike of 1912, when housewives and operatives blended and mixed to form a great human chain of strikers, issues of the home merged and overlapped with those of the workplace. Who could tell where the outrage of low wages ended and the "lash of youthful hunger" began? By what alchemy were poor health, child mortality, and filthy streets separated from shop-floor issues of overwork, poor conditions, and declining wages? Linking arms and pressing their claims shoulder to shoulder, proletarian women gave a totality to their lives, which they themselves defined as "bread and roses."

It was, of course, a slogan of hope rather than description, yet it was also an expression of possibility, not simply thought up but thought out, as women sought new sources of support and pressed their needs on an increasingly insecure municipality. Not only did proletarian women hold different thoughts, they also thought in different ways. The very opacity of those ways, as well as the possibilities and visions they produced, suggest as well the deep terrain on which power was both exercised and contested. Rather than a search for order, progressive reform might more fruitfully be explored as a contest over the "ordering of things," of identities and definitions, of images and perceptions, of concepts and meanings—what Clifford Geertz might describe as a "struggle for the real."[48] Increasingly articulated in a discourse of efficiency and order, progressivism brought forth nonetheless a politics of disorder and disordering, the kind of disordering, for example, that could prompt a ninety-year-old Lithuanian woman to tell her granddaughter's friend, "No, I never worked very much. I just did bits of mill work, and pieces of this and that."

Notes

1. Anonymous Lithuanian mill operative, interview by author, Lawrence, Massachusetts, June 1980.

2. Jeanne Boydston, "To Earn Her Daily Bread: Housework and Antebellum Working-Class Subsistence," *Radical History Review* 35 (1986): 8.

3. See especially Boydston, "To Earn"; Christine Stansell, "Women, Children, and the Uses of the Streets: Class and Gender Conflicts in New York City, 1850-1860," *Feminist Studies* 8 (Summer 1982): 309-37; Judith Smith, *Family Connections: A History of Italian and Jewish Immigrant Lives in Providence, Rhode Island, 1900-1940* (Albany: State Univ. of New York Press, 1985), see especially chapter three, 35-82.

4. Myrna M. Breitbart and Martha A. Ackelsberg, "Terrains of Protest: Reappropriation of Space and Transformation of Consciousness in Urban Struggle," unpublished paper, 24. See also Ackelsberg, "Women's Collaborative Activities and City Life: Politics and Policy," in Janet Flamming, ed., *Political Women: Current Role in State and Local Government*, vol. 8 of *Sage Yearbooks in Women's Policy Studies* (Beverly Hills, Calif.: Sage, 1984), 242-59.

5. Natalie Davis, "'Women's History' in Transition: The European Case," *Feminist Studies* 3 (Spring/Summer 1976): 83-93.

6. In New England, the ratio of males to females among foreign-born whites was 95.2 to 100 in 1890, 97.5 in 1900. For the same periods in Massachusetts, the ratio was 91.1 and 92.6. In Lawrence, the sex ratio among foreign-born whites was 82.1 in 1890,

93.0 in 1900. Yet even in 1910, at the height of immigration among the so-called new immigrants, sex ratios in Massachusetts favored women by a slim margin, 99.5. The only exception to this pattern was among the Polish between 1910 and 1920. Statistics here based upon Dianne L. Siergiej, "Early Polish Immigrants to Lawrence, Massachusetts: European Background and Statistical Profile" (Masters thesis, Tufts University, 1977), 186-95. Massachusetts, and especially Lawrence, was an exception to national patterns, suggesting the importance of female employment opportunities in determining immigrant destinations and in shaping the region's immigrant experience.

7. W. J. Lauck, "The Significance of the Situation at Lawrence: The Condition of the New England Woolen Mill Operative," *Survey* 27 (1911-1912): 1772-73. Immigration Commission, "Woolen and Worsted Goods in Representative Community A," *Immigrants in Industries, Part 4: Woolen and Worsted Goods Manufacturing, Immigration Commission Reports,* X, 61st Congress, 2d sess., Doc. 633 (Washington, D.C., 1911), 756.

8. Fourteen percent of southern Italian women in Lawrence's mills had prior factory experience, compared with 0.9% of the men, suggesting the appeal that textile centers held for many families and the important role that female labor played in family decision making. Immigration Commission, "Woolen and Worsted Goods," 270.

9. Louise Seymour Houghton, "Syrians in the United States," *Survey* 26 (1908–1909): 484, 486, 487-88.

10. "Detailed Expenditures for Food of Two Families and of Three Lodgers, by Race, August and October, 1911," in Charles P. Neil, *Report on Strike of Textile Workers in Lawrence, Massachusetts in 1912,* 62d Cong., 2d sess., Senate Doc. 870 (Washington, D.C., 1912), 82-83. In a city plagued by the overproduction of woolen cloth, it would take her three to six weeks to buy her husband a woolen suit and three to five weeks to buy herself a new suit ("Detailed Expenditures," 179e).

11. While Lithuanian and Polish immigrant women were employed to cook, clean, launder, and sew for boarders to supplement income, the French (77 percent), Syrians (42 percent), and southern Italians (38 percent) relied directly on the mill earnings of children and wives. See Donald B. Cole, *Immigrant City: Lawrence, Massachusetts, 1845-1921* (Chapel Hill: Univ. of North Carolina Press, 1963), 72; Robert E. Todd and Frank B. Sanborn, *Report of the Lawrence Survey* (Lawrence, Mass., 1912), 54-60; Siergiej, "Early Polish Immigrants," 69; and Immigration Commission, "Woolen and Worsted Goods," 784.

12. *New York Call,* Jan. 15, 1912.

13. Smith, *Family Connections,* 83.

14. Mrs. Brown and Olga Veckys, interview by author, October 18, 1981.

15. Annie Rogosz, activist file no. 023, author's possession. This file contains the names of 120 women active during the Lawrence Strike of 1912. Individual names were recorded (along with biographical materials) from contemporary accounts as well as oral histories, vital statistics, and census manuscript schedules for 1912.

16. In two half-blocks in Lawrence's Everett neighborhood, city investigators found collective living a common and "dangerous" practice. In three of the five tenements, multiple family groupings lived side by side, and 20 percent of these families consisted of three or more households. Todd and Sanborn, *Report of the Lawrence Survey,* 67, 68, 88. Lawrence as a whole ranked in the top 10 percent among American cities for residents per house, slightly exceeding eight persons for every dwelling and one and one-half residents for every room.

17. Quoted in Ardis Cameron, "Neighborhoods in Revolt: Wage-Earning Women

and Worker Militancy in Lawrence, Massachusetts, 1845-1912" (Ph.D. diss., Boston College, 1986), 265.

18. Elizabeth Vilkaite, interview by author, Aug. 1981.

19. Todd and Sandborn, *Report of Lawrence Survey,* 68.

20. Ezilda Murphy, interview by Clarissa A. Poirier, June 27, 1979, Oral History Project, Folder No. 48, Immigrant City Archives, Lawrence, Massachusetts.

21. See Ardis Cameron, "Bread and Roses Revisited: Women's Culture and Worker Militancy in Lawrence, Massachusetts," in Ruth Milkman, ed., *Women, Work, and Protest: A Century of Women's Labor History* (London: Routledge & Kegan Paul, 1985), 50-51.

22. Dora Swartz, interview by author, Aug. 12, 1981.

23. Quoted in Cameron, "Bread and Roses Revisited," 48.

24. Antonietta Carpinone, interview by author, Oct. 25, 1981.

25. Consiglia Teutonica, interview by author, Sept. 6, 1981.

26. Quoted in Cameron, "Bread and Roses Revisited," 52.

27. Amelia Stundza, interview by Jonas Stundza, June 7, 1979, Folder No. 25, Oral History Project, Immigrant City Archives, Lawrence, Massachusetts.

28. Robert Darnton, *The Great Cat Massacre and Other Episodes in French Cultural History* (New York: Vintage, 1985), 193. See also Michel Foucault, *The Order of Things: An Archeology of the Human Sciences* (New York: 1973).

29. Victor Turner, *Dramas, Fields and Metaphors: Symbolic Action in Human Society* (Ithaca: Cornell Univ. Press, 1974), 45-57, 272-98.

30. See Cameron, "Bread and Roses Revisited."

31. For women of the popular classes, such differences have been located in the division of labor by sex, whereby female obligations and responsibilities center on care of the home and family. This focus creates a sense of rights that, according to Temma Kaplan, provides "motive force for actions different from those Marxist or feminist theory generally try to explain." Temma Kaplan, "Female Consciousness and Collective Action: The Case of Barcelona, 1910-1918," *Signs: Journal of Women in Culture and Society* (1982): 545. Kaplan argues that the scope of female consciousness among popular women focuses on female duties as "gatherers and distributors of scarce resources in the community." See also Kaplan, "Class Consciousness and Community in Nineteenth-Century Andalusia," *Political Power and Social Theory* 2 (1981): 21-57.

32. Breitbart and Ackelsberg, "Terrains of Protest," 11.

33. Mary Ryan, *Womanhood in America: From Colonial Times to the Present* (New York: Viewpoints, 1975), 45.

34. Christine Stansell, "The Origins of the Sweatshop: Women and Early Industrialization in New York City," in Michael H. Frisch and Daniel Walkowitz, eds., *Working-Class America: Essays on Labor, Community, and American Society* (Urbana: Univ. of Illinois Press, 1983), 78-103.

35. Amelia Stundza, interview by Jonas Stundza, Immigrant City Archives, Lawrence, Massachusetts, no. 24, 7 June 1979, and follow-up interview by author, June 1980.

36. *Lawrence Tribune,* Feb. 28, 1912.

37. Consiglia Teutonica, interview by author, August 1981.

38. Much to the disappointment of its Protestant directors, the YWCA saw 2500 "mealers" between Monday and Saturday, but only a handful on Sunday. *YWCA Records,* Feb. 1907 to Mar. 1913, Sept. 25, 1911. Immigrant City Archives, Lawrence, Mass., 137-38.

39. Quoted in Cameron, "Bread and Roses Revisited," 44.

40. Lawrence City Mission, "Sixth Annual Report to the Patrons and Families of the Lawrence City Mission," City of Lawrence, 1865, 15-16; *12th Annual Report,* 1871, Lawrence City Doc. 1880-1895, 1886; *Lawrence Evening Tribune,* May 14, 1902; *Lawrence Journal,* Oct. 30, 1886.

41. Clark Carter, *Yearly Reports,* Lawrence City Mission, 1921, 4.

42. Stansell, "Women, Children," 312-13.

43. *Lawrence Tribune,* June 4, 1904.

44. This Lithuanian expression literally refers to policemen, but was used by several Lithuanian and Russian women to mean "official outsiders," those responsible for alien laws and "troubles." Translation courtesy of William Walkowitz. Olga Veckyte, interview by author, Oct. 18, 1981.

45. Susan M. Kingsbury, ed., *Labor Laws and Their Enforcement: Charles E. Parsons, Mabel Parton, Mabelle Moses, and "Three Fellows"* (New York: Arno and the New York Times Reprint Series, 1971), 198.

46. Anna Marino, interview by author, Aug. 8, 1981.

47. *Lawrence Tribune,* March 13, 1912.

48. Cliffort Geertz, *The Interpretation of Cultures* (New York: Basic, 1973), 316.

6

Reconstructing the "Family": Women, Progressive Reform, and the Problem of Social Control

EILEEN BORIS

"The best interests of the child," "the rights of biological motherhood,"[1] and the protection of the home and family from market relations are doctrines that in 1988 justified the New Jersey Supreme Court ruling on surrogate motherhood in the notorious Baby M case. These doctrines also illuminate the contradictory legacy of Progressive Era reform. Progressives employed these ideas to reconstruct the "family," as the nineteenth century gave way to the twentieth.

Judges joined social workers, feminists, and other reformers to intervene in family life in order to maintain the family unit and protect motherhood, domesticity, and children. Makers and administrators of public policy would expose private, intimate life to public scrutiny; they would curb tenement homework, end child labor, provide workmen's compensation, trace deserting husbands, and assist mothers so that they could stay at home with their children. As one state factory inspector put it, the "privacy of the home" must succumb to a "stronger duty," the public interest, which would "rescue . . . all homes, and make the necessary division between home and workplace."[2]

Women reformers played a key role in this activist use of the state, relying on an alternative set of values derived from women's sphere to reconstruct public life in accordance with their own ideal of womanhood. In the process, they improved the material conditions of working-class women and families and created new professional roles for themselves.[3] Their dependence on cultural ideas that associated women with "female" traits of nurturance, altruism, piety, and domesticity grounded women reformers in a discourse similar to the one that called upon such traits to argue for female inferiority and subordination rather than gender equality.

Although these cultural ideals could support a public policy that protected women from men, they reinforced the dependent status of women in the economy and the polity. Women reformers valued motherhood equally with working-class women, but reformers attached a different meaning to the word that made it difficult for women from other racial and ethnic groups or social classes to live up to. Working-class women, for their part, would use the structures built or supported by women reformers for their own ends.

A major issue in Progressive Era historiography is the problem of social control. Who defined the family—its constituent parts, its unities and conflicts, and the relations of members to each other, the economy, or other institutions in the society? Whose understanding of motherhood, breadwinning, or the best interests of the child shaped judicial decisions, legislation, and administrative directives? In other words, how did the family serve as a terrain for ideological and political struggle?

The family is treated as a unified whole both by liberal interpretations of progressives (humanitarians cleaning up the ravages of industrial capitalism) and by radical condemnations of progressives (social controllers who imposed Americanization on a supposedly passive immigrant working class).[4] Such interpretations assume that the genders and the generations have the same interests. In particular, many adherents to the social control thesis condemn the state as a paternalistic parent, forgetting that women reformers lobbied for and then staffed many of the "paternalistic" programs that sought to fulfill the needs of the disadvantaged for housing, education, pure food, and other basic necessities, though at the expense of their rights to self-determination or self-definition.[5]

A new generation of scholarship presents a more complex picture, allowing reinterpretation of social control as an interactive process in which "clients" are anything but passive: they demand divorces, mothers' pensions, and an end to child abuse.[6] While some of this literature romanticizes the nurturing and communal ethos of reformers, it nonetheless views the social programs and legal decisions of the period as complex and contradictory, a product of struggle between classes, genders, and racial and ethnic groups.[7] Rather than condemning reformers for neglecting the rights of the immigrant working class, this interpretation lauds the emphasis of reformers on needs over rights as part of an alternative "female" value system, according to the theories of psychologist Carol Gilligan.[8]

The regulation of industrial homework was a state policy that exemplified the attempt to shield the family from the marketplace and protect women from men. Through their active role in shaping state policy, women reformers, as well as working-class women, tried to improve the lives of women and their families. By the turn of the century, prominent women reformers were organizing public intervention that supported the ideological separation between public and private spheres, consequently reinforcing treatment of women as dependents rather than as autonomous individuals. Thus, the progressives attempted to mitigate the impact of capitalist industrialization by consciously or unconsciously stabilizing the social order, in which reconstructing the family was a central component.

To that end, women reformers actively sought to save the home from the factory. Testifying at hearings in 1915 to amend the New York State constitution, settlement house head resident Mary Simkhovitch typified the attitude of a generation of women reformers toward tenement homework. She called for the prohibition of manufacturing in the home because "it is, of course, a wholly unstandardized type of business," with long hours and low wages. Behind her criticism lay the distinction between home and workplace that was an inheritance from the Victorian past: "I speak of it as a business rather than a home because we know very well these homes have the form but not the substance of home when the time has to be given entirely to this work."[9] What Simkhovitch added to this conventional notion was the state's responsibility to maintain homes as homes, saving them from the exploitative social relations of the factory. Home assembly of artificial flowers and finishing of clothes was on the increase in immigrant neighborhoods, and the existing licensing system checked only for sanitary conditions; the unstandardized nature of the work made it almost impossible to regulate the hours and wages of homeworkers. Simkhovitch therefore sought to empower the state to abolish homework through a constitutional amendment, thereby subjecting the private home to public action.

Such an amendment was needed because the New York Court of Appeals, in *In Re Jacobs* (1885), had invalidated an 1884 act prohibiting cigar manufacturing in tenement houses. The court reasoned that such a law deprived a man of his right to property without improving the public health. Freedom within the home and its sanctity were central to the reasoning of the judges: "It can not be perceived how the cigarmaker is to be improved in his health or his morals by forcing him from his home and its hallowed associations and beneficient influences, to ply his trade elsewhere."[10]

As feminist Rheta Childe Dorr commented on this case in 1912, "the tradition [of the innate sacredness of the home] is strongest in strong men.

It sways legislatures and the courts, which, being composed entirely of men . . . have no more than a theoretical knowledge of Home." She stood squarely for the separation of home from workplace when she argued: "*In this day the presence of manufacturing in a home turns that home into a factory.*"[11] Furthermore, the fact that the home should be distinct from the factory did not mean that it lay beyond the police power of the state, a concept reformers developed to justify social welfare and labor legislation.[12]

The *Jacobs* case reflected the tendency of the courts to regard the home as private and therefore not subject to state intervention, an "absence" of the law from a legally defined private sphere that feminist legal theorists Nadine Taub and Elizabeth Schneider explain "has contributed to male dominance and female subservience."[13] By regarding the home as separate from the polity and the economy, courts ratified not only existing power relations within families but the relationship of different family members to the larger society. Thus, when it came to tenement homework, the fiction of the sanctity of the home obscured the ways that the home existed as part of both the polity and the economy. Also hidden was how the sexual division of labor within the families (where women were responsible for unpaid family labor) intersected with employer needs to encourage homework.

In tenement cigarmaking (where Bohemian immigrants predominated), whole families, led by the male head of household, bunched and rolled tobacco; *Jacobs* assumed that men, as independent actors, had the right to contract and, as heads of households, to determine activities in their home. Technology and union organization, however, would soon lead to a decline in tenement cigarmaking.[14] But the *Jacobs* decision held for all tenement homework, not just cigarmaking, in which a family-wage labor system prevailed and men joined their wives and children in homework. By the turn of the century, tenement homework was dominated by mothers and their children, especially Italians in the New York City garment trades.[15] After voters defeated the 1915 constitution, which contained a sweatshop amendment, New York reformers had to wait until the New Deal and an expanded understanding of the police power of the state to pass a homework law that allowed the industrial commissioner to prohibit home manufacturing of goods.

A more limited law passed in 1913, prohibiting tenement-made infant's clothes, dolls, and food items, was sustained in *People of the State of New York v. Balofsky* (1916). Arguing for the constitutionality of this law, the New York State Factory Investigating Commission contended: "What was considered an undue interference with the individual, then, is to-day recognized as a proper regulation by the State. The strong individualized tendencies of the period when the Jacobs case was rendered have given way to an appreciation of the rights of society as a whole and to the necessity for its protection and preservation."[16] Such a statement does not merely reflect the progressives' positive attitude toward the use of the state but, in the context of who did homework and why, also reveals the gender dynamics that lay behind the notion of "protection and preservation." While the commission's brief appends evidence of the health hazards posed by tenement manufacture—its dangers to the consumer and thus to public welfare—it cites women and children as the beneficiaries of such regulation because they were the homeworkers.

Freedom of contract might apply to men, as made clear in *Lochner v. New York* (1905), but other interests could prevail when regulating the labor of women and children. Thus, Josephine Goldmark of the Consumers' League compiled evidence for the famous Brandeis brief in *Muller v. Orgeon* (1908) that showed the negative impact of long hours at industrial occupations on women's bodies, including their reproductive capacities. In a decision that upheld shorter hours for women, the Supreme Court accepted such evidence out of a desire to protect its ideas of motherhood. As Justice Brewer wrote for the majority: "That woman's physical structure and the performance of maternal functions place her at a disadvantage in the struggle for subsistence is obvious . . . and, as healthy mothers are essential to vigorous offspring, the physical well-being of a woman becomes an object of public interest and care in order to preserve the strength and vigor of the race." This interpretation demonstrates the consequences of women's reform efforts based on female difference when entered into a judicial system not under women's control.[17] Women reformers' arguments for protective labor legislation, including their own understanding of motherhood, denied the simple dichotomy between public and private life found in *Jacobs* and similar decisions that overturned labor legislation. That women reformers tapped into the same symbols as judges suggests the difficulties of redefining the existing discourse when relying on its key term: woman as mother.[18]

Testimony in 1912 before the New York State Factory Investigating Commission—which the Women's Trade Union League (WTUL), the Consumers' League of New York, and other women's reform organizations had lobbied for in the wake of the Triangle Shirtwaist Fire—reveals the concepts of home, motherhood, child life, and work embodied in the 1913 tenement homework law. Newspaper reports on the commission's hearings present the attitudes of both the general public and homeworking mothers themselves. Under the bold-type subheadline "Give Fathers Living Wages," the *New York Globe* reported Florence Kelley as arguing for absolute and sweeping prohibition of tenement homework. The secretary of the National Consumers' League, a major formulator of labor standards legislation for women, rebutted those who claimed that taking homework away from women would cause suffering. Calling for state intervention, Kelley asserted: "The trade took the cloak and suit work away from the homes. The union took the cigar making away. The legislature can ultimately take it all away, and conditions will be better for it. The men say 'let us get out of this slavery, and we will take care of our own women and children.' Let us give them a chance." Kelley saw homework as undermining the standards of factory workers. In testimony that captured the complex understandings of her generation of (white) women reformers, she associated living wages not only with sexually defined roles, in which men supported families through wages and women through mothering, but also with economic independence for women without children (and presumably without men): "Factory conditions which will give living wages to men will eliminate the necessity of the home work for women and children. I mean in the case of families where the father is able-bodied. I would provide a pension for widows just as Colorado has done. Then I would give the factory work to detached women. The deliberately idle men I would send to the workhouse for the week-end, as Judge Lindsey does, just to remind them of their obligations."[19]

Such a defense of the family wage, which went hand in hand with a belief in the man's obligation to support his wife and children, reflected the dominent gender system of the Progressive Era.[20] Nonetheless, it also suggests the woman-centered analysis that these reformers brought to industrial life, how they based their programs on the real situation of women and not on abstract principles of equal rights.[21] The reformers' goal was not to keep women from the workplace but to end exploitation and insure that mothers could perform their nurturing work; thus, reformers connected the end of tenement homework with the establishment of mothers' pensions and child support laws. That mothers' pensions were underfunded and failed to provide a caretaker's grant, forcing those "worthy" enough to receive a pension to work for wages as well, stemmed from larger political forces over which reformers exercised little control.[22]

As much as the reformers championed the working-class mother, the chasm of class separated them from those who worked in the tenements. Kelley, who also linked compulsory education laws and education scholarships (to replace income lost from child laborers) with the abolition of homework, confessed to the commission: "If [children] were allowed to go to school they would at least be assured of a hot luncheon and the services of the school nurse and doctor,"[23] an attitude that reflects a general condemnation of tenement home life. Others directly attacked the mothering practices of tenement workers. Newspapers sensationalized the issue by repeatedly reporting testimony of child abuse; as far away as Wheeling, West Virginia, and Sioux Falls, Iowa, people read "Where Babies Work" and were told that "the mothers are often forced to beat the children in order to keep them at work but it is that or starve."[24] Child-labor investigator Mary Britton Miller told one reporter: "The average Italian mother watches the growth of a child, not with a view to becoming old enough to receive an education, but with a hungry eagerness for her to reach the age when she can be put into use as a wage-earning home slave." Miller recalled one truant boy explaining: "Our mothers makes us stay at home to work and licks us when we don't." Such mothers, she claimed, were stunting their children's minds, turning them into "slow, uncomprehending machines."[25]

Other investigators were more sympathetic to the homeworking mother. The *New York Evening Mail* editorialized: "Do the mothers of children force their babies to work at night because they wish to see them suffer? Do they like to whip their children to keep them at toil when they should be asleep? No. It is simply not to be believed. The mother heart is still the resting place of love and tenderness, in the ghetto as well as everywhere else. It is the mother's instinct to guard well the slumber of her child. These mothers of the slum are not by nature less kind than others. They are themselves the victims of the system of toil which they force upon their children."[26]

Elizabeth Watson, the chief investigator on homework for the Factory Investigating Commission, understood that homeworkers, who were responsible for home and children, could not be good housekeepers or mothers. Because "every instant taken from the work means loss of money," homeworking mothers would leave their homes dirty, prepare whatever was easiest to eat, buy what was convenient, even if more expensive, and neglect or manage children "with one hand" while assembling flowers with the other. Rarely receiving more than five or six hours' sleep, these women experienced a profound stretch out of the working day that made them, in Watson's words, "irritable and rough"[27] with their children.

Like Mary Dreier of the WTUL, one of the Factory Investigating

Commissioners, Mary Britton Miller, called for more charity as a substitute for homework.[28] She was in a minority in also demanding day nurseries and kindergartens so that mothers could go out to work. Dr. Annie S. Daniels of the New York City Infirmary for Women and Children agreed that if mothers had to earn wages, they should work in factories, with their children in day nurseries. Like most other reformers, however, she preferred to increase income by raising the male wage or providing income supplements so women could stay home.[29]

Fathers were not free from blame in Britton Miller's portrait of child abuse: "It is a question of saving the bodies and the souls and the minds of thousands of children . . . And it might drive the fathers to work . . . They are shiftless and lazy and often drunkards." Miller would rely on the law "to attend to them [the fathers] in some way. And the children should be rescued at any cost." Not all the investigators were so harsh toward the fathers in such families. In her report for the Factory Investigating Commission, Elizabeth Watson concluded, "the family budgets . . . show that the budget is small, *not* because the father is lazy, but because his daily wage is not sufficient to carry him through the dull season of his industry."[30]

What did homeworking mothers think of the attempt to prohibit their labor? Sources are more indirect, consisting of comments made to investigators and photographs of homeworkers. Mary Britton Miller appeared enraged that the mothers were "ingenious and resourceful in evading the school law and tricking the truant officers and the Judges." She painted a portrait of tenement mothers manipulating the judicial system by relying on their "wretched appearance"—that is, on their very poverty—as evidence of how much they needed the help of their children. Poor mothers were able to win over judges through the "sucking sound of drawn breath," their very hunger. Other investigators reported on the mutuality of the tenements, where those on the first floor would warn those living above of the coming of the inspector in time to hide any evidence of child labor.[31]

While reformers condemned homework for depriving children of fresh air and play, parents saw the streets as more dangerous to the welfare of their children. One father told documentary photographer Lewis Hine: "It's better than running the streets." Another said, "It is better for the children to learn something useful to do." Some families turned work into play. One former homeworker recalled, "It was like a game. Visiting kids would sit down and link in our house. Whoever did the most would get some extra snack or candy or fruit." Children proudly told investigators of their contribution: "Me was des helping mama," one injured child explained. Mothers boasted of their children's skills. "See how smart she is," said one mother of a seven-year-old embroidering stems of flowers. "I show her how and right away she makes them." Though reformers argued that mothers neglected their children, photographs taken with the goal of exposing the horror of tenement homework reveal the opposite: mothers gather with their children, hold them on laps, rock cradles, and sit beside them.[32] The work that middle-class reformers saw as a demoralizing element of domestic life was embraced by immigrant women and their families as a strategy for family survival. Sharing with the reformers the assumption that mothers should stay home with their children, but unable to live on the wages of their men, immigrant families at certain points of their life cycles accepted the exploitative conditions of homework as necessary, even if they complained when prices became too low. From the perspective of these families, immigrant women were fulfilling their roles as mothers by taking work into the homes. Thus, the debate was not over the role of women as mothers but over the responsibility inherent in that role and the means taken to fulfill it.

In this context, the same language held different meanings for different speakers. Judicial and legislative support of protective labor legislation relied upon the dominent cultural ideals of womanhood; women reformers justified state intervention in private life on the basis of protecting motherhood. Though reformers defined motherhood as a positively valued nurturing activity and judges reinforced their own notion of women's place, the actions of both nonetheless demonstrate that the private sphere never really existed for economically disadvantaged families, often also considered racially or culturally inferior. After all, women of color and working-class white women had to labor for others and could not fulfill the dictates of "true womanhood." In addition, protective labor legislation generally excluded those occupations—domestic service and agriculture—in which most women of color labored.[33]

The campaign to save the home from the factory by ending tenement homework embodied the reformers' idea of home, which included the male breadwinner and nurturing mother, though it also envisioned both homes and factories as places free from degradation. The gender system behind such public policies justified women's subordinate place in the labor market, which was central to the inability of mothers to support their children without assistance from men or the state.[34]

While the state in the nineteenth century sought primarily to defend the privacy of the family (except in the cases of the destitute or slave), by the early twentieth century the state was actively reconstructing the family in order to preserve gender-based obligations. Women reformers emphasized the needs of women and children and challenged the individualism of the marketplace, which devalued women's mothering activities. They sought to protect mothers, children, and women's sphere by restricting the rights of husbands, fathers, and capital rather than by empowering women, even if some women became active agents in the process.[35] As Martha Minow has argued in a different context, "to the extent that 'rights consciousness' animated the reform efforts, it was a consciousness of elite reformers seeking to limit the rights of parents and enlarge the rights or powers of the state." Yet a needs consciousness also pervaded the policies of these women reformers who sought to improve the material conditions of women and their children.[36]

What some historians have labeled social control can therefore be more accurately interpreted as an intervention into families on the part of the state and professional experts, mediated by the gender, class, race, and ethnicity of both family members and interveners. This process was more interactive than the concept of social control suggests. Women, regardless of their social position, were hardly passive in their relation to reformers or courts. They sought to fulfill their own ideas of motherhood, nurturing, and family life. Indeed, motherhood stood at the corner of Progressive Era discourse about the family, even though middle-class women reformers and male judges differed from working-class ethnic women (and even from each other) in their understanding of both the ideal and the reality of motherhood.

Saving the family from the marketplace, protecting the best interests of the child, and upholding the rights of mothers are concepts that continue to shape public policy toward families. That this policy is muddled in its intentions and contradictory in its consequences reflects the ambivalent legacy of Progressive Era reform. Committed to their vision of the self-sufficient family in the era of the large corporation, progressives sought to shield the home from the corrosive influence of external material and social changes. At the same time, however, progressives created a central role for the state in organizing and regulating the internal dynamics of family life. In this sense, the recent controversy over the Baby M case is an outgrowth of Progressive Era tension between an adherence to the traditional ideal of family privacy and a new belief in the need for public action to preserve the nuclear family.

Notes

This paper is a shortened version of one presented at the Conference on Women in the Progressive Era. The original included an additional case study on divorce, desertion, and child support written by Peter Bardaglio, who jointly developed its theoretical framework. I would like to thank him for all his efforts. Support for this work came from a Faculty Research Grant, Department of History, Howard University, and a Howard University Research Grant for the Humanities, Social Sciences, and Education.

1. "Excerpts from Decision by New Jersey Supreme Court in the Baby M Case," *New York Times* Feb. 4, 1988, B6.

2. Mary O'Reilly, "Sweat-Shop Life in Pennsylvania," in International Association of Factory Inspectors of North America, *Ninth Annual Convention* (Cleveland, Ohio: Forest City Printing House, 1895), 68. See the valuable discussion of progressives and family policy in Richard Busacca and Mary Ryan, "Beyond the Family Crisis," *Democracy* 2 (Fall 1982): 83-86.

3. John H. Ehrenreich, *The Altruistic Imagination: A History of Social Work and Social Policy in the United States* (Ithaca: Cornell Univ. Press, 1985), 34–36; Barbara J. Harris, *Beyond Her Sphere: Women and the Professions in American History* (Westport, Conn.: Greenwood, 1978), 118-119; and Walter I. Trattner, *From Poor Law to Welfare State: A History of Social Welfare in America,* 2d ed. (New York: Free Press, 1979), 190-205.

4. For liberal interpretations, see Roy Lubove, *The Struggle for Social Security, 1900-1935* (Cambridge, Mass.: Harvard Univ. Press, 1968); and Eric Goldman, *Rendezvous with Destiny* (New York: Knopf, 1952). For examples of social-control interpretations, consult Anthony M. Platt, *The Child Savers: The Invention of Delinquency* (Chicago: Univ. of Chicago Press, 1969); Christopher Lasch, *Haven in a Heartless World: The Family Besieged* (New York: Basic, 1977); and Barbara Ehrenreich and Deirdre English, *For Her Own Good: One Hundred Years of the Experts' Advice to Women* (Garden City, N.Y.: Anchor/Doubleday, 1978). Social controllers differ in their judgments of reformer and expert actions.

5. David Rothman, "The State as Parent: Social Policy in the Progressive Era," in Willard Gaylin et al., *Doing Good: The Limits of Benevolence* (New York: Pantheon, 1978), 69-95; see also Rothman, *Conscience and Convenience: The Asylum and Its Alternatives in Progressive America* (Boston: Little, Brown, 1980).

6. See Linda Gordon, "Family Violence, Feminism, and Social Control," *Feminist Studies* 12 (Fall 1986): 453-78; Eli Zaretsky, "The Place of the Family in the Origins of the Welfare State," in Barrie Thorne with Marilyn Yalom, eds., *Rethinking the Family: Some Feminist Questions* (New York: Longman, 1982), 188-224; Martha May, "'The 'Problem of Duty': The Regulation of Male Breadwinning and Desertion in the Progressive Era," in Institute for Legal Studies, Legal History Program, *Working Papers* 1 (Feb. 1986); Joanne Goodwin, "Gender and Early Social Welfare Policy: The Case of Mothers' Pensions in the U.S." (Paper delivered at the Social Science History Association, St. Louis, Mo., Oct. 1986); Martha Minow, "'Forming Underneath Everything That Grows': Toward a History of Family Law," *Wisconsin Law Review* (1985): 819-98.

7. For a fuller analysis, see Eileen Boris and Peter Bardaglio, "The Transformation of Patriarchy: The Historic Role of the State," in Irene Diamond, ed., *Families, Politics, and Public Policy: A Feminist Dialogue on Women and the State* (New York: Longman, 1983), 70-93; and "Gender, Race, and Class: The Impact of the State on the Family and the Economy, 1790-1945," in Naomi Gerstel and Harriet Gross, eds., *Families and Work* (Philadelphia: Temple Univ. Press, 1987), 132-51.

8. Carol Gilligan argues that women have a different set of ethical norms. While her work is ahistorical, it may very well describe some aspects of the ethical system of women

reformers in the Progressive Era. See Carol Gilligan, *In A Different Voice: Psychological Theory and Women's Development* (Cambridge, Mass.: Harvard Univ. Press, 1982). Linda Kerber responds to Gilligan's theory, with a warning for historians in "Some Cautionary Words for Historians," in "On 'In A Different Voice': An Interdisciplinary Forum," *Signs: A Journal of Women in Culture and Society* 11 (Winter 1986): 304-10.

9. "Meeting of Committee on Industrial Relations. Constitutional Convention," June 9, 1915, in Series No. 640, Papers of the Constitutional Convention of 1915; Working Files of Committees, box 14, New York State Archives, Albany, N.Y., 83–84; see also Committee of Labor Legislation and the Constitutional Convention of New York State, "Proposed Constitutional Amendments," ibid., box 13.

10. *In Re Jacobs*, 98 N.Y. 98, 113 (1885). For one analysis of this case, see William E. Forbath, "The Ambiguities of Free Labor: Labor and the Law in the Gilded Age," *Wisconsin Law Review* (1985): 795-96.

11. Rheta Childe Dorr, "The Child Who Toils at Home," *Hampton Magazine* 28 (Apr. 1912): 183.

12. See Ernst Freund, *The Police Power* (Chicago: Callaghan, 1904).

13. Naudine Taub and Elizabeth M. Schneider, "Perspectives on Women's Subordination and the Role of Law," in David Kairys, ed., *The Politics of Law: A Progressive Critique* (New York: Pantheon, 1982), 118.

14. See Dorothee Schneider, "The New York Cigarmakers' Strike of 1877," *Labor History* 26 (Summer 1985): 325-50; New York State, Bureau of Labor Statistics, "Tenement Cigarmaking in New York City," *Thirteenth Annual Report*, 1895 (Albany: Wynkeop Hallenbeck Crawford, 1896); and Edith Abbott, "Employment of Women in Industries: Cigar-Making," *Journal of Political Economy* 15 (Jan. 1907): 1-25.

15. For one study of Italians in New York homework, see Cynthia R. Daniels, "Between Home and Factory: Homeworkers and the State," in Eileen Boris and Cynthia R. Daniels, eds., *Homework: Historical and Contemporary Perspectives on Paid Labor at Home* (Urbana: Univ. of Illinois Press, 1989), 13-32; see also Mary Van Kleeck, *Artificial Flower Makers* (New York: Survey Associates, 1913).

16. On the power of *Jacobs*, see Ruth Shallcross, *Industrial Homework: An Analysis of Homework Regulation Here and Abroad* (New York: Industrial Affairs, 1939), 45-47; and "Brief on Law Prohibiting Certain Manufacture in Tenements," State of New York, *Fourth Report of the Factory Investigating Commission, 1915* (Albany: J.B. Lyon, 1915), 1: 382-84. On the judicial shift, see Eileen Boris, "The Quest for Labor Standards in the Era of Eleanor Roosevelt: The Case of Industrial Homework," *Wisconsin Women's Law Journal* 2 (1986): 53-74.

17. *Muller v. Oregon*, 208 U.S. 412 (1908). See the discussion in Norma Basch, "The Emerging Legal History of Women in the United States: Property, Divorce, and the Constitution," *Signs: A Journal of Women in Culture and Society* 12 (Autumn 1986): 112-15; Boris, "Quest for Labor Standards," 56; Frances E. Olson, "The Family and the Market: A Study of Ideology and Legal Reform," *Harvard Law Review* 96 (1983): 1556-57; Alice Kessler-Harris, "Protection for Women: Trade Unions and Labor Laws," in Wendy Chavkin, ed., *Double Exposure: Women's Health Hazards on the Job and at Home* (New York: Monthly Review, 1984), 139-54. For analysis of the women's reformers' use of the courts, see Sybil Lipschultz, "Social Feminism and Legal Discourse, 1908-1923," in Martha Albertson Fineman and Nancy Sweet Thomadsen, eds., *At the Boundaries of Law: Feminism and Legal Theory* (New York: Routledge, 1990), 209-25.

18. For more on this problem, see Eileen Boris, "The Power of Motherhood: Black and White Activist Women Redefine the 'Political,'" *Yale Journal of Law and Feminism,* 2 (Fall 1989): 25-49.

19. "Forbid Home Work and End Child Labor," *New York Globe,* Dec. 7, 1912, clipping in scrapbook, "New York Factory Investigating Commission, 1912-1913," box 57, Papers of the National Child Labor Committee, Library of Congress, Washington, D.C.; hereafter called "Scrapbook."

20. For analysis of both the family wage and the problem of male support, see Martha May, "The Historical Problem of the Family Wage: The Ford Motor Company and the Five Dollar Day," *Feminist Studies* 8 (Summer 1982): 399-424; and May, "Problem of Duty.'"

21. The most persuasive analysis along these lines is Kathyrn Kish Sklar, "Florence Kelley and the Integration of 'Women's Sphere' into American Politics, 1890-1921" (Paper delivered at the Organization of American Historians, Los Angeles, Calif., Apr. 1986).

22. For one case study, see Joanne Goodwin, "Mothers in Poverty: A Gender Analysis of Mothers' Pensions, 1911-1929" (Paper delivered at the Seventh Berkshire Conference on the History of Women, Wellesley College, Wellesley, Mass., 1987).

23. "Forbid Home Work," *New York Globe.*

24. For a history of child abuse, see Elizabeth Pleck, *Domestic Tyranny: The Making of American Social Policy against Family Violence from Colonial Times to the Present* (New York: Oxford Univ. Press, 1987); "Where Babies Work," *Wheeling News,* Jan. 7, 1913; and "Child Labor Horrors," *Sioux Falls Argus-Leader,* Jan. 16, 1913, in Scrapbook.

25. "Home Work in the Tenements Makes Children Slaves. Saw Mothers Who Were Merciless Taskmasters," *Star* Jan. 4, 1913, in Scrapbook.

26. "The Cry of the Children for Protection," *New York Evening Mail,* Dec. 7, 1912, editorial, in Scrapbook.

27. Elizabeth C. Watson, "Report on Manufacturing in Tenements in New York State," *Second Report of the Factory Investigating Commission,* 1913 (Albany: J.B. Lyons, 1913), 1: 695-97.

28. "Women Hope to Get Law to Save Children. Tenement Home Work Should Be Abolished; Miss Dreier Says. Reduces Factory Wages. Consumers League Officials Praise Factory Commission's Accomplishments," *New York Sun,* Dec. 8, 1912, in Scrapbook.

29. "Manufacturing in Tenements," in *Second Report,* 1: 113. In another context, Florence Kelley pointed to European day care projects with approval; see Kelley, "Married Women in Industry," *Proceedings of the Academy of Political Science* 1 (1910): 90-96.

30. "Homework in the Tenements," *Star.* See also *Home Work in the Tenement Houses of New York City,* reprint of Appendix VII to "Preliminary Report of the New York State Factory Investigating Commission, Submitted to the Legislature, March 1, 1912" (Albany: J.B. Lyons, 1912), 581-84.

31. See "Home Work in the Tenements," *Star;* and Elizabeth C. Watson, "Home Work in the Tenements," *Survey* 25 (Feb. 14, 1911): 3-12.

32. Notes for photographs 2812, 2881, 2829, in "Tenement House Scrapbook," lot 7481, and notecard file drawer, National Child Labor Committee Collection, Prints and Photographs Division, Library of Congress, Washington D.C.; Judith E. Smith, *Family Connections: A History of Italian & Jewish Immigrant Lives in Providence, Rhode Island, 1900-1940* (Albany: State Univ. of New York Press, 1985), 50, 54–56; and Edward Markham, "The Sweat Shop Inferno," *Cosmopolitan* 42 (Jan. 1907): 330. For another description of "good times," see Mary Alden Hopkins, "Children in Bondage:

Turning Children's Homes into Factories," *Good Housekeeping Magazine* 56 (June 1913): 748.

33. For an extension of this point, see Nancy Breen, "Shedding Light on Women's Work and Wages: Consequences of Protective Legislation" (Ph.D. diss., New School for Social Research, 1989).

34. Though too mechanical in its analysis, see Mimi Abramovitz, *Regulating the Lives of Women: Social Welfare Policy from Colonial Times to the Present* (Boston: South End, 1988), 30-40, 181-213.

35. See Linda Gordon, *Heroes of Their Own Lives: The Politics and History of Family Violence* (New York: Viking, 1988).

36. Martha Minow, "We, the Family: Constitutional Rights and American Families," *Journal of American History* 74 (Dec. 1987): 976.

7

Law and a Living: The Gendered Content of "Free Labor"

ALICE KESSLER-HARRIS

> What could possibly be more contemptible than the question: "What is the least sum on which an honest girl can keep body and soul together and escape disgrace?"
> —Florence Kelley[1]

Supreme Court decisions are frequently unpopular. Yet few have faced the storm of national derision that confronted the April 1923 opinion handed down in *Adkins v. Children's Hospital.* By a vote of five to three (Brandeis abstaining), the Court negated the constitutionality of a Washington, D.C., law that provided minimum wages for women and minors. With its act the Court also placed in jeopardy the minimum wage legislation of thirteen other states.[2]

Newspaper editorials, public meetings, and placards denounced the decision. Mary Anderson, head of the Women's Bureau, called it "nothing short of a calamity."[3] Samuel Gompers declared it to be a "logical next step in perfecting the doctrine that those who cannot help themselves shall not be helped."[4] The *New York World* ran a cartoon that depicted Justice George Sutherland handing the document to a woman wage earner, with the caption: "This decision, madam, affirms your constitutional right to starve."[5] In the immediate aftermath of the decision, the National Women's Trade Union League called a conference to stave off what it feared would be a "a wholesale reduction of wages for more than 1,500,000 women and girls."[6] The "greatest wrong" in the decision, as Gompers and others pointed out, was that in describing labor as a commodity to be bought and sold, Sutherland had likened "the labor of a woman to the purchase of a shinbone over the counter to make soup."[7] Henry Seager, respected professor of economics at Columbia University, fulminated that the decision "represents a menace to the stability of our established institutions vastly more serious than that of socialists, communists, bolshevists, or any other group of 'labor agitators.'"[8] Many opponents of the decision either described the Court's power to declare laws unconstitutional or urged that it be severely restricted. Henceforth, they suggested, six or seven justices, rather than a bare majority of five, should be required to repudiate any state law.[9]

The response might have been louder because the decision was apparently so unexpected. Fifteen years earlier, in *Muller v. Oregon,* the Court had accepted the principal that women's health was a proper subject of state concern and therefore of state regulation.[10] In the wake of that decision, most industrial states had taken it upon themselves to regulate the hours and working conditions of women and minors. These laws, quintessentially progressive in that they attempted to redress the imbalances of rapid industrial growth, had withstood many legal challenges and, just a year after *Adkins,* were to survive another. Though states were more cautious when it came to regulating wages, thirteen states and the District of Columbia had enacted minimum wage laws before 1923. Each was grounded in the assumption that working women's needs for food, clothing, and shelter could be accurately determined and in the desire to maintain women's health and to protect their morals by establishing wages at a level "adequate to supply the necessary cost of living."[11]

Minimum wage laws varied from state to state. Some set wage levels. Others established regulatory commissions to determine appropriate wages. Some provided legal penalties for violators. Others relied on public exposure to inhibit transgression. They had weathered many challenges in state courts, and in 1917 the U.S. Supreme Court, in an equally divided vote, affirmed an Oregon Supreme Court decision to uphold a minimum wage law.[12] These successful defenses of minimum wage laws led one commentator to note in 1921 that "no successful attack can be anticipated upon the principle of these laws in view of the absolute uniformity with which they have been maintained in the different states when pressed to a decision in the court of last resort."[13] Moreover, minimum wage laws were popular. Even after *Adkins,* states like Massachusetts and Washington continued to enforce their statutes, hoping to evade legal challenges; others, like New York, passed new laws.[14] Why then had the Court so unexpectedly countered what seemed like a well-established trend?

The answer may lie in the competing paradigms embedded in the issue of minimum wages for women. Decisions about minimum wages were grounded both in legal precedents around labor and in those around women. Watching the judiciary confront these issues reveals the vital importance of the idea of gender differences in the Progressive Era. Looking at the evolution of the relationship between a doctrine grounded in changing theories of labor and one that rested on separate spheres may tell us something about the relationship of gender differences to other influential ideas in the construction of law and social policy. As we examine the roots of *Adkins,* we begin to understand something of how the gendered content of ideas governed an important set of political and judicial decisions and, not inadvertently, laid the groundwork for incorporating nineteenth-century notions of workers' dignity and independence into the judicial system.

Minimum wage legislation derived its rationale from the gendered arguments used to gain passage of other regulatory legislation.[15] Its purpose, as the title of the Oregon act makes clear, was "to protect the lives and health and morals of women and minor workers . . ." or, as the District of Columbia Act put it, "to protect women and minors from conditions detrimental to their health and morals, resulting from wages which are inadequate to maintain decent standards of living."[16] As such, it was firmly rooted in progressive notions of women's separate sphere. Wage-earning women, in the familiar words of *Muller v. Oregon,* deserved protection because the "two sexes differ in structure of body, in the functions to be performed by each, in the amount of physical strength, in the capacity for long-continued labor . . . in the capacity to maintain the struggle for subsistence."[17] The widely accepted notion that women were mothers of the race provided more than adequate justification for the court to regulate women's working lives. But although the courts in earlier decisions had accepted sex differences as a reasonable basis for restraining the freedom of women and employers to contract earlier decisions, and would continue to rely on them, it rejected the idea in *Adkins.*

In so doing, the Court simply affirmed what had been well established by 1923, namely that an individual's freedom to contract was not subject to restraint by the state, unless the public welfare was affected. The decision was rooted in nineteenth century arguments over free labor. As Justice Sutherland noted, freedom of contract, while not absolute, was "the general rule, and restraint the exception."[18] But the idea of free labor was not gender neutral, and therein lay the difficulty. The Court, in this decision, insisted that women were individuals within the meaning of the law and thus overturned two decades of precedent that had held that the requirements of gender difference superseded the right to freely contract their services. How had the two, so carefully reconciled for a generation, come into conflict?

We need to step back for a moment. Two alternative conceptions of "free labor" had contested in the 1870s. The first, deriving from the early republic, had taken root in the period before the Civil War and, by the postwar period, was championed by such working class advocates as the Knights of Labor. In this view, labor was free when it had the capacity to participate independently in civic life. But that capacity inhered in the dignity and independence of the working person and therefore assumed that each person had equal rights or access to economic self-sufficiency. This doctrine of equal rights embodied at least a theoretical social quality that, workers and their representatives held, could not be sustained if workers were reduced to permanent wage-earning status. Implicit, in this view was the notion that only economic independence could guarantee effective self-representation and the perpetuation of a democratic republic. The idea of free labor as it evolved in the nineteenth century thus assumed that, in order to participate effectively in the polity, workers required at least the possibility of escape from wage labor into self-directed employment.[19]

From this conception of free labor women as individuals were virtually excluded. They were not expected to be members of the polity in the same sense as men, nor was their wage work expected to offer access to independent judgment. In the eyes of male workers, women's wage labor, while dignified and offering access to self-support, ought not to lead either to independence or to self-sufficiency. Rather, just as men's free labor was predicated on their capacity to support a family, so women's was assumed to sustain the family labor of men. As family members, women participated in the polity through their menfolk. Their wage work was encouraged only in occupational fields and at moments in the life cycle that did not violate customary conceptions of free labor. For women's wage work to threaten the male's capacity to be free was a problem, just as it was a problem if women's wage work undermined the capacity of either men or women to be effective family members. The American labor movement had engaged in debates on this issue since at least the 1830s, when male trade unionists protested the employment of female labor. The result of hiring women, skilled workers then thought, would be to impoverish "whole families and benefit none but the employers." They urged women to adopt strategies that would qualify them for "the more sober duties of wives, mothers and matrons."[25] The idea of free labor reified the idea of separate spheres, discouraging women from participating in wage work except in ways that would help to maintain family lives.

But labor had rules that did not necessarily derive from families. In the late nineteenth century, a dramatic acceleration in the process of industrialization threatened possibilities for self-directed employment for men as well as for women. While the defenders of free labor confronted the challenges of a debilitating and all-encompassing wage system with such innovations as cooperative producer associations and political action, a new generation of industrialists and entrepreneurs battled them at every turn.[21] Eager for a rapid transformation of control into their own hands and anxious to maximize the possibilities of cheap labor, entrepreneurs treated workers as individuals, each capable of negotiating and each protected by the Fourteenth Amendment's prohibitions on deprivation of property. Labor's freedom, they suggested, with the concurrence of the courts, inhered only in its right to freely contract to sell itself.

This view, commonly known as freedom of contract, challenged labor's notions of putative social equality and threatened the economic independence from which it derived. Within this perspective, equal rights were embedded in the capacity of each individual to compete freely. Workers (male and female) were free only to enter into contracts to sell their labor without restraint. In this position, entrepreneurs were joined by the courts. As a matter of formal and legal principal, the courts, beginning in the 1880s, ignored the vulnerable position of workers and turned the Fourteenth Amendment's prohibition against depriving citizens of life, liberty, and property on its head. Consistently, the courts interpreted freedom of contract as a ban on state efforts to restrict the rights of employers to offer even the most debilitating working conditions. The courts thus effectively snuffed the political vision of free labor. Valiant battles of workers' organizations could not prevent this development. With a few specific exceptions, the doctrine outlawed protective legislation for workers, depriving them of state intervention while employers were left free to impose their own conditions of work.[22] The crack in this system was gender.

The effort to limit labor's expectations by means of freedom of contract expressed the stake of a rapidly industrializing society in cheap and available labor. While theoretically the tendency of such a system was to pull women into the labor force as individuals, there remained some question as to whether they were "protected" by the Fourteenth Amendment as men were. For the same assault on free labor that had undermined notions of work as the locus of dignity relied upon, and perpetuated, the idea of the family as an economic unit and as the source of values by which a new generation of laborers would be raised. If, on the one hand, this provided a large pool of "cheap labor," on the other, even the most hard-boiled advocates of freedom of contract could not be insensitive to the problem that women who were treated as individuals for the purposes of the workplace still needed to fulfill demanding roles as family members. Work roles that undermined the working-class family by destroying women's health or fertility or encouraging women to compete for male jobs could easily destroy the golden egg that produced cheap labor.

Advocates of freedom of contract differed from the champions of free labor on virtually every score. Yet both agreed to some sense of separate spheres. The content of women's roles differed for each. Labor's conception was rooted in the belief that effective civic participation demanded workplace dignity that in turn rested on an ordered and comfortable family life. Business's conception derived from the desire to preserve the family as an economic unit that could provide incentives to stable and loyal work-force participation. Either way, ideas of gender difference defined women as family members whose work roles were secondary. Ideally, at least, this led to no contradiction for male workers: women, seen either as individuals who competed with them for jobs or as family members on whose household labor they relied, belonged at home. But for employers, placing women in separate spheres meant that they had to treat them simultaneously as individuals with a sacrosanct freedom of contract and as family members in whom they and the state had a special interest. It was this contradiction that the courts were called upon to resolve in the minimum wage cases.

By 1908, the courts had successfully responded with regard to hours. Under pressure from coalitions of women workers, reformers, and trade unions, legislatures and courts had legitimized the now familiar device of making women "wards of the state." But what worked for hours had special consequences when applied to wages. Regulating hours, as the Supreme Court noted in *Adkins,* had "no necessary effect on the heart of the contract, that is, the amount of wages to be paid and received."[23] The minimum wage, in contrast, touched its core. It was designed to defend freedom of contract by ensuring that women who could not otherwise survive did not undermine an ideology that relied on the fiction of a worker's liberty to negotiate fair terms of labor. At the same time, the minimum wage threatened the idea of freedom of contract by clearly identifying some workers as lacking in appropriate liberty. Tracing the resolution of this dilemma will tell us something of how ideas of gender difference helped to construct social reality. In one of the wonderful ironies of history, judicial decisions and the legal system contributed to definitions of female difference that in the end threatened the idea of the free labor market they were meant to protect.

The progressive attempt to accommodate gender invigorated a free labor debate that had been all but lost. Arguably, it helped to alter the terms of the debate. In creating sex as a category outside the common expectation of labor and law, the courts opened the door to an evaluation of the proper relation of the state to labor as a whole.[24] The language with which this struggle was enacted tells us something about the centrality of separate spheres in the lives of men and women and also about its competing functions. It enables us to watch how the notion of separate spheres first confronted and eventually helped to break down the pernicious idea of freedom of contract.

Let us begin with the case of Quong Wing, a Chinese laundryman who, in the winter of 1911-12, petitioned the United States Supreme Court for relief. Quong Wing, a male, had sued the treasurer of Lewis and Clark County, Montana, to return the ten dollars he had paid for a license to take in hand laundry. The Montana law, as cited by Justice Oliver Wendell Holmes in the Supreme Court decision, "imposed the payment upon all persons engaged in the laundry business, other than the steam laundry business, with a proviso that it should not apply to women so employed where not more than two women were employed."[25] Because the law applied to all laundries except steam laundries, it taxed small enterprises while exempting large ones, and because it applied to all persons who worked in hand laundries except women who worked alone or in pairs, it in effect taxed men who did what was considered women's work. There can be little doubt that the state meant to tax Chinese men, while exempting women and large operators, for, as Justice Holmes observed in his opinion for the Court, "hand laundry work is a widespread occupation of Chinamen in this country while on the other hand it is so rare to see men of our race engaged in it that many of us would be unable to say that they had ever observed a case."[26] Yet Quong Wing did not charge racial discrimination—an issue he might well have won. Instead, he charged sexual discrimination—and lost. The Supreme Court upheld the Montana statute because, as Holmes put it,

> If the state sees fit to encourage steam laundries and discourage hand laundries, that is its own affair. And if again it finds a ground of distinction in sex, that is not

> without precedent. . . . If Montana deems it advisable to put a lighter burden upon women than upon men with regard to an employment that our people commonly regard as more appropriate for the former, the Fourteenth Amendment does not interfere by creating a fictitious equality where there is a real difference. The particular points at which that difference shall be emphasized by legislation are largely in the power of the state.[27]

This case was not the first to identify gender difference as a legal category.[28] But, unlike the rationales for restricting women's working hours, on which the Court drew and which were rooted in the presumed physical disadvantage of women and the social benefits of legislation, the Court here asserted an arbitrary power to discriminate between men and women—not a new phenomenon but one that it did not even seek to justify except as a matter of legislative choice. *Quong Wing* thus extended *Muller*'s standard of sex as an appropriate classification to assert a state's right to define which sex differences could be taken into account. In imposing a new standard for legislative review, the case raises many issues, among them how readily gender "difference" is deployed under circumstances that would have explicitly precluded ethnic "difference," and the content of the "distinction" or "difference" to which the Court so blithely refers but makes no attempt to define. But for our purposes the most interesting question is the way in which the decision illuminates the social meaning of men's and women's wages.

The decision in *Quong Wing* suggests that the "common regard" (or popular perceptions of women's roles) is determinative in legislative choice as to which differences shall be emphasized. But surely that is a problem. If we take seriously Justice Holmes's comment that "the particular points at which that difference shall be emphasized by legislation are largely in the power of the state," then we have little choice but to view gender difference as an idea with a political content that moves people to behave in certain kinds of ways—in short, as an ideological construct. The decision tells us quite clearly that male and female job choices, and the earnings that result, are subject to regulation to bring them into line with the "common regard." A look at the evidence suggests the ideological level at which gender entered the debate.

In 1912, the common regard held that women belonged in families. Employers freely (and largely falsely) expressed the belief that women did not need incomes equal to those of men because they could rely on families to support them. More subtly, in the common regard, questions of masculinity entered into every decision on wages. For men, the wage encompassed family support; for women, it tended to incorporate only the self-support of a single person. This was made clear by New York State's Factory Investigating Commission of 1912. Eager to establish a case for the minimum wage, it asked several thousand employers to estimate what wage would be "required to support in health and working efficiency" the following categories of workers:

> A young woman of 16 to 18 years, living independently.
> A young man of 16 to 18 years, living independently.
> An adult woman living independently.
> An adult man living independently.
> A normal family containing one man at work, one woman, doing her own housework, and three children under 14 at school.[29]

No question about women supporting others was ever asked. Rather, the opposite assumption was made, namely that it was appropriate for women to derive part of their support from families. This assumption found its way into *Adkins,* in which Justice Sutherland objected to the District of Columbia law because it failed to take account of "the cooperative economies of the family group, though they constitute an important consideration in estimating the cost of living, for it is obvious that the individual expense will be less in the case of a member of a family than in the case of one living alone."[30]

The wage might thus appropriately order the relations between the sexes. As a relative, not an absolute, phenomenon, the wage can be read in terms of how women stretched their earnings and in terms of such larger meanings as independence or power in the family. It can illuminate social conceptions of womanhood and their relationship to gendered structures that extend far beyond the wage itself. How the wage "images" women—like the role it plays in fixing relationships between men and women—tells us something about how structures of difference are maintained and used. For if the common regard legitimized a lower wage for women and negated women's articulated experience about what it cost to live and help support a family, it also set the stage for the struggle over whether a minimum wage was socially desirable and economically legitimate.

Because the battle was hard fought, the price of maintaining separate spheres was high. It took the form of a vicious and clearly ideological attack on women as workers that exaggerated their "natural" attachment to the home and belittled their ability to earn wages. The popular imagination conjured up pictures of wage-earning women who were helpless, dependent, weak, handicapped, ignorant, delicate, and exploitable. Portraits of wage-earning women depicted them as greedy and lazy as well. They had, it was said, a "natural longing for recreation . . . adornment" and luxury. At the same time, women lived in a world where unscrupulous employers did not hesitate to subject them to conditions "akin to slavery" and thus leave them vulnerable to peculiar dangers that threatened to lure them into vice and immorality. These conditions prevented them from living in "decency" or from enjoying "healthy and normal lives," and they inhibited the peace of a "satisfied mind" and a "wholesome existence." Worse, they threatened the "health and well-being" of future mothers and therefore held "the strength of the nation hostage."[31] While these images expanded on those evoked to justify shorter hours for women but not for men, their consequences were not at all alike.

In the debate over the minimum wage, both sides had a stake in maintaining wage differentials, and so both resorted to this imagery. The terms of the debate thus contributed to depicting women in the extreme language of childhood and vulnerability. For example, both sides saw women as inefficient workers who lacked training. Proponents of the minimum wage argued that wage earners could be divided between those who "are earning what they receive or more" and those "whose services are worth little or nothing."[32] Even sympathetic reformers like Florence Kelley held that too many untrained and unskilled women flooding the job market depressed women's wages. To raise wages required educating and training women to be more efficient and effective workers. That this had not happened as a natural result of the market was perceived as the result of differences women's character.

Women were depicted as being in competition with each other. Like the notion that women workers were inefficient, the idea that female competition reduced wages pervaded the imagery. One side described women as "undutiful daughters" who tempted by luxurious living, allowed their mothers to overwork themselves while they sought riches in the factory or department store. This view also imagined dissatisfied wives not content to live on their husbands' earnings. Though sympathetic to the minimum wage, the other side constructed a picture of "women whose earnings are supplemented from other resources" and who are therefore a "constant drag on the wage level and offer formidable competition to the growing thousands of women dependent on their own labor for support. . . ."[33] The circular logic of this argument appears when we place it in the form of a syllogism: Women do not earn enough, therefore they live with others, therefore they reduce the level of wages for all women, therefore women do not earn enough.

Another explanation was that women chose the wrong jobs. For example, opponents of the minimum wage suggested that women could easily save money and achieve mobility if they were willing to become domestic servants. Such jobs were widely available. But women, objecting to the endless hours, close supervision, and live-in conditions, frequently refused them. In view of their willingness to turn down these jobs, a minimum wage would only reinforce women's worst qualities, rewarding the inefficient without benefiting those who were oriented toward hard work and mobility. On the other side of this coin, a picture of women's inability to advance themselves could yield an argument for state aid, as illustrated by the belief that they were in occupations not reachable in the normal course of trade union organization. "A great deal can be said for minimum wage laws and laws limiting the hours of labor for women," asserted feminist Crystal Eastman, who normally opposed special laws for women only, "on the ground that women's labor is the least adapted to organization and therefore the most easily exploited and most in need of legislative protection."[34] Women who selected jobs that restricted their ability to bargain collectively and were, therefore, incapable of securing a fair return on their wages constituted, according to some labor leaders, "a helpless class of labor, broken in spirit." "Practically impossible to organize under existing conditions," they might be more readily organized once their "broken spirit had been reinforced by a minimum wage."[35]

Women were represented as people with weak characters. Opponents of a minimum wage suggested that legislation would increase immorality because it would give extra money to frivolous, unworthy people. Those who favored a minimum wage argued that weak women would succumb to vice and prostitution at the least temptation and needed higher wages to enable them to resist.[36] Neither argument seemed to have much to do with reality. Of the fifteen experts who responded to the New York Factory Investigating Commission's question as to whether women's low wages yielded prostitution, twelve attributed prostitution to low family incomes, not the low wages of the woman worker. Still, the commission concluded that one of the dangers of low wages for women was vice and immorality, and a persistent demand of its nonexpert witnesses for a "wage that a woman could live on, and live right."[37]

Public debates over the minimum wage, arguments for and against it in a series of court cases, and the judicial decisions made in such cases built on these portraits. Both sides drew vivid pictures of women's helplessness in relation to work and wages in order to make a case for their positions. Those opposed to the minimum wage, and who might have relied on more complex descriptions of women's lives, chose instead to defend the wage system. Regulating the wage, in their view, would restrict the market, ignore supply and demand, reduce profits, and drive employers out of business. In the legal imagination, at least, free enterprise vied with family roles as the salvation of America. To save women might require a regulated wage; to save America required freedom of contract. The woman's wage became an arena for playing out struggles that ranged far beyond domesticity.

Arguments against the minimum wage were predicted heavily on the assumption that employers paid a "natural" wage that was the equivalent of the service rendered—that women were worth no more than what they earned. The neoclassical economic theory on which such arguments rested held the worker responsible for his or her place in the job market. In a free market, workers who could freely sell their labor earned the economic value of what they produced. Employers hired workers at different levels of wages calculated to reflect the value of the product created as well as the supply of workers willing to accept the wages offered. If women tended to work on low-value products (garments, paper towels, boxes, textiles, and shoes, for example), that was not the employers' fault, but a result of women's choices. Business could not pay more than "natural" wage without threatening the profits that enabled it to survive. If women's wages tended to be low, the logical explanation lay in a persistent assertion of a woman's "difference." A regulated minimum wage that forced employers to "supply individual needs . . . in excess of what the employee earns or is worth"[38] would be disastrous. From this flowed a series of questions: Should the wage be determined not by the value of the services rendered but by the cost of supporting women? Should industry be required to cover the deficit in women's wages? Was there a constitutional question implicit in the issue of "whether an employer may be compelled to pay the cost of maintaining the employee whose full services he voluntarily uses in the conduct of an enterprise?"[39] Since no employer would stay in business without profits, would attempts to regulate wages (as a function of the cost of supporting women rather than the value of the services they rendered) not drive employers out?

Circumventing the idea of freedom of contract by exacerbating women's weakness and helplessness transformed the debate. Freedom of contract rested on the notion that the wage was an abstraction—the product of agreement between employer and employee. The argument over the minimum wage, because it was gendered, exposed the social issues embodied in the wage and thus kept alive a social meaning on which defenders of free labor had insisted. The progressives connected the wage argument to hours suggesting that if women's wages were so low as to undermine their childbearing and rearing capacities, then the state as a whole would suffer because its future citizens would be weak and without good discipline and values. Under those circumstances, freedom of contract would threaten the "future of the race." For the courts to accept this argument required suspending wage theory and arguing for redistribution of income according to norms of social justice that recalled the ideals of advocates of free labor.

In focusing so heavily on separate spheres, protagonists and antagonists alike begged the question of social justice in the industrial sector, evoking fears that the extreme solutions required to compensate for women's weakness might threaten the free market. Thus, the argument over wages placed the judiciary squarely in the position of deciding whether to concede separate spheres to women in order to redistribute income sufficiently for women to maintain families (granting some credence to the older free labor ideology and enabling women to keep open possibilities for gendered action) or whether to sustain freedom of contract in the face of the apparent threat to families. The conundrum that this posed is revealed in the language and arguments used during the course of the debate.

First, the debate raised the issue of the appropriate relationship between male and female wages. If the natural wage was a male wage, and women's wages were low because they "could not earn a wage," then attempts to create an arbitrary minimum for women and not men would threaten the balance between male and female spheres. The alternative would be to raise male wages. But this begged the issue of whether a state that could impose a minimum wage could not also impose a maximum. Some who agreed that the public welfare was menaced by low wages for women had to concede that it was equally vulnerable to low male wages. For if higher wages were necessary to health and morality—if a law fixing wages was a health law—surely then it was desirable for both men and women. If benefits claimed for women were given to men after all, then whole families would benefit. As one commentator put it, "If . . . a minimum wage law for women is constitutional because it tends to provide the race with healthy moral mothers, so would a minimum wage law for men, because it would tend to provide the race with strong honest fathers."[40] Once opened, that pandora's box could only produce a case for a higher wage for all.

Closely related to the issue of health was that of morality. One of the basic arguments for minimum wages was that women with insufficient incomes were regularly tempted into amorous relationships or even into prostitution in order to make ends meet. Raising this issue involved not only questions of male morality but those of women's character as well. As Justice Sutherland put it, "It cannot be shown that well paid women safeguard their morals more carefully than those who are poorly paid." He added, "If women require a minimum wage to preserve their morals, men require it to preserve their honesty."[41] The same kind of logic served the purposes of an Arkansas judge who dissented from his colleagues in believing the minimum wage to be unconstitutional. The wage, he argued, was not an issue of health and morality at all:

> Wealth, at least to the extent that it affords ease and comfort, is the goal of all mankind, regardless of sex, and failure of its attainment often brings discontent and unhappiness, but I am unwilling to say that women's health or virtue is dependent upon financial circumstances so as to justify the State in attempting to regulate her wages. Her virtue is without price in gold. She may become the victim of her misplaced affections and yield her virtue, but sell it for money—no. When she falls so low as that it is only from the isolated helplessness of her shame and degradation.[42]

If women could not earn their keep, then society, not women, would pay the cost of women's low wages. Again, women who worked were depicted as mere parasites who imposed a financial burden on the state and on other industries. Women's low wages, in this view, were nothing less than a "menace to public welfare." As Felix Frankfurter put it in the famous case of *Stettler v. O'Hara*, "Industries supporting male workers were being drawn upon to assist in supporting women workers engaged in other industries, which were refusing to carry their cost." Frankfurter, defending Oregon's minimum wage law, argued that the immediate effects of women's low wages were to impose financial burdens on the state, " which threatened excessive and unremunerative taxation." Women's wages, he argued, were a "community problem—a problem affecting the state in its pervasive entirety."[43]

The degree to which arguments over women's wages threatened freedom of contract emerges most forcefully in the suggestion that depictions of women's difference that fueled a demand for the minimum wage would in the end raise false expectations as to the distribution of income and property. These expectations could not, according to some, be met under the limits of the Constitution, for they required "A to give part of his property to B."[44] Such an action would deny individual rights, destroy natural competition, and evoke the spector of social revolution. Minimum wage legislation, in the words of a June 1917 commentator, was "a new expression of the paternalistic and socialistic tendencies of the day. It savors of the division of property between those who have and those who have not, and the leveling of fortunes by division under governmental supervision. It is consistent with the orthodox socialist creed, but it is not consistent with the principles of our government which are based upon the protection of individual rights."[45]

Champions of the minimum wage did not deny that individual rights were endangered by regulation. Rather, they argued that individual rights could not be allowed to supersede the rights of "women who must labor in order to live. It would seem," noted Justice Wendell Stafford, who had been part of the majority in the original District of Columbia Supreme Court decision that upheld the constitutionality of minimum wages, "that the right of this class to live on a barely decent level, and the right of the public to have them so live, should outweigh the right of those who do not need to work in order to live, and who therefore are merely asserting a right to earn money and thereby accumulate property."[46]

The idea that weak women were at some level responsible for undermining a cherished principle of government was echoed and expanded by court decisions at all levels beginning in 1917. It finally became a key argument for invalidating the minimum wage. From 1912 to 1923, the minimum wage was more or less sustained. But by 1917, tensions provoked by the emphasis on gender difference became apparent. Writing for the District of Columbia Supreme Court in the penultimate round of *Children's Hospital v. Adkins*, Justice Josiah A. Van Orsdel declared that "legislation tending to fix the prices at which private property shall be sold . . . places a limitation upon the distribution of wealth, and is aimed at the correction of the inequalities of fortune which are inevitable under our form of government, due to personal liberty and the private ownership of property. These principles are embodied in the Constitution itself."[47]

Imposing a minimum wage was thus the equivalent of using the police power to "level inequalities of fortune." Van Orsdel made his own economic bias clear: A wage based upon competitive ability is just, and leads to frugality and honest industry, and inspires an ambition to attain the highest possible efficiency, while the equal wage paralyzes ambition and promotes prodigality and indolence. It takes away the strongest incentive to human labor, thrift and efficiency, and works injustice to employee and employer alike, thus affecting injuriously the whole social and industrial fabric."[48]

"No greater calamity," he continued, could befall the wage-earners of this country than to have the legislative power to fix wages upheld. It would deprive them of the most sacred safeguard which the Constitution affords. Take from the citizen the right to freely contract and sell his labor for the highest wage which his individual skill and efficiency will command, and the laborer would be reduced to an automaton—a mere creature of the state. It is paternalism in the highest degree . . . it is but a step to a legal requirement that the industrious, frugal, economical citizen must divide his earnings with his indolent, worthless neighbor . . . . it will logically, if persisted in, end in social disorder and revolution."[49]

Under the circumstances, to defend women's differences required what some perceived as an attack on first principles. Advocates of the minimum wage had coached their arguments in exaggerated assertions about the traditional roles of women. But to maintain those roles at the expense of freedom of contract would, in the view of a conservative judiciary, undermine the principle of individual rights and the economic system itself. To accommodate the pressure would jeopardize the wages of men and of other women, the profits of industry, and the free enterprise system. Minimum wages, in short, would so alter the role of the state as to produce nothing less than the dreaded disease of sovietism.[50]

Faced with a sharp conflict between two ideological systems, one had to give way. If women were to continue as paid workers, the courts could either deny the importance of gender differences or negate freedom of contract. As it turned out, the Supreme Court chose to sustain freedom of contract by declaring the minimum wage "to be wholly beyond legislative discretion."[51] Divided five to three (with Brandeis abstaining because his daughter had been involved in preparing the brief), the court declared that gender differences had come to the vanishing point, that there was no reason therefore to abrogate freedom of contract, and that the minimum wage was unconstitutional.

To some observers, it appeared that the court had done an "anomalous somersault." A closer view reveals the decision to have been a logical consequence of the contradictions produced by the way in which women's differences had been incorporated into the social meaning of the wage. Speaking for the majority, Sutherland evoked the underlying issues as he saw them: free enterprise was arrayed against motherhood. He concluded that free enterprise had to be preserved, even at the cost of wiping out the separate spheres. The wage, he asserted, was based on a "just equivalence of the service rendered," not on the need of the worker. No matter how pressing, the need of the worker could not avail. "The ancient inequality of the sexes," he declared in a much quoted paragraph,

> has continued with diminishing intensity. In view of the great—not to say revolutionary—changes which have taken place. . . . in the contractual, political, and civil status of women, culminating in the Nineteenth Amendment, it is not unreasonable to say that those differences have come almost, if not quite, to the vanishing point. . . . While the physical differences must be recognized in appropriate cases, and legislation fixing hours or conditions of work may properly take them into account, we cannot accept the doctrine that women of mature age, *sui juris,* require or may be subjected to restrictions upon their liberty of contract which could not lawfully be imposed in the case of men under similar circumstances.[52]

Castigating those who did not pay attention to employers' needs and acknowledging that a woman was worth little in the free labor market, he attacked the statute for failing to "require that the wage have any relation to the reasonable value of the workers' services."

Bold as the decision was, it might have been expected. It built upon what was implicit in Holmes's opinion in *Quong Wing.* Holmes had asserted that the existence of sexual difference (or separate spheres) was the legitimate province of the state to define. In his view, sexual difference was a legitimate classification for legislators. By 1923, in a new political environment, the Supreme Court stymied by the tension between attributions of gender difference and an economic system that assumed freedom of contract, chose to take the opposite position. It simply defined sexual difference as less important.

But the issue was not easily put to rest. The rhetoric of the debate and the reality of women's lives conspired to keep it alive. In the dissents to *Adkins* and in the protest that ensued, a strong appeal to social justice, rooted in family and domestic life, persisted. Dissenting Chief Justice Robert Taft, for example, disagreed with the majority decision because "it is not the function of this court to hold Congressional acts invalid simply because they are passed to carry out economic views which the Court believes to be unwise or unsound."[53] To others, it violated simple principles of social justice. "It demeans humanity," said Samuel Gompers, that "women and girl wage earners are to be bought over the counter."[54] Confusion reigned over the Court's consistent affirmation of gender difference when it came to hours and working conditions and its equally consistent opposition to sex-based classifications when wages were at stake. Case after case came to the Supreme Court, only to be turned back.[55] But by 1937 the Court once again reestablished an interest in women's difference as the opening wedge of a fight for social justice.

In *West Coast Hotel Co. v. Parrish,* the Court reversed itself. Chief Justice Charles Evans Hughes, speaking for the Court, rejected a freedom of contract defense against minimum wage legislation because "the Constitution does not speak of freedom of contract. It speaks of liberty. . . . But the liberty safeguarded is liberty in a social organization which requires the protection of law against the evils which menace the health, safety, morals and welfare of the people." Speaking in the language of nineteenth-century advocates of free labor, he denied any "absolute" freedom of contract and argued that liberty did not imply "immunity from reasonable regulations and prohibitions imposed in the interest of the community."[56] What were the interests of the community? They resided in protecting those parties that did not stand upon an equality and therefore in protecting women's economic bargaining power.

Calling upon *Muller v. Oregon,* and repeating the words of *Quong Wing* that only a "fictitious equality" existed between men and women, the Court argued, in overturning *Adkins,* that women "are relatively defenseless against the denial of a living wage." Low wages were "detrimental to their health and well being" and "cast a direct burden for their support upon the community." Echoing Holmes's insistence on the state's right to determine where difference should be emphasized, the Court castigated selfish employers for disregarding the public interest, noted the anguish of the economic depression, and asserted that the "relative need" of women "in the presence of the evil, no less than the evil itself is a matter for legislative judgment."[57]

But the premonitions of Van Orsdel, Sutherland, and others had not been misplaced. For, though Chief Justice Hughes used gender differences to highlight the state's interest in "the exploitation of a class of workers who are in an unequal position with respect to bargaining power and are thus relatively defenseless against the denial of a living wage," he explicitly utilized female difference as the entering wedge for judicial decisions about others in need.[58] In so doing, he ensured that a new definition of liberty would prevail. Less than three years later, the Court relied on its decision in *West Coast Hotel* to sustain the constitutionality of the Fair Labor

Standards Act, which legislated minimum wages for men and women. But it abandoned sex difference as the crucial criterion for undermining freedom of contract. In *United States v. Darby,* the case that affirmed the FLSA and cleared the path for the social legislation of the modern period, the Court transcended gender and argued that "it is no longer open to question that the fixing of a minimum wage is within the legislative power."[59]

How can the shift be explained? Part of the answer lies in the change in social conditions in the fourteen years between the two decisions. Sutherland, in dissent from the majority in *West Coast Hotel,* tried once again to make the case that there was no longer any reason why women "should be put in different classes in respect of their legal right to make contracts. Nor should they be denied, in effect, the right to compete with men for work paying lower wages which men may be willing to accept."[60] This argument carried little weight in the Depression climate. But much of the shift in Court opinion lay in the way that language about women and agitation around them demonstrated the evident social purposes of such legislation. By the 1930s, when public opinion was once again ready to consider the search for social justice as part of the legitimate end of government, the idea that women constituted a separate and deserving class could and did serve to illustrate the rigidity of old doctrines of freedom of contract. Attention to gender difference had kept alive the possibility that all workers deserved state protection. As Justice Harlan Fiske Stone put it in his dissent from the Court's final attempt to preserve the sanctity of freedom of contract in *Morehead v. New York,* "In the years which have intervened since the Adkins case. . . . we have had opportunity to perceive more clearly that a wage insufficient to support the worker does not visit its consequences upon him alone; that it may effect profoundly the entire economic structure of society and, in any case, that it casts on every taxpayer, and on government itself, the burden of solving the problems of poverty, subsistence, health and morals of large numbers in the community."[61]

Looking at the struggle over the mimimum wage should convince us that, whatever the realities of gender differences, the idea of difference constitutes the cultural context within which debates over workplace aspirations and expectations are shaped. As difference remains embedded in the wage, so it is hidden in other arenas of social policy. But in the Progressive Era, gendered ideas contested with other systems of thought to produce the compromises that yielded familiar legislation. If we think about legislation this way, we might learn something about how ideas are institutionalized into law and public policy. For as Justice Holmes put it in

1912, "The particular points at which [sex] differences shall be emphasized by legislation are largely in the power of the state." The progressives fully understood and utilized that idea.

Notes

This essay was first published in *A Woman's Wage: Historical Meanings and Social Consequences* (Lexington: Univ. Press of Kentucky, 1990).

1. Quoted in Florence Kelley, *Women's Work and War* 1 (July 1918): 3.

2. The other states were Arizona, Arkansas, California, Colorado, Kansas, Massachusetts, Minnesota, North Dakota, Oregon, Texas, Utah, Washington, and Wisconsin. Bills were under consideration in Missouri, Ohio, New Jersey, and New York. For a summary of minimum wage legislation to 1919, see Lindley D. Clark, "Minimum Wage Laws of the United States," *Monthly Labor Review* 12 (Mar. 1921): 1-20.

3. "Calls Wage Ruling by Court a Calamity," *New York Times*, Apr. 12, 1923, 11. See also "The Minimum Wage Law," editorial, *New York Times*, Apr. 11, 1923, 20; and "Freedom of Contract," *St. Louis Post-Dispatch*, Apr. 10, 1923, 18. For contrary opinions with different reasoning, see "The Minimum Wage Decision," *Milwaukee Journal*, Apr. 10, 1923, 8; and "The Minimum Wage Decision," *Washington Post*, Apr. 10, 1923, 6.

4. "Minimum Wage Law for Women Is Void," *New York Times*, Apr. 10, 1923, 23.

5. *New York World*, Apr. 11, 1923, 13.

6. "New Wage Decision Stirs Women to Act," *New York Times*, Apr. 11, 1923, 13.

7. "Labor Leaders Hit Wage Law Decision," *New York Times*, May 16, 1923, 5; and "Gompers Assails Wage Decision as Reactionary," *St. Louis Post-Dispatch*, Apr. 10, 1923, 1.

8. Henry R. Seager, "The Minimum Wage: What Next? A Symposium," *Survey* 50 (May 15, 1923): 216.

9. "Mr. Untermyer on the Minimum Wage Decision," *American Federationist* 30 (May 1923): 408; see also opinions quoted by Seager in "Minimum Wage"; Barbara Grimes, "Comment on Cases," *California Law Review* 11 (1923): 361; and "Minimum Wage Ruling Attacked," *New York Evening Post*, Apr. 10, 1923, 1.

10. *Muller v. Oregon*, 208 U.S. 412 (1908).

11. *Adkins v. Children's Hospital*, 261 U.S. 525, 546 (1923). For background, see Judith Baer, *The Chains of Protection: The Judicial Response to Women's Labor Legislation* (Westport, Conn.: Greenwood, 1978); Susan Lehrer, *Origins of Protective Labor Legislation for Women: 1905-1925* (Albany State Univ. of New York Press, 1987); and Elizabeth Faulkner Baker, *Protective Labor Legislation with Special Reference to Women in the State of New York*, Columbia University Studies in History, Economics and Public Law, 16 (New York: Columbia Univ. Press, 1925).

12. *Stettler v. O'Hara*, 243 U.S. 629 (1917).

13. Clark, "Minimum Wage Laws," 5. In addition to Oregon, the highest courts of Minnesota (*Williams v. Evans* et al., 139 Minn. 32 [1917]); Arkansas, (*State v. Crowe*, 130 Ark. 272 [1917]); Massachusetts (*Holcombe v. Creamer*, 231 Mass. 99 [1918]); and Washington, (*Spokane Hotel v. Younger*, 113 Wash. 359 [1920]), had all explicitly sustained such legislation. See Rome G. Brown, "Oregon Minimum Wage Cases," *Minnesota Law Review* 1 (June 1917): 471-86.

14. In part, the relatively low level of opposition reflects the fact that many states excluded from coverage industries in which female labor was most crucial. For example,

Texas excluded agriculture, domestic service, and nursing. Arkansas excluded cotton factories and fruit harvesting.

15. Baker, *Protective Labor Legislation*, 101-2, writing in 1924, raises the question of whether this gender-based strategy might not in retrospect have been a mistake. After all, Sutherland struck down the law in part because, he argued, women were no longer different from men. In addition, the Court had sustained a law protecting the health of male workers in *Bunting v. Oregon*, 243 U.S. 426 (1917).

16. Cited in *Settler v. O'Hara* et al., 69 Ore. 519 (1914), 519; and in *Adkins v. Children's Hospital*, 261 U.S. 525 (1923), 525.

17. *Muller v. Oregon*, 208 U.S. 412, 422 (1908).

18. *Adkins v. Children's Hospital*, 261 U.S. 546 (1912).

19. For the pre–Civil War notion, see Eric Foner, *Free Soil, Free Labor, Free Men: The Ideology of the Republican Party before the Civil War* (New York: Oxford Univ. Press, 1970). For legal development in the Gilded Age, see William Forbath, "The Ambiguities of Free Labor: Labor and the Law in the Gilded Age," *Wisconsin Law Review* (1985): 767-817.

20. John B. Andrews and W.D.P. Bliss, *History of Women in Trade Unions* (1911; reprint, New York: Arno, 1974), 47, 48.

21. The struggle is chronicled in such books as Leon Fink, *Workingmen's Democracy: The Knights of Labor and American Politics* (Urbana: Univ. of Illinois Press, 1983); and Brian Greenberg, *Worker and Community: Response to Industrialization in a Nineteenth Century American City, Albany and New York, 1850-1884* (Albany: State Univ. of New York Press, 1985).

22. Exceptions to a worker's right to freedom of contract generally included only occupations, such as railroad workers, miners, and seamen, in which public health and safety were at risk. Where private health was concerned, as in the case of bakers and cigarmakers, courts generally refused to support state intervention.

23. *Adkins v. Children's Hospital*, 261 U.S. 554 (1923). This led one commentator to observe that "the idea of the opinion seems to be that somehow the Constitution entitles the employer of such benefits as he may derive from the independent resources of possible women employees" (Thomas Reed Powell, "The Judiciality of Minimum Wage Legislation," *Harvard Law Review* 37 [1924]: 565).

24. Leon Fink, "The New Labor History and the Powers of Historical Pessimism: Consensus, Hegemony, and the Case of the Knights of Labor," *Journal of American History* 75 (June 1988): 115-36, argues that the idea of free labor retained much of its zest long after the corporate attack dropped. John Diggins, "Comrades and Citizens: New Mythologies in American Historiography," *American Historical Review* 90 (June 1985): 614-38, argues, in contrast, that the corporate image had won over most workers by the late 1880s. My own sense is that the issue of gender kept the question alive into the 1930s.

25. *Quong Wing v. Kirkendall*, 223 U.S. 59, 62 (1912).

26. Ibid., 63.

27. Ibid. In a dissenting opinion, Justice Joseph P. Lamar denied that difference could be so arbitrarily used. "The individual characteristics of the owner do not furnish a basis in which to make a classification for purposes of taxation," he declared (64-65).

28. The best known case is, *Bradwell v. Illinois*, 16 Wall 130 (1873), in which Justice Miller, speaking for the Court, argued that the privileges and immunities protected by the Fourteenth Amendment did not supersede state laws—in this case the Illinois law that reserved membership in the bar to men. But it is Justice Bradley's concurring opinion that is

widely cited, for Bradley chose to broaden the Illinois Supreme Court's assertion that Bradwell was properly deprived access to the bar because she was a *married* woman and thus could not be bound by contracts. According to Bradley, "the civil law has always recognized a wide difference in the respective spheres of man and woman. Man is, or should be, woman's protector and defender. The natural and proper timidity and delicacy which belongs to the female sex evidently unfits it for many of the occupations of civil life" (132). See also Leslie Friedman Goldstein, *The Constitutional Rights of Women: Cases in Law and Social Change* (New York: Longman, 1979), 45–51; Leo Kanowitz, *Sex Roles in Law and Society: Cases and Materials* (Albuquerque: Univ. of New Mexico Press, 1973), 42–46.

29. New York State, *Fourth Annual Report of the Factory and Investigating Commission* (Albany: S.B. Lyon, 1915), 1: 25: Hereinafter referred to as FIC.

30. *Adkins v. Children's Hospital,* 261 U.S. 555-56 (1923).

31. See the testimony of John Mitchell, Norman Hapgood, Edward Bates, and Albertus Nooner, published in the FIC *Fourth Report,* 1: 706, 769, 777, 780; and the testimony of Mary Simkhovitch, Frederick Whitin, and Martha Falconer in Appx. III: 414, 410, 394.

32. *Morehead v. New York ex rel Tipaldo,* 298 U.S. 587, 590 (1936).

33. Testimony of Harry Allen Overstreet and Roger Babson in FIC, *Fourth Report,* 1: 730, 790.

34. Crystal Eastman, "Equality or Protection," *Equal Rights* 15 (Mar. 1924): 156.

35. Testimony of Tim Healey and Homer Call in FIC, *Fourth Report,* 1: 771, 770; Helen Marot (774) had an opposite perspective. In "Equal Rights Amendment," *American Federationist* 45 (Mar. 1938): 245, William Green noted, "Women with centuries of homework and with traditions of legal wardship as a background do not find it as easy to establish voluntary collective bargaining with the employer as men workers."

36. Testimony of Maude Miner, James Brown Reynolds, and Frederick Whitin, in FIC, *Fourth Report,* 1, Appx. III, 410, 412, 416.

37. Testimony of Charles Augustus Yates, New York State, *Factory Investigating Commission, Syracuse Hearings* (Albany: S.B. Lyon, 1911), 1097.

38. Brown, "Oregon Minimum Wage Cases," 478.

39. Powell, "Judiciality of Minimum Wage Legislation," 545.

40. National Consumers League, *The Supreme Court and Minimum Wage Legislation* (New York: New Republic, 1925), 204. Elizabeth Baker argued: "Both men and women need a living wage in order to live. A sub-living wage for men is perhaps the largest single cause of the entrance of their wives and children into gainful employment; thus the argument of prescribing the payment of the living wage by law may prove to be as strong for one sex as for the other." Baker, *Protective Labor Legislation,* 424-25.

41. *Adkins v. Children's Hospital,* 261 U.S., 556.

42. *State v. Crowe,* 130 Ark. 272, 285 (1917).

43. Brief of Defendant in Error, U.S. Supreme Court, Records and Briefs, *Stettler v. O'Hara,* October term 1916-17, Docket nos. 25 and 26, A12. See also testimony of Timothy Healey and Edward T. Devine, FIC, *Fourth Report,* 1: 771, 697; as well as the discussion of these issues in Irwin Yellowitz, *Labor and the Progressive Movement in New York State: 1897-1916* (Ithaca: Cornell Univ. Pres, 1965), 131-35.

44. Ellis Brief, U.S. Supreme Court, Records and Briefs, *Adkins v. Children's Hospital,* October term 1922, Docket nos. 795 and 796, Ellis Brief, 43.

45. Brown, "Oregon Minimum Wage Cases," 486.

46. Transcript of D.C. Supreme Court Opinion, June 6, 1921, U.S. Supreme Court, Records and Briefs, *Adkins v. Children's Hospital,* June 5, 1921, October term 1922, Docket nos. 795 and 796, 42.

47. Van Orsdel opinion, *Adkins v. Children's Hospital,* 284 Fed. Rep. 613, 617 (1922).

48. Ibid., 621.

49. Ibid., 623.

50. This was countered by a supporter who argued, "If we fail to give adequate remedy to real oppressive conditions, the people will turn to other economic systems for remedies." *Adkins v. Children's Hospital,* State of Wisconsin, Amicus Curaie, Records and Briefs, 14.

51. Barbara H. Grimes, "Constitutional Law: Police Power; Minimum Wage for Women," in National Consumers' League, *Supreme Court,* 107.

52. *Adkins v. Children's Hospital,* 261 U.S. 553.

53. Ibid., 562; Taft reasoned: employees wih the lowest pay are not equal to employers; they are subject to the overreaching of harsh and greedy employers; the result is the evils of the sweating system.

54. "Gompers Assails Wage Decision as Reactionary," *St. Louis Post-Dispatch,* Apr. 10, 1923, 1.

55. In *Radice v. New York,* 264 U.S. 292 (1924), the Court sustained legislation that prohibited women from working at night. Other cases that turned back attempts to establish minimum wages included *Murphy v. Sardell,* 269 U.S. 530 (1925), for Arizona; *Donham v. West Nelson Co.*, 273 U.S. 657 (1927), for Arkansas; and *Morehead v. New York ex rel Tipaldo,* 298 U.S. 587 (1936), for New York. For commentary on Morehead, see Robert L. Hale, "Minimum Wages and the Constitution," *Columbia Law Review* 36 (Apr. 1936): 629-33.

56. *West Coast Hotel Co. v. Parrish,* 300 U.S. 379, 391, 399 (1937). Note the shift in imagery here. Where earlier discussions had described women as a burden on the community, Hughes argued that "the community is not bound to provide what is in effect a subsidy for unconscionable employers" (399). Sutherland, dissenting, repeated at length his defense of freedom of contract as affirmed by *Adkins,* concluding somewhat plaintively, "We do not understand that it is questioned by the present decision" (406).

57. Ibid., 400.

58. Ibid. 399. Hughes quoted an earlier Court decision to the effect that "if the law presumably hits the evil where it is most felt, it is not to be overthrown because there are other instances to which it might have been applied" (400).

59. *U.S. v. Darby,* 312 U.S. 125 (1940). Kanowitz, *Sex Roles,* 190, notes that "the cases relied on by the Court in Parrish were all cases that make no distinction between the sexes insofar as the constitutionality of the states' regulation of the employment relationship was concerned." cf. *West Coast Hotel.* Kanowitz also notes that the Court's decision in *Darby* signified its belief that in *Parrish* it had upheld a minimum wage in general, not one for women only (468).

60. *West Coast Hotel,* 411, 412.

61. *Morehead v. New York,* 635.

8

Hull House Goes to Washington: Women and the Children's Bureau

MOLLY LADD-TAYLOR

During the Progressive Era, women reformers lobbied the federal government to assume responsibility for children's welfare. Historians have investigated the ideology and careers of elite women reformers, but little is known about the role working-class and rural women played in the formation of public policy.[1] What impact did new federal programs have on ordinary women? Did they benefit or lose as the authority of the federal government increased? An examination of the operation of the U.S. Children's Bureau, the first government agency to be headed and staffed almost entirely by women, illuminates the relationship between women reformers, working-class and rural mothers, and the state.

Established in 1912, the Children's Bureau operated as the women's branch of the federal government in the 1910s and 1920s. It gave professional women a place in the government—eight years before they were able to vote—and enabled them to shape public policy directly. The Children's Bureau had close ties to settlement houses, women's clubs, and individual mothers, and it gave them all a voice in the federal government. However, the Bureau did not receive unanimous support for all of its activities; some women were estranged by the agency's conception of child welfare and resented the government's intrusion into their lives.[2]

The two principal campaigns of the Children's Bureau, improving infant health and regulating child labor, illuminate the dual character of the Progressive Era state, which both advocated social justice and enforced social control. Although it grew out of the movement to curtail child labor, the Bureau is best remembered for its leadership role in promoting child health. The agency acted as an advocate for powerless women and children, and it led a broad-based movement to combat infant mortality, which culminated in the passage of the nation's first social-welfare measure, the Sheppard-Towner Maternity and Infancy Act of 1921. At the same time, the Bureau lobbied for and then enforced child-labor legislation, imposing reformers' views of childhood on an unreceptive working class. Although the federal agency published thousands of pages on child-labor legislation and administered the 1916 Keating-Owen Act during the nine months it was in operation, the Children's Bureau could not generate significant grass-roots support for child-labor reform.

The drive to create a federal bureau to compile and disseminate information about children was spearheaded by settlement house residents, clubwomen, and opponents of child labor. The idea originated in 1903 with Florence Kelley, secretary of the National Consumers' League, and Lillian Wald, nurse and founder of New York's Henry Street Settlement. Both women had been active in the child-labor movement and, as settlement residents, had witnessed firsthand poor women's need for child-rearing information and health care for their families. President Theodore Roosevelt supported their efforts, and the National Child Labor Committee, organized in 1904 to investigate child labor and lobby for stronger laws against it, drafted a bill. In 1909, the White House Conference on the Care of Dependent Children endorsed the idea of an agency for children, and hearings commenced. Opposition to the bill came primarily from manufacturers hostile to the regulation of child labor and from conservatives who saw the bureau as an invasion of family life. Social workers, reformers, and women's clubs who supported the bill insisted that children needed protection. Wald noted with irony that Congress appropriated federal funds to protect crops and livestock but not children. On April 8, 1912, six years after the first bill was introduced in Congress, President William Howard Taft signed the Children's Bureau bill into law.[3]

The creation of the Children's Bureau was an important symbol of federal interest in child welfare, but its limited budget and small staff suggest that Congress intended it to be merely symbolic. Housed in the Department of Commerce and Labor, the Children's Bureau was originally conceived as a research agency designed to "investigate and report . . . upon all matters pertaining to the welfare of children and child life among all classes of our people." The law specifically mentioned infant mortality, juvenile delinquency, "dangerous occupations," "accidents and diseases," and legislation affecting children. With an initial appropriation of $25,640 and a predominantly female staff of fifteen, the Bureau had fewer resources than many private child-welfare organizations, leading some reformers to doubt that it could be a significant factor in reform. They underestimated the Bureau's first director, Julia Lathrop.[4]

For women reformers, the appointment of Hull House resident Julia

Lathrop as first chief of the Children's Bureau was a triumph equal to the creation of the Bureau itself. Lathrop was the first woman to be appointed head of a federal agency, and her appointment was a recognition of women's efforts in the formation both of the Bureau and of their unique interest in child welfare. A graduate of Vassar College and longtime resident of Hull House, Lathrop was the first woman member of the Illinois State Board of Charities and a leader in the fight for the juvenile court and for better care for the mentally ill.[5]

As a visible, if not very powerful, woman in a high government position, Lathrop had to contend with congressional opponents—and even some Children's Bureau friends—who doubted women's administrative abilities and dismissed the women on the Bureau staff as unwomanly spinsters. Like her fellow settlement residents, Lathrop advanced women's influence in government without explicitly challenging women's sphere. She operated successfully in the male political world and never married or had children, yet she portrayed child welfare as being above politics and maintained that motherhood was "the most essential of employments." Lathrop's emphasis on women's maternal role and her denial of female career ambition allowed the Children's Bureau to extend its influence without appearing to do so.[6]

In its early days, the Children's Bureau functioned more like a social settlement than a government bureaucracy. Like Hull House residents, Children's Bureau workers were concerned with the physical, psychological, and economic well-being of the "whole" child. Lathrop shared Jane Addams's belief in the reciprocal dependence of the classes and tried to resolve social conflicts by building relationships that crossed classes and cultures. While settlement residents gave money and acted as nurses or midwives for neighborhood women, Lathrop and her staff frequently sent money for food or clothing out of their own pockets to needy women who wrote to them. These actions, which formed an integral part of the Bureau's baby-saving campaign, led to women's loyalty and appreciation of the federal agency and to their enthusiastic support of its work.[7]

An impressive political strategist, Lathrop designed a program for the Children's Bureau that both protected children and safeguarded women's role in the government. Anxious to defend the Bureau from its detractors and to justify its expansion, Lathrop determined that the Bureau's initial activity should avoid controversy while building public support for the new agency. Interpreting the bill's open-ended language regarding the "welfare of the children" broadly, Lathrop emphasized issues that affected all women and not just the poor. Although the Children's Bureau was originally identified with child-labor reform, Lathrop decided that its first focus should be infant health. She felt that conservatives who opposed investigations into child labor could hardly object to research on infant health. The Bureau's birth registration campaign and investigations into the causes of infant mortality were therefore designed to build support for the agency while gathering information considered necessary for further reforms. "I think there is no antagonism to the work which the Bureau has undertaken in birth registration and in making an inquiry into infant mortality," Lathrop wrote Wald in 1913. "Of course, as time goes on the Bureau will necessarily be compelled to deal with matters which are less generally acceptable. . . . I am on the whole rather glad that it has begun with a small staff and a small appropriation, but in the course of the next few years I think it should increase rapidly."[8]

Lathrop also used her extensive network of contacts among women's clubs, college graduates, scholars, and politicians to build public support for the Children's Bureau. When Congress tried to limit the Bureau's 1914 appropriations to $25,000 (the minimum allowed by law), she mobilized club women and reformers to lobby their congressmen and convinced newspapers and magazines such as the *Ladies' Home Journal* to write favorable articles about the Bureau's work. As a result, the agency received an appropriation of $139,000, over five times greater than that of the previous year.[9]

Combating infant mortality was not, as some historians have implied, inherently less controversial than regulating child labor.[10] Although saving babies' lives had obvious appeal, Lathrop's strategy of focusing on infant health had three additional advantages over concentrating on child labor. First and foremost was that, as a new movement, the child-health campaign had not yet developed a strong opposition. Child-labor reform was associated with radicalism, for labor organizations had spoken out against child labor as early as the 1870s and 1880s. According to Jane Addams, Hull House residents (who had had their first lobbying experience with the 1893 Illinois child labor law) were sharply criticized for their attempt to restrain manufacturers. By 1900, twenty-eight states had some kind of child labor legislation, and businessmen had mobilized to fight the laws. In contrast to child-labor reform, baby-saving did not become a political campaign until the Children's Bureau took on the issue in 1913. Although physicians and public health reformers had been concerned about infant mortality for many years—the American Association for the Prevention of Infant Mortality was established in 1909—it was not until health reformers entered politics and demanded government appropriations and federal involvement in infant health care that the baby-saving campaign developed a significant opposition.[11]

A second strategic advantage of the baby-saving campaign was that the Children's Bureau women did not have to compete with men for its leadership. The mostly male National Child Labor Committee established itself as leader of child-labor reform before the Children's Bureau was created, and Lathrop believed it had a paternalistic and condescending attitude toward the Bureau staff.[12] Yet few male reformers presumed to speak for women on such intimate matters as maternal and infant health, and the women of the Children's Bureau were allowed to emerge uncontested as leaders of the Progressive Era baby-saving campaign. Finally, while child-labor reform was primarily popular among the middle class, the infant-health campaign had the potential for bringing together women "among all classes of our people," since wealthy and poor mothers alike feared their children would die.

The decision to focus on infant mortality reflects not only Lathrop's political acumen but also her concern about the nation's infant death rate, one of the highest among industrialized nations. In 1915, 10 percent of all infants and almost 20 percent of black children in the birth registration area (where statistics were collected) died before their first birthday. Lathrop viewed the baby-saving campaign as part of a broad movement for child health and welfare rather than as an issue separate from child-labor reform. For example, birth registration was as essential to the enforcement of child-labor legislation and compulsory school attendance as it was to the prevention of infant death and disease.[13] Lathrop hoped that the Bureau's birth registration drive, child care bulletins, and infant mortality studies would generate a women's movement demanding child-welfare reform.

The Bureau's infant mortality studies, which relied not on death records but on interviews with mothers about their living children, were both innovative sociology and a useful organizing tool. According to assistant Bureau chief Lewis Merriam, the goal of the studies was not to "conduct investigations for the sake of investigations but to conduct investigations which will aid in the improvement of the condition of children."[14] The first study, conducted in 1913 in Johnstown, Pennsylvania, a steel town with a large immigrant population, was followed by seven other investigations. Federal agents worked closely with women's clubs, parent-teacher associations, the clergy, and the press to develop contacts in each community. The Children's Bureau was convinced that almost every mother would help with the study if she knew that "her testimony may be helpful to other mothers rearing children" and instructed investigators to appeal to women "on the ground that the Bureau recognizes mothers and plans to build its future work to a considerable extent on their advice, testimony, and cooperation." Conscious of the need to win women's support and sensitive to the intimate nature of the questions, the agency employed only women investigators. Interviewers were instructed not to ask about illegitimate births or about income from boarders or private charities if doing so would offend or injure the reputation of any woman.[15]

The public's enthusiastic response to the infant mortality investigations demonstrated that the issue of child health hit a responsive chord among the nation's women. In Johnstown, only two of the 1,553 mothers visited refused to be interviewed. Indeed, many women complained because the visitors had not brought along child-rearing information and because they were interested only in babies born in 1911, and not in other children. As the Children's Bureau staff had hoped, women's individual interest in the health of their children developed into collective action. Even before the results of the first study were made public in 1915, infant-welfare activity in Johnstown increased. Local women organized an infant-welfare exhibit, a baby-welfare station, and little mothers' classes for older children in the summer of 1914.[16]

The Children's Bureau investigations into infant mortality reflected the ambiguity of progressive reform, combining a concern with economics and the environment with a cultural bias in favor of the middle class. Interviewers focused on social and economic issues, such as improved housing conditions, sanitation, sewage, income, and access to medical care. Although they omitted questions about alcoholism and venereal disease, which conservatives considered leading causes of infant deaths, the agency's bias in favor of middle-class home life and child-rearing methods was evident in the inquiries about "superstitious" health practices and cultural variations in diet.

The Bureau's most dramatic finding was the sharp correlation between poverty and infant mortality. Researchers in Johnstown found that a child whose father earned under $521 a year was almost twice as likely to die as one whose father earned over $1,200 and that deaths were 40 percent higher in homes that did not have running water. According to Lathrop, the Johnstown study demonstrated that infant mortality resulted from "a coincidence of underpaid fathers, overworked and ignorant mothers, and those hazards to the life of the offspring which individual parents cannot avoid or control because they must be remedied by community action."[17]

Despite its conclusion that poverty was a chief cause of infant mortality, the Bureau stressed educational solutions rather than structural economic change. Although they concluded that household help, free or moderately priced prenatal and nursing care for poor women, and a family wage that enabled mothers to stay at home with their children would help save babies' lives, investigators focused on the problem of maternal ignorance.[18] "Poverty usually means low standards and ignorance on the part of the mother," read the Manchester, New Hampshire, report, "while ample income makes possible the attainment of higher standards, better medical attention, and greater knowledge in the care of the baby."[19] Prevented by political realities and the agency's narrow mandate from working for economic change, the Children's Bureau staff emphasized maternal education, which they hoped would make an immediate difference in women's lives.

Like the infant mortality studies, Bureau publications on *Infant Care* and *Prenatal Care* reflected both the progressive faith in science and efficiency and its interest in reform. Although the bulletins assumed that women had access to adequate health care, pure milk, and a "standard of life . . . high enough to permit a woman to conserve her strength for her family," author Mary West recognized that most mothers could not attain this ideal. West, a widowed mother of five, intended the bulletins to answer women's desperate need for child-rearing information while promoting "scientific" child-rearing methods she considered superior to traditional ways. On the one hand, the bulletins promoted modern conceptions of proper nutrition and cleanliness, cautioned against cuddling and spoiling the baby, and stressed the importance of feeding by the clock. On the other hand, they included money- and time-saving tips, useful information on food preparation and treatments for minor illnesses, and motherly common sense. The claim that children should have a room (or at least a bed) of their own and should drink a quart of milk a day probably increased the anxiety of many poor mothers. At the same time, it led others to expect these things for their children. Like the rest of the Children's Bureau staff, West hoped that insisting on a minimum standard of child welfare would lead women to demand child-welfare services for their own families.[20]

The public's enthusiastic response to the pamphlets showed that well-off and poor women all over the country read and tried to follow the Children's Bureau advice. Lathrop noted in 1914 that demand for *Prenatal Care* "exceeded all expectations"[21] and complained that fulfilling requests for pamphlets required the full-time services of one member of the Bureau's small staff—and sometimes the services of three or four. Lathrop, West, or another member of the Children's Bureau staff responded to every one of the thousands of letters they received from women across the United States. They tried through the mail to provide rural women with the emotional support and practical assistance that as settlement workers, they had offered in person to urban women. In addition to sending advice, encouragement, and occasionally money out of their own pockets, the Bureau staff prevailed upon local charities, women's clubs, and the Red Cross to donate layettes, food, money, and nursing care to needy mothers. Offering sympathy, advice, and even material assistance from afar, the government agency thus substituted for distant relatives and friends. Lathrop comforted an expectant Wyoming mother of two who lived sixty-five miles from a doctor and was "filled with perfect horror at the prospects ahead"[22] by sending encouraging letters, money, and medical care. The mother replied that the doctor sent by the Bureau was "so good and dear [that] One can not help *loving* her, and wanting her to stay all the time. It has certainly been a wonderful two days for me."[23]

Even women who hated and distrusted private and public charities saw the federal Children's Bureau as a friend. A pregnant mother of three from Chicago wrote a bitter letter to the government complaining that she was abused by her husband and that local charities refused to help her. Yet after Lathrop wrote her a sympathetic letter and sent Alice Hamilton of Hull House to visit, the woman wrote again to apologize for the tone of her earlier letter. Hamilton, she wrote, had been so supportive, "so different from the other people I have met."[24] Perhaps because the federal Children's Bureau was not allowed to dispense (or withdraw) money or material assistance, women were not intimidated by the government's power.

Women's personal allegiance to the Children's Bureau was central to the success of its baby-saving campaign. As a result of the contact they had with the Bureau through infant-health conferences, letters, and participation in the infant-mortality studies and birth registration campaign, thousands of mothers volunteered to help the Children's Bureau "in any way."[25] Fifteen hundred clubwomen helped with the Bureau's campaign for birth registration in 1914. Two years later, women's clubs working with the federal Children's Bureau organized more than two thousand National Baby Week observances across the country. By 1918, eleven million women served on more than seventeen thousand committees that weighed and measured preschool children as part of national Children's Year. A major achievement of the Bureau's baby-saving campaign was inspiring communities to establish permanent health clinics and birth registration programs. These services were funded and administered by local governments, allowing the federal Children's Bureau to stay within its mandate of research and education, to preserve its role as children's advocate, and to minimize public distrust of the federal government. In the context of traditional skepticism about federal power, the Bureau's lack of administrative authority had certain advantages.[26]

The Children's Bureau's dramatic success as an advocate for children contrasted with its efforts to enforce child-labor regulations during the same period. In one sense, the 1916 Keating-Owen Act was a great advance for child-welfare reformers and the Children's Bureau: it established a national minimum standard of protection for child workers and put federal authority behind child-labor regulation. Using the interstate commerce clause, Keating-Owen prohibited children under fourteen from working in mills, factories, or canneries and prevented those under sixteen from working in mines or quarries. Children under sixteen years old were prohibited from night work and from laboring more than eight hours a day. Congress placed the administration of the Keating-Owen Act within the Department of Labor, which in turn delegated the responsibility to the Children's Bureau. The passage of a federal child-labor law not only marked a stronger national commitment to the protection of children but gave women in the federal government real administrative authority for the first time. The $150,000 allocated for the bill's enforcement surpassed all previous appropriations to the Children's Bureau and enabled Lathrop to bring in fellow Hull House resident Grace Abbott to direct the new Child Labor Division.[27]

The limitations of the Keating-Owen Act were many. The minimum standard of protection fixed by federal law was weaker than that established under many state child-labor laws. While New York set minimum standards for children's health and level of education, for example, no such provisions were in the federal law. Moreover, the federal bill covered only about 150,000 workers, making no provision for the majority of child wage-earners in home industries, agriculture, and the street trades. The stipulation of thirty days as the period of time children were forbidden to work on a product before it was shipped—labeled a "joker" clause that nullified the purpose of the law by an indignant reformer—gave a loophole to manufacturers who made shipments at thirty-day intervals, periodically hiring and firing children to keep within the letter of the law. Worst, supporters' hopes that the child-labor law would be a stepping-stone to further reform were dashed when the Keating-Owen Act was declared unconstitutional within only nine months of its enactment.[28]

While the Children's Bureau's baby-saving campaign mobilized a grass-roots movement and brought much-needed information and health services to women in rural areas, the short-lived Keating-Owen Act neither grew out of nor led to broad-based support among the working class. The Bureau staff united with mothers from every region and social class to demand greater community attention to children's health, challenging the belief of many husbands and male politicians that prenatal and well-baby care was a luxury. Despite the support social workers, educators, labor leaders, and physicians gave the Keating-Owen Act, the child-labor law pitted poor families and manufacturers against the Children's Bureau, which enforced the law. Because only poor children worked for wages and only a minority of child wage-earners were covered by Keating-Owen, the fight to regulate child labor affected women differently, dividing rather than uniting women of different classes and regions.

Both the infant-health and child-labor reform movements operated from a cultural perspective often at odds with working-class and farm mothers. The standards advocated by health reformers often clashed with working-class child-rearing practices, while child-labor reform challenged traditional views regarding the needs of children and the importance of work. Yet, although the baby-saving campaign offered a service that working-class and farm mothers could accept or refuse, the child-labor law imposed privation on working-class parents. Because it deprived poor families of much-needed income without providing them with a viable substitute for lost wages, Keating-Owen often increased rather than reduced hardship, exacerbating the tensions between the child-welfare views of the reformers and the cultural values and economic needs of working-class and immigrant families.

As children's advocate, the Bureau staff viewed child labor legislation as part of a larger movement that included infant and prenatal health care, compulsory schooling, mothers' pensions, and a family wage. Jane Addams, mentor to both Lathrop and Abbott, recognized as early as 1893 that passage of child-labor legislation would "in many cases work hardship" and spoke before mothers' meetings and working women's clubs to convince mothers of the "ultimate benefit"[29] of the Illinois child-labor law. However, as administrators working within a government bureaucracy, the Children's Bureau staff did not have the luxury or time to organize working-class support for the 1916 Keating-Owen Act; the "tremendous task of administration"[30] required all their efforts. Obliged to enforce an inadequate law rather than educate the public or lobby for other child welfare reforms, Lathrop and Abbott were caught between their administrative responsibilities and their broader progressive principles of advocacy for the poor.

Even before the enactment of the Keating-Owen Act, the Children's Bureau efforts to regulate child labor differed significantly from its baby-saving campaign. Child-labor reformers had published reams of propaganda, such as socialist John Spargo's sensationalist *The Bitter Cry of the Children* (1906), before the Bureau was established in 1912. Perhaps to compensate for the voluminous and often sensationalist propaganda available to the public, Children's Bureau publications on child labor were dull. Evoking the authority and objectivity of the federal government, they tried to minimize the controversial nature of the subject and protect the vulnerable Children's Bureau from the enemies of reform. While the agency's innovative infant mortality investigations came alive with stories of hardship gleaned from personal interviews with mothers, its studies of state child-labor laws and employment certificate systems compiled tedious and previously printed information gathered from school and employment records.[31]

Despite Lathrop's efforts to avoid politicizing the four-year-old Children's Bureau, the passage of the Keating-Owen Act inevitably put the agency in the midst of controversy. The Bureau staff tried to downplay public perception of federal authority but maximize its influence by cooperating with state child-labor inspectors and local manufacturers. The Bureau accepted work permits issued by the states in order to build support for the federal law and to avoid the expense of issuing certificates at both the state and the national level. However, the Bureau's readiness to work closely with state inspectors exacerbated the already cool relations between the government agency and the National Child Labor Committee. Despite the agency's attempt to cooperate with business, most manufacturers continued to oppose the child-labor law. Moreover, the bureau's conciliatory attitude toward industrialists angered labor organizations such as the Atlanta Federation of Trades.[32]

Enforcement of the Keating-Owen Act was a dfficult task, and Abbott directed most of the Bureau's resources to southern states with child-labor standards below the federal law. The Bureau hired federal agents to inspect working conditions in factories and to issue employment certificates to child wage earners. Because birth registration statistics were inadequate, the job of verifying children's ages was nearly impossible. In North and South Carolina, for example, less than 1 percent of young applicants for work permits had birth certificates. Bibles, life insurance policies, and medical examinations frequently conflicted with school records, the proof of age considered most reliable by federal inspectors. Overwhelmed with the difficult task of determining children's ages, Bureau agents often looked with suspicion on parents of child wage earners, who they believed would lie to obtain work permits for their children. As a result, some children probably lost jobs because they looked younger than they were or because they weighed less than the eighty pounds considered standard for a fourteen-year-old. During the same period that the Bureau's Maternity and Infancy Division helped poor mothers obtain money, clothing, and nursing care, the Child Labor Division rejected child workers' proof of age and denied their families' requests for assistance. The Bureau staff's respect and understanding for poor women was evident in their letters to mothers concerned about their children's health, but it was missing from their correspondence on the Keating-Owen Act. Although they expressed sympathy for parents who lost income as a result of the child-labor law, staff members did not contact local agencies to help these parents and suggested no other means of assistance.[33]

Thousands of mothers wrote appreciative letters to the Bureau in response to its child-rearing bulletins in 1917 and 1918, but the relatively few letters from working-class men and women concerning the Keating-Owen Act usually complained about hardship caused by the law. Some, such as the request for a work permit made by a Georgia widow and mother of two whose fifteen-year-old son had lost his job, suggest that even women who were unhappy with the child-labor law were familiar with the Bureau's baby-saving campaign and continued to look to the agency for help.[34] A South Carolina woman, while not doubting that the women of the Children's Bureau were "sincere," complained that they were ignorant of the impact of the law. "We can never boast of Free America again so long as a few men are allowed to make laws to oppress the poor laboring people,"[35] she wrote.

Many of the letters concerning the Keating-Owen Act were written by fathers, attorneys, or even manufacturers purportedly concerned about their employees. A father of ten who earned only $1.35 a day complained that his daughter was sent home from work because she did not weigh the requisite eighty pounds (although her mother weighed only ninety pounds).[36] Another angry father accused the Bureau of taking the "wrong side of the matter"[37] after it refused to accept the family Bible as evidence of his son's age. "I do not know weather [sic] you have given it a Serious thought or not of how many bread Winners this [law] means to put upon the Streets of our town with no way of support only to go Hungry and naked,"[38] protested a disabled miner and father of nine. Yet Bureau officials insisted that the agency had no "discretion" in individual cases. Rather than helping these families find alternative means of support, officials maintained that there was nothing they could do.[39]

The June 1918 Supreme Court decision declaring the Keating-Owen Act unconstitutional was a bitter blow for child-labor reformers. According to Lathrop, the Children's Bureau was "embarrassed"[40] by the Court's five-to-four decision that the child-labor law was an invasion of states' rights and an unlawful extension of the interstate commerce clause. Nevertheless, the agency was encouraged by Oliver Wendell Holmes's vigorous dissent, and it continued to agitate for child-labor reform. One month after the Supreme Court decision, the War Labor Policies board voted to make the standards of the child-labor law a condition of federal contracts. The Children's Bureau played an instrumental role in securing a second federal child-labor law, passed in 1919 but declared unconstitutional three years later, and it lobbied vigorously for a child-labor amendment to the Constitution.[41]

Despite their efforts on behalf of child-labor reform in the 1920s, the women of the Children's Bureau were increasingly constrained by their positions inside the government. The agency had been brought into existence by the Progressive Era women's movement, and it depended on that movement to support its efforts at reform. Yet in the 1920s, when conservative opposition weakened the Bureau's allies, the staff's long-standing conviction that child-welfare reform depended on protecting the Bureau compelled them to compromise with political opponents and to play down their advocacy of reform.[42]

Although it presaged hard times to come, the defeat of the Keating-Owen Act was not a significant setback for the Children's Bureau. The defeat of the child-labor law was demoralizing, but it was only one component of the Bureau's child-welfare program and did not yet affect its other efforts. Indeed, the Court's decision came during the Children's Year of 1918, arguably the height of the federal baby-saving campaign. The Children's Bureau and the Women's Committee of the Council for National Defense received a special appropriation to designate the second year of the war as Children's Year. Eleven million women worked with the Bureau to organize baby clinics and to weigh and measure preschool children. Also in 1918, Representative Jeanette Rankin introduced the first maternity and infancy protection bill into Congress. Passed in 1921 on the crest of progressive reform, the Sheppard-Towner Maternity and Infancy Act was the first "women's" bill to pass after women won the vote, as well as the first federal social-welfare legislation. Unlike the Keating-

Owen Act, Sheppard-Towner survived two constitutional challenges—only to be defeated by a coalition of physicians and right-wing organizations who convinced Congress to cut off Sheppard-Towner funds in 1929.[43]

The fortunes of the child-labor reform and infant-health movements appeared to diverge during the Progressive Era because Lathrop made a strategic decision to separate them in order to build support for the Children's Bureau, yet separate strategies were ineffective in the 1920s. Opposition to the infant-health campaign mobilized after the passage of the Sheppard-Towner Act and gained momentum with the defeat of the child-labor amendment. Although women reformers continued to lobby for both the child-labor amendment and Sheppard-Towner appropriations, the conservative political climate and the disarray of women's organizations in the post-suffrage era made it difficult for them to defend the Children's Bureau (and themselves) from increasingly virulent conservative attacks. Not until the emergence of a new reform coalition in the 1930s were the child-welfare programs championed by Progressive Era reformers reestablished by law.[44]

The Children's Bureau left women reformers with an ambiguous legacy. On the one hand, the agency staff worked with working-class and rural mothers in a broad-based campaign to eliminate infant mortality and to get the federal government to assume responsibility for child welfare. On the other hand, it administered a child labor law which many working-class families considered hurtful. Female reformers in government functioned both as advocates for poor mothers and as administrators of the (sometimes injurious) policies that affected them, and their contradictory role made conflict with grass-roots mothers inevitable. The uneasy relationship between the Children's Bureau women and their constituents conveys a useful lesson for feminists in politics today.

Notes

1. See Ellen Fitzpatrick, *Endless Crusade: Women Social Scientists and Progressive Reform* (New York: Oxford Univ. Press, 1990); Robyn L. Muncy, *Creating a Female Dominion in American Reform, 1890-1930* (New York: Oxford Univ. Press, 1991); Lela Costin, *Two Sisters for Social Justice* (Urbana: Univ. of Illinois Press, 1983); Allen Davis, *Spearheads for Reform: The Social Settlements and the Progressive Movement, 1890-1914* (New York: Oxford Univ. Press, 1967), and *American Heroine: The Life and Legend of Jane Addams* (New York: Oxford Univ. Press, 1973); Kathryn Kish Sklar, "Hull House in the 1890s: A Community of Women Reformers," *Signs* 10 (1985): 658-77. Molly Ladd-Taylor, *Raising a Baby the Government Way: Mothers' Letters to the Children's Bureau, 1915-1932* (New

Brunswick, N.J.: Rutgers Univ. Press, 1986), explores the impact of grass-roots women on welfare policy. For an overview of progressivism, see Arthur S. Link and Richard McCormick, *Progressivism* (Arlington Heights., Ill.: Harlan Davidson, 1983).

2. The best work on the Children's Bureau remains Nancy Pottishman Weiss, "Save the Children: A History of the Children's Bureau, 1903-1918" (Ph.D. diss., University of California, Los Angeles, 1974). See also Muncy, *Creating a Female Dominion*; Jacqueline Parker and Edward M. Carpenter, "Julia Lathrop and the Children's Bureau: The Emergence of an Institution," *Social Service Review* 55 (Mar. 1981): 60-76; Dorothy Bradbury, "The Children's Advocate: The Story of the United States Children's Bureau, 1903-1946," n.d., Martha May Eliot Papers, Arthur and Elizabeth Schlesinger Library on the History of Women in America, Radcliffe College, Cambridge, Mass.; James Johnson, "The Role of Women in the Founding of the United States Children's Bureau," in Carol V.R. George, ed., *"Remember the Ladies": New Perspectives on Women in American History* (Syracuse: Syracuse Univ. Press, 1975), 170-96; and Louis J. Covotsos, "Child Welfare and Social Progress: A History of the United States Children's Bureau, 1912-1935" (Ph.D. diss., University of Chicago, 1976).

3. See Johnson, "Role of Women," 185; and House Committee on Labor, *Hearings on H.R. 4694, A bill to establish in the Department of Commerce and Labor a Bureau to be known as the Children's Bureau,* 62d Cong., 1st sess., May 12, 1911.

4. Law establishing the Children's Bureau, quoted in Children's Bureau, *Prenatal Care,* Publication no. 4 (Washington, D.C.: GPO, 1913), 2. According to Jacqueline Parker and Edward Carpenter, the budget of the National Child Labor Committee was $46,803.66 in 1909. The Better Babies Bureau of the *Woman's Home Companion* received $30,000 in 1913. See Parker and Carpenter, "Julia Lathrop," 61, 75n.

5. Edward T. James, Janet Wilson James, and Paul Boyer, eds., *Notable American Women* (Cambridge, Mass.: Belknap, 1971), 2: 370-72.

6. *Congressional Record,* 67th Cong., 1st sess., June 29, 1921, 8759. See also Julia Lathrop, "Highest Education for Women," *Journal of Home Economics* 8 (Jan. 1916): 1-8. Alexander McKelway of the National Child Labor Committee doubted women's administrative abilities. See Costin, *Two Sisters,* 105-6.

7. See Jane Addams, *Twenty Years at Hull-House* (New York: Signet, 1960), 90-118.

8. Parker and Carpenter, "Julia Lathrop," 67-70, 74.

9. Weiss, "Save the Children," 179-85.

10. Ibid., 239.

11. See Addams, *Twenty Years,* 153; and Walter I. Trattner, *Crusade for the Children: A History of the National Child Labor Committee and Child Labor Reform in America* (Chicago: Quadrangle, 1970). On the early campaign against infant mortality, see Richard A. Meckel, *Save the Babies: American Public Health Reform and the Prevention of Infant Mortality, 1850-1929* (Baltimore: Johns Hopkins Univ. Press, 1990).

12. Costin, *Two Sisters,* 105-6.

13. See Bureau of the Census, *Historical Statistics of the United States, Colonial Times to 1970* (Washington, D.C.: GPO, 1975), pt. 1: 57; and Parker and Carpenter, "Julia Lathrop," 67.

14. Quoted in Weiss, "Save the Children," 185.

15. "Memorandum for Field Agents," Mar. 27, 1913, Children's Bureau Records, Central Files, 1914-1940, Record Group no. 102, File 11-421, National Archives, Washington, D.C. (hereafter cited as CB). See also "Instructions to Agents" (for Manchester,

N.H.), n.d., CB, File 11-312-1. For an analysis of the Bureau's infant mortality studies, see Molly Ladd-Taylor, "Mother-Work: Ideology, Public Policy, and the Mothers' Movement, 1890-1930" (Ph.D. diss., Yale University, 1986).

16. See Children's Bureau, *Infant Mortality: Results of a Field Study in Johnstown, Pa., Based on Births in One Year,* Publication no. 9 (Washington, D.C.: GPO, 1915), 6; Weiss, "Save the Children," 191; and "Report of Infant Welfare Work Carried on in Johnstown, Pa. during the Summer of 1914 by the Associated Charities," CB, File 11-419.

17. Children's Bureau, *Infant Mortality in Johnstown,* 53, 22.

18. See, for example, Children's Bureau, *Infant Mortality: Results of a Field Study in Waterbury, Conn., Based on Births in One Year,* Publication no. 29 (Washington, D.C.: GPO, 1918), 33.

19. Children's Bureau, *Infant Mortality: Results of a Field Study in Manchester, N.H., Based on Births in One Year,* Publication no. 20 (Washington, D.C.: GPO, 1917), 71.

20. Children's Bureau, *Prenatal Care,* 6; see also Children's Bureau, *Infant Care,* Publication no. 8 (Washington, D.C.: GPO, 1914).

21. Julia Lathrop to William B. Wilson, Jan. 12, 1914, CB, File 6007.

22. Mrs. A.P., Wyoming, to Julia Lathrop, Oct. 19, 1916, CB, File 4-3-0-3. This and similar letters to the Children's Bureau are reprinted in Ladd-Taylor, *Raising a Baby.*

23. Mrs. A.P., Wyoming, to Julia Lathrop, Nov. 21, 1916, CB, File 4-3-0-3.

24. Mrs. H.B. to Children's Bureau, Feb. 28, 1916, and Mrs. H.B. to Julia Lathrop, Mar. 20, 1916, CB, File 4-2-0-3. Reprinted in Ladd-Taylor, *Raising a Baby,* 148-53.

25. Mrs. A.P., Wyoming, to Julia Lathrop, Nov. 21, 1916, CB, File 4-3-0-3.

26. Grace Abbott, "Ten Years' Work for Children," *North American Review* 218 (Aug. 1923): 189-200.

27. See Costin, *Two Sisters,* 103; "An Act to Prevent Interstate Commerce in the Products of Child Labor, and for Other Purposes," reprinted in Children's Bureau, *Administration of the First Federal Child-Labor Law,* Publication no. 78 (Washington, D.C.: GPO, 1921), 174-76.

28. See Trattner, *Crusade,* 128-32; Children's Bureau, *First Federal Child-Labor Law;* and J.W. Root to Julia Lathrop, Nov. 25, 1916, CB, File 25-0. For a survey of state laws, see Children's Bureau, *Child Labor Legislation in the United States,* Publication no. 10 (Washington, D.C.: GPO, 1915).

29. Addams, *Twenty Years,* 153.

30. Quoted in Weiss, "Save the Children," 261.

31. Compare John Spargo, *The Bitter Cry of the Children* (1906; reprint, Chicago: Quadrangle, 1968), with Children's Bureau, *Administration of Child Labor Laws: Part 1, Employment Certificate System New York,* Publication no. 17 (Washington, D.C.: GPO, 1917), and Children's Bureau, *Child Labor Legislation.*

32. See Coston, *Two Sisters,* 104-6; Trattner, *Crusade,* 133-34; and G.F. Bell to W.B. Wilson, June 23, 1917, CB, File 25-0-2.

33. See Children's Bureau, *First Federal Child-Labor Law;* Abbott, "Ten Years' Work," 195-96; Weiss, "Save the Children," 263; and W.H.S. to Richard E. Byrd, Dec. 20, 1917, CB, File 25-2-1-1.

34. Mrs. J.A., Augusta, Ga., to Children's Bureau, Mar. 8, 1918, CB, File 25-4-1-1.

35. Mrs. C.N., South Carolina, to Grace Abbott, June 3, 1917, CB, File 25-2-1-1.

36. S.H. to Labor Department, Sept. 11, 1917, CB, File 25-4-1-1.

37. J.A.R. to M.E., Gardner, N.C., Mar. 15, 1918, CB, File 25-4-1-1.

38. T.P., Bevier, Mo., to Children's Bureau, Sept. 13, 1917, CB, File 25-2-1-1.

39. Grace Abbott to S.H., Sept. 26, 1917, CB, File 25-4-1-1.

40. Julia Lathrop to Mrs. James Rae Arneill, CB, File 6011.

41. Trattner, *Crusade,* 134-42; and Costin, *Two Sisters,* 110-15, 151-58.

42. In her study of the Women's Bureau, Judith Sealander, *As Minority Becomes Majority: Federal Reaction to the Phenomenon of Women in the Work Force, 1920-1963* (Westport, Conn.: Greenwood, 1983), esp. 3-11, sensitively describes the tension between women's "insider" status in government and their "outsider" role as advocates of reform.

43. Abbott, "Ten Years' Work," 129. On the Sheppard-Towner Act, see Molly Ladd-Taylor, "Federal Help for Mothers: The Rise and Fall of the Sheppard-Towner Act," in Susan Reverly and Dorothy O. Helly, eds., *Connected Domains: Beyond the Public/Private Dichotomy in Women's History* (Ithaca, N.Y.: Cornell Univ. Press, in press). J. Stanley Lemons, *The Woman Citizen: Social Feminism in the 1920s* (Urbana: Univ. of Illinois Press, 1975); and Sheila Rothman, *Woman's Proper Place: A History of Changing Ideals and Practices, 1870 to the Present* (New York: Basic, 1978); Muncy, *Creating a Female Dominion;* Meckel, *Save the Babies.*

44. See Susan Ware, *Beyond Suffrage: Women in The New Deal* (Cambridge, Mass.: Harvard Univ. Press, 1981).

9

Working It Out: Gender, Profession, and Reform in the Career of Alice Hamilton

BARBARA SICHERMAN

The career of Alice Hamilton (1869-1970) at first sight defies conventional wisdom about women's professional achievements in the Progressive Era. While most women were concentrated in sex-segregated or sex-typed work, Hamilton specialized in industrial toxicology, a branch of public health that studies poisons in the workplace. Public health was "women's work" in the field of medicine, but Hamilton spent most of her professional life in the male world: she attended a coeducational medical school, worked in a research lab, investigated dusty lead factories and copper mines, and in 1919 became Harvard's first woman professor, though not, she observed, the first who deserved the position.[1]

If Hamilton worked mainly with men, her career was not built on a traditional male model in which personal advancement and the approval of professional peers were central to self-definition. She was not untouched by ambition, but her aspirations took a different turn. Shaped by the service ethic that propelled so many women of her generation, but also trained as a laboratory scientist, Hamilton constructed her career in ways that permitted her to move between worlds that at first seemed irreconcilable. In her work, she chose a path that mediated between profession (mainly male) and reform (mainly female), between "objectivity" and "advocacy"; an unlikely blend of "crusader and scientist,"[2] a prominent public health leader aptly called her. She was, on the one hand, an exacting professional committed to scientific canons in advancing knowledge of industrial diseases. On the other, she defined for herself a mission of service dedicated to improving workers' health. Although she went to Harvard, her reference group remained the female reform network of Hull House, the National Consumers' League, and the Children's Bureau.

Hamilton entered medicine at a time of transition. Women had been successfully practicing medicine for several decades, and with their admission to prestigious coeducational medical schools in the 1890s, their professional prospects seemed to be increasing. But physicians of Hamilton's generation could not take their opportunities for granted. Their autobiographies tell stories of discrimination, some humorous, some painful, all reminders of women's second-class status in the profession.[3] Even women like Hamilton who rejected the medical separatism of their predecessors still tended to view themselves and the world through the prism of gender. Hamilton did not think of herself as a "woman doctor," but when she claimed that women were wiser and more empathic than men and had their own distinctive contributions to make, she formulated her objectives in the language of women's sphere. She always maintained that, contrary to her expectations, her sex enhanced her industrial work and that factory owners more readily tolerated suggestions about employees' health from a woman than from a man. Whether correct in this assumption or not—and she probably was correct—the way she framed the issue, like the way she constructed her career, suggests the continued potency of gender.[4]

Hamilton's career exemplifies the paradox of the progressive generation of women, a paradox rooted in gender. Growing up in the late Victorian era, when gender stereotyping was probably at its peak, adolescent girls and young women confronted behavioral norms that were to all appearances tightly bounded by gender and class. Indeed, standards of womanliness, sexual purity, and gentility seemed to be growing more, rather than less, confining. These prescriptions coexisted with new educational and vocational opportunities that enabled middle- and upper-middle-class white women to transcend many of the limitations of their gender and class position. As they struggled to integrate new options with traditional standards of womanliness, many women of Hamilton's generation felt a shared sense of female possibility that propelled them to unprecedented achievement in the public sphere. For the ambitious, the debilitating aspects of gender stereotyping were often counterbalanced by a new sense of female selfhood based for most on some mix of personal aspiration and shared gender consciousness.

To their work these daughters of the middle and upper-middle classes brought the obligations of service considered appropriate to their class and gender. In time, Jane Addams and others who left protected homes to live in city space among the poor and foreign-born largely transcended traditional notions of noblesse oblige, individual charity, and moral absolutism. How they transmuted traditional values into new social and political norms, even as they gained a large measure of personal freedom, is the heart of their story. In her classic text *Twenty Years at Hull-House,* Addams described her transformation—and that of a generation—from cultural dilettante to effective agent of social change. For Addams, settlement life had reciprocal benefits: it provided women of the privileged classes with a steadying realism and sense of purpose, even as it authorized them to put their knowledge to practical use. Addams took an anthropological view of her neighbors, whose experiences she interpreted as part of an entire way of life. But she balanced objectivity with empathy. Her genius was her ability to render with sympathy people who were ordinarily alien to her middle-class readers: teenage prostitutes, ward bosses, shoplifters. Addams's difference from an earlier generation of charity visitors is exemplified by her effort to keep herself honest: she took along a neighborhood woman whenever she spoke about Hull House.

As settlement residents turned to improving their districts and protecting their neighbors from the worst consequences of modern urban and industrial life, they endorsed a variety of social welfare programs modeled after those already in place in Europe. Constituting the dominant force in American settlements, women thus found themselves in the vanguard of the social justice wing of the progressive movement.[5] By creating their own institutions (the settlements) and running important private and public agencies that addressed urgent social problems (the National Consumers' League, the Children's Bureau), women developed a base from which they could direct their own political agenda, often in alliance with congenial men.[6] To these activities they brought a vision of collective female action on behalf of the poor, especially the least protected among them, women and children.

Women may have been especially prepared to advance collective solutions to the problems of urban and industrial life because of their historic exclusion from the American tradition of individualism. Growing up without the entitlement to public leadership that was the birthright of their brothers, women like Addams struggled for years before finding ways to authorize their large ambitions. Politically, this exclusion was most blatant in the denial of suffrage on the grounds that women's interests were subsumed under the family and were therefore represented by husbands.[7] Given the high degree of gender consciousness in the late nineteenth century, manifested variously but insistently in the temperance, social purity, and suffrage movements, it is not surprising that many women concluded that men did not represent their interests and that women had to act on their own behalf. Moreover, professional women (who for the most part remained single, living usually with other women, sometimes in female communities) were often exempt from the obligations of traditional family life, a circumstance that undoubtedly strengthened their enthusiasm for social welfare, as did the radicalizing tendencies of communal life.

The collective journey of a generation may be charted in numerous individual transformations, and it is here that biography can help to elucidate social trends. Hamilton's career—the way she defined it and the way she worked it out—brings to light a great deal about the objectives and trajectories, personal and political as well as professional, of her generation. Hamilton's career aspirations, her conception of her work, and her politics were all shaped by considerations of gender. Her apparent singularity makes the correspondences even more compelling. Because she worked in integrated settings, it is possible to compare her activities and responses with those of male colleagues. Stretching the gender system about as far as it would go, at least in terms of career, Hamilton's life also reveals the degree to which that system affected female subjectivity. Defining activities as gender-appropriate was not unique to the progressive generation, but the formulations provided by Hamilton and her cohort help locate female consciousness at a precise historical moment. They also enable identification of the differences between progressives and the generation that followed, which by and large rejected the progressive synthesis on gender.

Alice Hamilton was the second of four sisters born in the span of six years to a prominent family from Fort Wayne, Indiana. The family culture fostered intellectual achievement and moral earnestness in its daughters, even as it engendered a sometimes constraining sense of gentility. Noted for being bookish, the girls were educated mainly at home, with an emphasis on classical languages, the "great" works of English literature, and standard Protestant texts. The Hamiltons were also inward-turning; except when they attended the First Presbyterian Church, Alice and her sisters played only with the large band of nearby cousins. Unambiguously, the family culture promoted a tradition of singlehood that was then a precondition for a successful career; of the eleven female cousins, only the youngest married, an extreme even in a generation known for its low marriage rates. Altogether, the intellectual and moral stakes in this largely female family were high: Alice's sisters each had a career, and although only one of their closest female cousins succeeded in leaving Fort Wayne, all had serious aspirations.[8]

From an early age, Alice Hamilton was determined to make her life count. Like so many progressive women, the key to her aspirations was finding meaningful work. Impelled in part by the family's deteriorating finances, she decided in her teens to become a physician, a career she thought more likely to satisfy her desire to be both independent and useful than nursing or teaching, the likely alternatives. Overcoming her family's initial objection—medicine was then a less prestigious profession than now—Hamilon went on to acquire an outstanding medical and scientific education: a medical degree in 1893 from the University of Michigan, where women constituted nearly 30 percent of her graduating class, followed by postgraduate work in pathology and bacteriology in Germany and at Johns Hopkins University.[9]

Like most of her female contemporaries, Hamilton entered medicine with a commitment to social service; by her late teens, her initial goal of becoming a medical missionary had given way to a desire to work with the poor—"Corner 375th St. & Slum Alley."[10] Inspired by the scientific enthusiasm of her Michigan professors, she opted instead for a full-time career in laboratory research, then an unusual choice for a woman *or* a man. The change was not without its difficulties. Like other women whose aspirations to do (and be) good were religiously inspired, Hamilton's path to "self" was often beset by feelings of "selfishness." In these circumstances, a career in science (so remote from patient care) seemed self-serving rather than altruistic. Although she gradually moved away from the religious observances of her youth, as a medical student she found her professors' disdain for religion distressing. But she welcomed the discipline of scientific inquiry; indeed, the Ann Arbor ethos of research and experimentation made her impatient with the old-fashioned conception of hospital work and narrow specialization in obstetrics and gynecology at the New England Hospital for Women and Children, where she later interned. She was fiercely critical of the limited clinical opportunities, the narrow training of her superiors, and their authoritarian treatment of the interns; altogether, she thought no male physician would tolerate such conditions. Hamilton's negative experience at the New England Hospital exemplified the increasingly problematic status of separate medical institutions at a time of changing professional standards.[11]

For more than a decade Hamilton struggled to find the right work. Her first job, as professor of pathology at the Woman's Medical School of Northwestern University, proved unsatisfactory; she had to rely on male colleagues at nearby medical schools for scientific materials for her teaching and research. The job was also short-lived; the school closed in 1902, a sign of shrinking opportunities for women physicians. Hamilton next worked as a bacteriologist at the new Memorial Institute for Infectious

Diseases in Chicago. She chose the position over the secretaryship of the newly formed Committee on the Prevention of Tuberculosis of the Charity Organization Society of New York, which she considered too unscientific despite its hefty salary. Besides, she did not wish to leave Hull House, where she had lived since coming to Chicago. At the institute, Hamilton laid the basis for a promising scientific career, publishing articles on such subjects as scarlet fever and antibodies. She concluded that she was only a "fourth-rate bacteriologist," a typically self-deprecating assessment (she served as president of the Chicago Pathological Society in 1911-12). Clearly, the laboratory did not enable her to fulfill the longing, expressed in her mid-twenties, to leave behind some "definite achievement, something really lasting . . . to make the world better."[12]

Hamilton found Hull House fascinating and companionable, but settlement life compounded her uncertainty. In the early years she did everything from starting a well-baby clinic to teaching basket weaving. On top of her job and family responsibilities, this dispersal of energy made her life seem "scrappy" and unfulfilled. She feared she would be classed by Addams, whom she intially idolized and always revered, as one of those educated people who was "utterly unable to put their knowledge into a form useful to simple people." Both then and later, Hamilton rejected for herself the role of "fireside fairy" that suited Addams but smacked of the traditionally unstructured and, to Hamilton, self-sacrificing lives of women. As she struggled to reconcile laboratory and settlement, Hamilton confronted two apparently different value systems: on the one hand, the emerging professional culture of science with its privileging of "pure" research; on the other, the settlement service ethic, which Addams later articulated in *Twenty Years at Hull-House,* a powerful critique of a purely intellectual culture. Longing to bring the two worlds together, to apply "pathology . . . to Polk street,"[13] Hamilton formulated her dilemma in the starkly polarized language of gender: knowledge or practice, science or service. Neither domain satisfied her fully.

In the end, Hull House provided the natural springboard for Hamilton's entry into industrial medicine. The environmental causes of disease, as of poverty, were readily apparent in a neighborhood where garbage lined the streets and open privies abounded. Hamilton took the lead in the settlement's public health work, participating in neighborhood investigations of typhoid and cocaine. She was also prominent in Chicago's early campaign against tuberculosis, a disease often contracted on the job. Her first article on occupational diseases appeared in 1908, a moment of burgeoning, if short-lived, American interest in industrial diseases.[14]

That year, through the Hull House connection, Hamilton became a member of the Illinois Commission on Occupational Diseases. In 1910, at the age of forty-one, she took charge of the commission's survey of industrial diseases.

Hamilton supervised the nine-month project and conducted the major research, a survey of lead poisoning, the first to combine field work and laboratory study. Her report, which documented 578 cases of lead poisoning, had an immediate impact. In 1911, Illinois passed its first occupational disease law, one of six states to do so. The same year, Hamilton became special investigator for the U.S. Bureau (later Department) of Labor. For the next nine years she conducted the pioneering investigations on which her reputation largely rests, first on lead poisoning in several industries and, during World War I, on poisoning in munitions factories. The collective impact of her work was dramatic, demonstrating the high morbidity and mortality rates of the lead and munitions industries.

From the start, Hamilton defined her objectives broadly. Her assignment was purely investigative: the federal government had no authority to enter plants, let alone to force compliance. She could rely neither on company officials (who denied danger) nor on union and medical records (the former nonexistent, the latter inadequate, if available at all). In her efforts to correlate medically diagnosed cases of illness with specific occupations, Hamilton pioneered in shoe-leather epidemiology, adapting the technique of the social survey, the paramount instrument of women reformers of the era. In workers' homes, and occasionally in saloons, she learned of company attempts to fool the "lady from Washington"; despite owners' denials, she also found lead on workers' clothing and in their kitchens. Insisting on going beyond the "cold, printed report," Hamilton did what she could to improve working conditions. Through the combined force of her meticulous research, persuasive powers, and no doubt also her charm, Hamilton had remarkable success in convincing factory owners and managers to institute safety measures. She also talked about industrial diseases wherever she could find listeners, most importantly among her medical colleagues, whom she took to task for ignoring lead poisoning.

In her forties, Hamilton found the life work that had previously eluded her, work that was "scientific only in part, but human and practical in greater measure."[15] She took pride in the pioneering nature of her early studies, when almost everything she learned was new and much of it "really valuable."[16] Amazed at management's casual attitude toward lead poisoning—"One would almost think I was inquiring about mosquito bites"—she attributed this form of class exploitation to the gulf between workers in the dangerous trades and their employers.[17] Full of self-doubt as a young woman, Hamilton found her voice by championing the mainly poor and foreign-born workers in the dangerous trades, "a class which is not really free."[18] The work as she defined it also permitted her to escape the constraints customarily imposed on women of her class without violating her own notion of femininity. Chafing at what she called "the tiresome tradition that a woman is something different and must be treated differently,"[19] she delighted in her ability to go anywhere and do anything a man could do. Although she chose to work for the most part in the world of men, by emphasizing the human side of science and by relying on personal persuasion as an instrument of change, she adopted a classically "feminine" strategy.

By this time, too, Hamilton had aligned herself with the social justice wing of the progressive movement. When she arrived at Hull House in the fall of 1897, she did not yet endorse the boycotting of sweatshop products, already a reform orthodoxy; her family's values, she later explained, were "right-wing Liberal, Godkin's Nation was exactly suited to my parents' ideas."[20] After a few years of living in the run-down immigrant neighborhood, Hamilton's social views broadened and her politics took a somewhat radical turn. Her observation of police brutality and the hardship caused by economic depression brought out her latent empathy with the poor, and what began, at least in part, as an adventure in "slumming" ended with a deep commitment to social justice. Like her colleagues, she became committed to public solutions for what had once been considered individual problems. She helped draw up for the National Conference of Charities and Correction recommendations for the minimum standards required by every American for a life of decency, including a living wage, an eight-hour work day, and the right to a home, a program adopted by Theodore Roosevelt in his abortive presidential campaign in 1912. In later years, Hamilton feared infringements on individual liberties, but, unlike some progressives, she never wavered in her belief in the ameliorative power of government. Although she criticized industrial capitalism and sometimes voted for the Socialist party, that faith kept her from joining the far left, even though she personally admired (and supported the defense funds of) radicals of various persuasions. Like Jane Addams, she was a pragmatist, "willing to accept half a loaf rather than no bread."[21]

By World War I, Alice Hamilton was the nation's foremost authority on lead poisoning and one of a handful of prominent specialists in industrial medicine. David Edsall, the dean of the Harvard Medical School who had a long-standing interest in industrial diseases and knew Hamilton personally, turned to her when he sought a specialist in industrial toxicology for the university's new degree program in industrial hygiene. The appointment went through quickly, once Edsall assured president A. Lawrence Lowell that Hamilton's studies "stand out as being unquestionably both more extensive and of finer quality than those of anyone else who has done work of this kind in this country. . . . I would emphasize the fact that she is greatly superior to any man that we can learn of for such a position."[22] Although flattered by the offer, Hamilton accepted with reluctance and only after securing the terms she wanted: a half-time position teaching industrial toxicology that left her free to pursue her own investigations and to return to Hull House each spring.[23]

At Harvard, Hamilton continued to hold to a conception of her work that transcended a narrow model of professionalism. As her field expanded and became more complex, her role changed from pioneer investigator to consultant, codifier, and troubleshooter. American knowledge about industrial diseases expanded in the 1920s, but enforcement lagged behind and workers still served as experimental guinea pigs for testing new chemicals. Hamilton's long-range goal was to establish an impartial bureau of experts to do what trained factory inspectors did in Europe. In the meantime, she maintained a constant vigilance, effectively serving as watchdog for the host of new diseases that kept pace with America's rapid expansion as an industrial nation. Hamilton not only followed up numerous requests from physicians, factory inspectors, and plant managers who sought help in identifying obscure cases of illness or improving factory conditions but she also kept after those in authority, urging them to do the right thing. Often she gained partial compliance, sometimes conspicuous success, as when she persuaded a chemist who worked for a shoe factory near Boston to forgo the use of benzene. Her two acclaimed textbooks, which incorporated her incomparable knowledge of European as well as American conditions, codified the field of industrial toxicology.

In addition to her individual efforts, Hamilton prodded others to take up the larger issues of investigating and controlling industrial diseases. She attempted, unsuccessfully for the most part, to raise funds for research and field studies from foundations. Ironically, her success was greatest with the presidents of several lead companies, from whom she secured a no-strings-attached grant for Harvard. The resulting landmark study demonstrated how lead was absorbed, stored, and eliminated from the body and developed the first effective treatment for lead colic. Hamilton was also in the forefront of those urging the surgeon general to call national conferences to address the dangers of two new substances used in industry, one on tetraethyl lead in 1925, the other on radium in 1928.[24] With Florence Kelley and the National Consumers' League, she orchestrated the early stages of the radium conference, soliciting support from the medical community to ensure action by the surgeon general. In the continued absence of government authority over industrial diseases, Hamilton considered these conferences the high point of voluntary cooperation between the federal government, medicine, industry, and labor.

Hamilton was one of the few individuals willing and able to work with all concerned parties, with the pro-business National Safety Council and the union-based Workers' Health Bureau, as well as physicians and public-interest groups. Most of her professional colleagues had a more restricted definition of their role. These differences were apparent in the dramatic case of the women employed by the U.S. Radium Corporation in Orange, New Jersey, who became ill while painting luminous dials on watches. Hamilton had to prod Cecil Drinker, professor of physiology and assistant dean of Harvard's School of Public Health, first to publish his findings and later to testify in court. Drinker and other Harvard colleagues had established radium as the cause of the terrible new disease that brought necrosis of the jaw and death to its victims. He thought his responsibility ended when he submitted his report to the company and changed his mind only after Hamilton informed him that the corporation had issued a false statement to the New Jersey Department of Labor—and after he learned that someone else planned to publish an article on the new disease. By contrast, Hamilton concerned herself with the plight of the victims and did everything she could to help them.[25]

Similarly, while Hamilton hoped that the tetraethyl lead conference would be "the pebble with which David will kill Goliath,"[26] Drinker was "much disquieted by the conference," which he feared might "result in much argument and little real intelligent action."[27] Drinker's position was that of the expert who questioned the advisability of bringing to a public forum matters he considered essentially scientific—that is, whether tetraethyl lead actually poisoned workers and polluted the environment. Hamilton did not question the assumption that experts should make final determinations about scientific questions; indeed, she insisted that they do so. But she had an abiding faith in the value of publicity in bringing about social change: "Nothing will win the fight but public opinion," she declared in the radium case. It was the quintessential belief of a generation of progressive reformers.[28]

In addition to taking a broader view of her work than did her colleagues, Hamilton refused to put purely professional concerns or even job security ahead of the obligations of citizenship as she saw them. Before coming to Harvard, she supported birth control and federal health insurance, both anathema to many physicians, and had been a pacifist during World War I. When colleagues challenged her views over the years, among them her advocacy of recognizing the Soviet Union and her appeal for clemency for Sacco and Vanzetti, she responded unequivocally. In December 1919, soon after Hamilton arrived in Boston, the major fund-raiser for the industrial hygiene program asked her to cease her fund-raising efforts for Quaker food and relief programs in Germany, where she had witnessed the devastating effects of famine the previous summer. Hamilton refused, explaining, "It would be quite impossible for me to enter into a relation with any institution if by so doing it was necessary for me to detach myself from purely human problems and to take no part in questions which are of the deepest importance to me as a human being, not as a member of a faculty or a physician or anything that represents but one side of me."[29]

At Harvard, Hamilton was a triple outsider—on the basis of her gender, her conception of her work, and her politics. In the manner of other institutions that sought to maintain an inexorably male image, Harvard attempted to render her invisible: she was not to appear in the Harvard Club, at football games, or on the commencement platform.[30] Hamilton's marginalization resulted from her professional priorities as well as her gender. Joseph Aub, a young physiologist and friend, attributed the tendency of his colleagues to "minimize her efforts" not only to her sex but also to prevailing academic disdain for practical achievement. It was laboratory rather than field work that carried academic prestige in the 1920s, and Hamilton's investigations and acclaimed textbooks counted for little next to experimental research. Although Hamilton felt isolated at Harvard, she had protected herself by insisting on the half-time position.[31] The university never promoted her, but she had greater visibility than her male colleagues; one specialist in industrial hygiene considered her too well-known to need an introduction, even to laypeople, "at least those who read." And a 1934 editorial on Hamilton's textbook, *Industrial Toxicology,* proclaimed, "The name Hamilton parallels the building up of the awareness and the study of poisoning in industry."[32] Moreover, Harvard proved useful to her: in view of declining government interest in industrial diseases in the 1920s, Hamilton's move to academe kept her at the center of her field.

Although Hamilton's conception of her work differed from that of her colleagues, it was not because she viewed professionalism as inimical to reform.[33] She was herself a consummate professional, for whom possession of a specific skill was vital to building a sense of confidence and personal efficacy. Indeed, she insisted on defining her field narrowly, disavowing expertise even on industrial dusts. She differed from her male colleagues in insisting that knowledge be applied to broad social goals and in using her expert status to enlist both medical and popular support for such efforts. If Hamilton did not reject professionalism as such, she disapproved of its narrowing tendencies. She was dismayed when women medical students turned down her appeal to investigate poisons in munitions plants during World War I because they believed they could gain better experience elsewhere. Hamilton's wartime encounter anticipated the changing priorities of young professional women, who in the 1920s were less likely to identify with women's causes or respond to the call to service that had animated her generation; thinking their opportunities secure, many defined their goals exclusively in terms of personal advancement.

Hamilton's efforts to mediate between the worlds of profession and reform sometimes involved her in a difficult balancing act: maintaining her professional credibility while working for social change. In the radium case, she refused to conduct a new investigation when Cecil Drinker withheld his data on the grounds that the corporation had commissioned his study, nor did she challenge his right to do so. But she kept after him until he conceded and even persuaded him to testify in court on behalf of the victims. At the same time, her professional ties might have made her more inclined than some reformers to trust the good will of medical colleagues. After the radium conference, the head of the Consumers' League of New Jersey criticized Hamilton for endorsing an investigation by the Public Health Service rather than holding out for more radical measures.

On balance, the tension between professional and reform commitments was a creative one for Hamilton, the role of mediator one that suited her temperament. If she was isolated at Harvard, she nevertheless exercised considerable influence within the profession and could appeal to those in positions of power, even as she worked to extend knowledge and control beyond the profession. When conflict existed, Hamilton sided with the reformers. In the jurisdictional wars between government agencies, she was often critical of the efforts of the Public Health Service to limit the Department of Labor's work in industrial medicine. When the Public Health Service attempted to absorb the infant and maternal health programs of the Children's Bureau in 1930, Hamilton joined with Grace Abbott and other reformers in their successful effort to keep the bureau intact.[34]

With reform colleagues, Hamilton worked to keep alive the larger progressive vision during the bleak postwar era. An important member of the women's reform and pacifist network, she had, as Dr. Hamilton of Harvard, greater expert standing than most of her female colleagues when testifying on such subjects as child labor, the eight-hour work day, the minimum wage, workers' compensation, protective legislation, and, with the advent of the depression, health insurance and old-age pensions. Women were not alone in endorsing these programs, but they kept a more radical edge into the 1920s than did men. Two factors, both gender-related, accounted for this tendency: women's marginal position in mainstream politics and employment and their organization into voluntary and professional associations with an interest in pursuing the progressive agenda.[35]

Like Hamilton, professional women in predominantly female settings tended to define their work broadly. Unlike their male counterparts, who often saw prevention as inimical to the interests of the profession, most women physicians embraced the cause of public health. The American Medical Women's Association endorsed health insurance and federal grants to states for maternal and infant health, programs opposed by the American Medical Association.[36] Women physicians and social workers thus exemplified the creative ways in which progressives transformed the older vision of "disinterested" reform that Paula Baker locates at the core of women's political tradition into new careers and new forms of public service.[37] The position of women professionals was less disinterested than has sometimes been claimed: they gained employment from the new social institutions and programs they helped to create, notably the Children's Bureau and the Sheppard-Towner program. But women's association with the poor was not only or even mainly a matter of self-advancement. Hamilton repeatedly turned down opportunities for job security and higher pay in order to do the work she desired, even though her choice left her in search of additional income. If the Children's Bureau provided jobs for women professionals, including physicians, under the guidance of Julia Lathrop and Grace Abbott, it also engaged in a broad-based program of investigation, education, and reform.

In many respects, the Children's Bureau represented the ultimate triumph of the woman-centered progressive vision in which experts, volunteers, and clients were linked in a common venture. The bureau oversaw child labor reform and maternal and infant health programs until they fell victim to the conservative politics of the 1920s. It provided reassurance as well as "expert" advice to women across the nation; letters from women and children who were poor and isolated provide ample testimony to the bureau's success in reaching out to a neglected population. The close relationship between professionals and volunteers (enlisted by the bureau to gather vital information for its innovative studies of infant and maternal mortality) was a key to women's effectiveness in the Progressive Era and stands in marked contrast with recent tension between these groups.[38]

The achievements of progressive reformers depended on this shared perception of women's special interests and on the ability to translate them into careers and public policy. Like Hamilton, many of the cohort negotiating womanhood at the end of the Victorian era found freedom in work, in female collectivity, and in associations that crossed class lines. More than any other, the settlement experience exemplified the unity of personal, professional, and political life. Jane Addams sometimes emphasized the congruence between Hull House and traditional female endeavors. Significantly, however, she repudiated self-sacrifice as a motive for settlement work, emphasizing instead the "subjective necessity" of settlements to women of the comfortable classes. Empowerment came with the acquisition of objective skills and the ability to use them on behalf of the disadvantaged. Reformers also gained exemption from many of the constraints of gender and class. Hamilton delighted in her ability to do "breakneck stunts" in the mines, to walk the streets at night, and to meet people of all races, classes, and reputations. She relished the irony of an encounter with a prostitute whom she had hoped to rescue (but found content in her work) and who thought Hamilton's work disgusting: "That is not the sort of thing I could possibly do."[39] No doubt Addams and other residents also enjoyed breaching traditional standards of gentility, such as collecting garbage (not "a lady's job," according to the neighborhood women) or appearing in the streets without hats.[40]

Reformers' emphasis on difference stands in seeming contrast to their often unconventional behavior, including their avoidance of marriage and motherhood. Historians have praised the institutional base erected by progressive women, while often assailing their recource to a gendered language that appears to reinforce essentialism. In this context, Linda Kerber's recent reminder of the problematic nature of "separate spheres," of the pitfalls of equating ideology with reality, mental boundaries with practical ones, is useful.[41] Progressive views on gender illustrate the problem. Gender consciousness propelled many women into the public sphere, where their activities often departed from traditional norms. Lacking an ungendered language, however, they interpreted these departures as "feminine." Although Hamilton never glorified the "eternal feminine," as Addams sometimes did, she too invoked gender to delineate work to which she thought women especially suited or to generalize differences in women's and men's behavior.[42]

The common notion that women might be especially suited to certain types of work derived not only from preconceptions about gender but also from observing the work women did. Hull House and the Children's Bureau depended on a largely female personnel, who often lived collectively and endorsed a common political agenda. Thus, practice influenced perception, and perception practice, in self-fulfilling prophecy. Hamilton knew men devoted to public health and welfare, but as a group men never seemed so insistently or deeply concerned with the problems that animated her female associates. It was difficult to express this sense of difference other than in terms of gender. To do so made reformers less sensitive to the ways in which gender continued to constrain women, but their gender consciousness encouraged the personal and political bonding necessary to their endeavor. The attraction of a model based on difference may also have resulted from progressive reformers' simultaneous sense of empowerment and marginality. To the degree that they were dispersed in the male world, they felt marginal and impotent, as Hamilton did at Harvard. By contrast, insofar as they defined their own agenda and created institutions that gave them authority, women felt empowered and central. Under such circumstances, the language of gender provided a scheme for ordering the world that was both useful and exhilarating.

For Hamilton, consciousness of difference also entailed recognition of the limits on women's authority. She was pessimistic about achieving genuine parity between the sexes and observed in her sixties, "My idea is that the American man gives over to the woman all the things he is profoundly disinterested in, and keeps business and politics to himself."[43] This perception was not a call for retreat, as women's effort to preserve an independent Children's Bureau indicates, but it reveals an underlying awareness of gender struggle that surfaced rarely. Women who transgressed accepted gender "boundaries" incurred outright hostility. When Addams claimed that European soldiers could be induced to conduct bayonet charges only when buoyed by a ration of rum, she called forth the wrath of outraged male patriots. Formerly a candidate for sainthood, Addams was castigated as "a silly, vain, impertinent old maid, who may have done good charity work at Hull House, Chicago, but is now meddling with matters far beyond her capacity."[44] The episode foreshadowed attacks on women in the 1920s as sexual deviants ("old maids") and as radicals whose political agenda was outside the mainstream. Julia Lathrop's work at the Children's Bureau was likened to that of Aleksandra Kollontai in the Soviet Union as an attack on the family.

The generation who came of age in the 1920s had little interest in maintaining a collective female identity. With the battle for suffrage won, and women's presence in the workplace apparently secured, the new generation sought advances in personal life and the removal of barriers to individual achievement. The heated debate over the Equal Rights Amendment reveals two distinct conceptions of womanhood and of politics.[45] Justifying the protective legislation they had worked so hard to secure, progressive opponents of the ERA stressed women's biological weakness and reproductive potential, grounds that had received legal sanction in *Muller v. Oregon* (1908), while similar laws for men had been invalidated by the courts. Where the pro-ERA National Woman's Party wanted freedom for individual women to seek the most advantageous employment, Hamilton and other opponents saw such freedom as a handicap to the majority of working women, a group disadvantaged by their concentration in the poorest paying (and sex-segregated) jobs and their assumption of the double burden of work and maternity.[46] Thus, despite the appeal to biology, opposition to the ERA hinged on class as well as gender considerations. In contrast to members of the NWP, as well as many of their own contemporaries (including some suffragists who capitulated to the racial and ethnic prejudices of the era), reformers identified themselves with what they perceived to be the interests of those who were economically deprived and culturally different. Those who had begun life as "protected" beings now counted themselves among the protectors. Although few reformers had a consistently class-based or socialist analysis, and many hoped to transcend a politics based on class difference, most linked their own fortunes with those of the socially deprived and often inarticulate groups among whom they lived and worked. The change from a united female front to concentration on individual sex equality in the 1920s largely excluded the concerns of working-class and black women from the feminist agenda as represented by the NWP.

The gender consciousness of progressive reformers helped them chart their way into new and daring political paths and life choices, but as the ERA debate reveals, it also marked out limits beyond which they would not go. While rejecting marriage and motherhood for themselves, they sidestepped but did not fundamentally challenge the gender system, especially belief in the sanctity of the home and the family wage and the incompatibility of careers and motherhood. On balance, the myths of gender probably helped more than they hindered the reformers. They were a source of personal empowerment to many middle- and upper-middle-class white women of the Progressive Era. To the degree that the mission of women like Hamilton derived from their sense of gender-appropriate activity, it left them free from the need to conform to political or professional norms defined by others. Their gender consciousness also promoted a progressive politics that, if it sometimes highlighted women's weakness, included all women within its purview.[47] Under such a banner, a generation of women attained unprecedented power in the public sphere. No other group of women has left such an indelible mark on American life.

Notes

The title is borrowed from Sara Ruddick and Pamela Daniels, eds., *Working It Out: 23 Women Writers, Artists, Scientists, and Scholars Talk about Their Lives and Work* (New York: Pantheon, 1977). I wish to thank Joan Jacobs Brumberg, Joan Hedrick, Mary Kelley, and Susan Ware for commenting on an earlier version of this essay. I would also like to thank Harvard University Press and W. Rush G. Hamilton for permission to publish material drawn from Barbara Sicherman, *Alice Hamilton: A Life in Letters* (Cambridge, Mass.: Harvard Univ. Press, 1984).

1. The career trajectories of progressive scientists and physicians, as well as patterns of "women's work," are analyzed by Margaret W. Rossiter, *Women Scientists in America: Struggles and Strategies to 1940* (Baltimore: Johns Hopkins Univ. Press, 1982); and Regina Markell Morantz-Sanchez, *Sympathy and Science: Women Physicians in American Medicine* (New York: Oxford Univ. Press, 1985).

2. C.-E.A. Winslow quoted in clipping, *Gazette, Montreal*, Sept. 16, 1931, Alice Hamilton Papers, Schlesinger Library, Radcliffe College, Cambridge, Mass.

3. See, for example, S. Josephine Baker, *Fighting for Life* (New York: Macmillan, 1939); and Bertha Van Hoosen, *Petticoat Surgeon* (Chicago: Pellegrini & Cudahy, 1947).

4. Linda K. Kerber, in "Separate Spheres, Female Worlds, Woman's Place: The Rhetoric of Women's History," *Journal of American History* 75 (June 1988): 9-39, has recently noted the problematic nature of the concept of separate spheres and of historical writing about it. In this essay, the term "separate spheres" denotes progressive thought on the subject. Similarly, the term "gender" denotes thinking about relationships between the sexes, as articulated by Joan Wallach Scott, *Gender and the Politics of History* (New York: Columbia Univ. Press, 1988), esp. 1-11.

5. Generalizations about progressive women in this essay refer principally to white, middle-class settlement workers and their allies in medicine and in social and child welfare work. Working-class members of the Women's Trade Union League and those attached to settlements, as well as black settlement leaders, often endorsed similar social welfare programs, but their life histories follow different trajectories.

6. On women's institutions, see Estelle Freedman, "Separatism as Strategy: Female Institution Building and American Feminism, 1870-1930," *Feminist Studies* 5 (Fall 1979): 512-29; on England, see Martha Vicinus, *Independent Women: Work and Community for*

Single Women, 1850-1920 (Chicago: Univ. of Chicago Press, 1985). See also Kathryn Kish Sklar, "Hull House in the 1890s: A Community of Women Reformers," *Signs* 10 (Summer 1985): 658-77.

7. On this point, see Ellen DuBois, "The Radicalism of the Woman Suffrage Movement: Notes toward the Reconstruction of Nineteenth-Century Feminism," *Feminist Studies* 3 (Fall 1975): 63-71; and Linda K. Kerber, "Can a Woman Be an Individual? The Limits of Puritan Tradition in the Early Republic," *Texas Studies in Literature and Language* 25 (Spring 1983): 165-78.

8. Material not otherwise cited is drawn from Barbara Sicherman, *Alice Hamilton: A Life in Letters* (Cambridge, Mass.: Harvard Univ. Press, 1984). The other basic source on Hamilton's life is her autobiography, *Exploring the Dangerous Trades* (Boston: Little, Brown, 1943). See also Barbara Sicherman, "Sense and Sensibility: A Case Study of Women's Reading in Late-Victorian America," Cathy N. Davidson, ed., *Reading in America: Literature and Social History* (Baltimore: Johns Hopkins Univ. Press, 1989), 201-25. On Hamilton's work, see Angela Nugent Young, "Interpreting the Dangerous Trades: Workers' Health in America and the Career of Alice Hamilton, 1910-1935" (Ph.D. diss., Brown University, 1982).

9. The objection of this patrician and literary family was probably as much a matter of class as of gender. Hamilton herself felt a disjunction between her class background and that of most of her fellow "hen medics," whom she found lacking in gentility.

10. Elizabeth Failing Conner, Diary, Monday, Feb. [20, 1888], Miss Porter's School Archives, Farmington, Conn.

11. Hamilton's early career aspirations and experiences are discussed in Sicherman, *Alice Hamilton*, 33-64; the situation at the New England Hospital, 64-87. Hamilton's position was not simply a defense of scientific medicine or an attack on women's institutions; she pointedly contrasted the New England Hospital with the Northwestern Hospital for Women and Children in Minneapolis, where she had previously interned. Nor was she alone in her criticisms: two years earlier, resident physician Bertha Van Hoosen, always more of a medical feminist than Hamilton, had criticized the hospital in similar terms. See also Virginia G. Drachman, *Hospital with a Heart: Women Doctors and the Paradox of Separatism at the New England Hospital, 1862-1969* (Ithaca: Cornell Univ. Press, 1984), 151-63; and Morantz-Sanchez, *Sympathy*, 174-79.

12. Alice Hamilton to Agnes Hamilton, March 8 [1894], Hamilton Family Papers (HFP), Schlesinger Library.

13. Hamilton's career crisis is treated in Sicherman, *Alice Hamilton*, 130-52. Hamilton also represented her parents' differences in gendered terms. She depicted her mother as a woman of "generous enthusiasms and indignations," her father as a rather remote intellectual whose hatred of sentimentality was "probably a wholesome factor in a household of women." *Exploring*, 30-31. While frequently resorting to such conventional formulations, the language in which she portrayed Hull House was sometimes "masculine." She found there a tough-minded approach to reform, a rejection of sentimentality, and an "impersonality" that she did not usually associate with women. These perceived qualities may have enhanced the settlement's appeal to her.

14. Interest came principally from middle-class labor reformers and academics, rather than physicians. It was centered in the U.S. Bureau of Labor, which began commissioning investigations of industrial diseases in the first decade of the century, and the American Association for Labor Legislation, whose director, John B. Andrews, conducted the study of

phosphorus poisoning that prompted passage of the landmark Esch Act of 1912 that effectively eliminated the use of white phosphorus matches. See David Rosner and Gerald Markowitz, "The Early Movement for Occupational Safety and Health, 1900-1917," in Judith Walzer Leavitt and Ronald L. Numbers, eds. *Sickness and Health in America: Readings in the History of Medicine and Public Health,* 2d ed., rev. (Madison: Univ. of Wisconsin Press, 1985), 507-21.

15. Hamilton, *Exploring,* 129.

16. Ibid., 121.

17. Ibid., 151.

18. Hamilton, "Industrial Diseases," *Charities and The Commons,* 20 (Sept. 5, 1908), 659. For a fuller account of her work before 1919, see Sicherman, *Alice Hamilton,* 153-83, 200-02, 209-11; and Hamilton, *Exploring,* chs. 7-9, 11-12.

19. Hamilton, *Exploring,* 216. In her life and work, Hamilton blended qualities assumed to divide along the fault lines of gender. Contemporaries and historians alike have been intrigued by the contrast between Hamilton's work and her persona and by her ability to combine seemingly opposite characteristics; to her friend Felix Frankfurter, for example, she represented "the finest combination of exquisiteness and expertness." Felix Frankfurter to Leo Mayer, Dec. 20, 1960, Felix Frankfurter Papers, Library of Congress.

20. "Speech at H.H. 50th Anniversary," Alice Hamilton Papers.

21. Quoted in Sicherman, *Alice Hamilton,* 360.

22. David L. Edsall to A. Lawrence Lowell, Dec. 20, 1918, Lowell Papers, No. 311, Harvard University Archives, Cambridge, Mass.

23. See Sicherman, *Alice Hamilton,* 209-10.

24. See David Rosner and Gerald Markowitz, "A 'Gift of God'?: The Public Health Controversy over Leaded Gasoline during the 1920s," *American Journal of Public Health* 75 (April 1985): 344-52; and Angela Nugent, "The Power to Define a New Disease: Epidemiological Politics and Radium Poisoning," in David Rosner and Gerald Markowitz, eds. *Dying for Work: Workers' Safety and Health in Twentieth-Century America* (Bloomington: Indiana Univ. Press, 1987), 177-91.

25. The radium case is extensively documented in the Raymond H. Berry Papers, reel 3, National Consumers' League Papers, Library of Congress, Washington, D.C. See especially Berry to Hamilton, Jan. 9, 1929, and Sicherman, *Alice Hamilton,* 281, 283, 312-15.

26. Alice Hamilton to Katherine B. Codman, May 17, 1925, HFP.

27. For Drinker's views, see Cecil K. Drinker to Alice Hamilton, May 18, 1925, Physiology Department Files, Harvard Medical Archives, Countway Library of Medicine, Boston, Mass.

28. In her own work, Hamilton disavowed the sensationalism of the muckrakers, preferring the technique of personal persuasion. Her policy enabled her to maintain access to the factory owners whose cooperation she needed; rarely was she barred from entering a plant. For Hamilton's work in the 1920s and early 1930s, see Sicherman, *Alice Hamilton,* chs. 7 and 8.

29. Alice Hamilton to Frederick C. Shattuck, Dec. 9, 1919, Shattuck Papers, Countway Library.

30. On efforts to render women scientists invisible, see Rossiter, *Women Scientists,* 160-217, passim; on Hamilton at Harvard, see Sicherman, *Alice Hamilton,* 4-5, 237-38, 262-66.

31. Penina Migdal Glazer and Miriam Slater, *Unequal Colleagues: The Entrance of Women into the Professions, 1890-1940* (New Brunswick: Rutgers Univ. Press, 1987), 145-60, correctly emphasize Hamilton's marginality at Harvard but overstate its importance to her. Because Hamilton constructed her career in ways that freed her from dependence on male colleagues, her situation differed from that of Florence Sabin, who was deeply hurt when she was passed over for appointment as head of anatomy at Johns Hopkins and the post went to one of her male students.

32. "Industrial Toxicology by Alice Hamilton," *[Detroit Medical News]*, Alice Hamilton Papers, 10.

33. In this essay "professionalism" refers to a commitment to the standards of one's profession; and "professionalization" connotes efforts to increase the authority of a profession.

34. On this dispute, see Lela B. Costin, *Two Sisters for Social Justice: A Biography of Grace and Edith Abbott* (Urbana: Univ. of Illinois Press, 1983), 145-48, 168-75. The battle was over turf: the Public Health Service wanted control over all "medical" issues, while the Children's Bureau wanted to retain oversight of all aspects of child welfare. The conflict was also a matter of commitment: from past experience women reformers had little illusion that the Public Health Service would devote much attention to maternal and child health. Although the Children's Bureau had recently been cut back because of the demise of the Sheppard-Towner program, the ability of reformers to prevent total defeat demonstrates the importance to women of having a separate institutional base.

35. Although their program collapsed in the mid-twenties, as the child-labor amendment died in the states and Congress refused to reenact the Sheppard-Towner Act, women reformers came into their own once again during the New Deal. The appointment of Frances Perkins as Secretary of Labor and the efforts of Molly Dewson, Eleanor Roosevelt, and others on behalf of social legislation marked the culmination of women's national political influence. When Hamilton retired from Harvard in 1935, the "old-girl" network found a place for her: as a consultant for her old department in the Division of Labor Standards, recently created by Perkins.

36. See the discussion of social medicine in Morantz-Sanchez, *Sympathy*, esp. 266-311.

37. Paula Baker, "The Domestication of Politics: Women and American Political Society, 1780-1920," *American Historical Review* 89 (June 1984): 620-47.

38. On the bureau, see Molly Ladd-Taylor, *Raising a Baby the Government Way: Mothers' Letters to the Children's Bureau, 1915-1932* (New Brunswick: Rutgers Univ. Press, 1986); and Jacqueline K. Parker and Edward M. Carpenter, "Julia Lathrop and the Children's Bureau: The Emergence of an Institution," *Social Service Review* 55 (Mar. 1981): 60-77. Lathrop defined the bureau's expertise as statistical rather than clinical, in part to avoid conflict with the medical profession.

39. Hamilton, *Exploring*, 91-92.

40. See Hamilton, *Exploring*, 91-93; and Jane Addams, *Twenty Years at Hull-House* (1910; reprint, New York: New American Library, 1960), 204. On British settlement workers, see Vicinus, *Independent Women*, 211-46. esp. 230.

41. Kerber, "Separate Spheres," 9-39. See also Jill Conway, "Women Reformers and American Culture, 1870-1930," *Journal of Social History* 5 (Winter 1971-72): 164-77.

42. Hamilton sometimes seemed to deprecate women's public achievements compared with those of men; she refused to review Mary Ritter Beard's *Woman as Force in History*

because she thought it made too many claims for women. Yet she identified the source of the problem as women's lack of equal professional opportunity: "So far men have never given us a fair field." Ultimately, she concluded that separate was not equal and that, at least in medicine, what women needed most was not separate institutions but internships in the best teaching hospitals. See Sicherman, *Alice Hamilton,* 3.

43. Transcript, meeting of May 15, 1932, p. 45, Recent Social Trends, in William F. Ogburn Papers, box 9, Joseph Regenstein Library, University of Chicago.

44. Quoted in Allen F. Davis, *American Heroine: The Life and Legend of Jane Addams* (New York: Oxford Univ. Press, 1973), 229.

45. On the ERA debate, see the very helpful discussion in Nancy F. Cott, *The Grounding of Modern Feminism* (New Haven: Yale Univ. Press, 1987), esp. 117-42; on Hamilton, see Sicherman, *Alice Hamilton,* 253-57, 384-85. Economic and class issues, as well as personal liberty, weighed heavily with Hamilton, who had more to do with male workers and unions than most women reformers. In the ERA debate Hamilton appealed, rather uncharacteristically, to the principle of the greatest good for the greatest number. Usually she was highly sensitive to the claims of the individual. Although she favored testing workers for exposure to poisons, she was reluctant to remove them from the source of their livelihood if they wished to continue work and posed no health threat to their fellow workers. While many of her colleagues supported prohibition and Herbert Hoover in 1928, Hamilton, who viewed prohibition as class legislation that discriminated against the poor, endorsed Al Smith. Since most physicians opposed prohibition, Hamilton's position may also have been influenced by her professional training.

46. In her own studies, Hamilton noted that lead caused sterility in both sexes, not only in women. In her arguments for protective legislation, however, she emphasized women's greater susceptibility to poisoning, the "more serious form" lead poisoning took in women, and the dangers of lead as a "race poison." But she argued not only from biology, for she also observed that the greater incidence of lead poisoning among women may have resulted from their presence in the poorest and worst paid industries. See Hamilton, *Women in the Lead Industries,* (Bureau of Labor Statistics, Bulletin no. 253, Washington, D.C., 1919); *Women Workers and Industrial Poisons* (Women's Bureau, Bulletin no. 57, Washington, D.C., 1926); "Protection for Working Women," *Woman Citizen* 8) Mar. 8, 1924): 17; "Protection for Women Workers," *Forum* 72 (Aug. 1924): 152-60. See also Vilma R. Hunt, "A Brief History of Women Workers and Hazards in the Workplace," *Feminist Studies* 5 (Summer 1979): 274-85; and Ruth Heifetz, "Women, Lead, and Reproductive Hazards: Defining a New Risk," in Rosner and Markowitz, *Dying for Work,* 160-76.

10

African-American Women's Networks in the Anti-Lynching Crusade

ROSALYN TERBORG-PENN

The height of the lynching era in United States history coincided with the Progressive Era, stretching from the mid-1890s to the early 1920s. Throughout the period, African-Americans took the lead in educating public opinion about what they described as mob rule. Although individuals in black communities contributed significantly to the outcry against lynching, it was national organizations such as the National Federation of Afro-American Women, the National Association of Colored Women (NACW), and the National Association for the Advancement of Colored People (NAACP) that took active roles in seeking legally to make lynching a crime. The coalition that resulted included men and women of both races, but African-American women, called "spokeswomen" in their communities, formed the backbone of the anti-lynching crusade. These women mobilized the grass roots, educated the wider society, raised funds, lobbied politicians, and pressed for interracial cooperation with white women.

Like many other movements of the times, the anti-lynching movement cannot be characterized as only a Progressive Era reform. Like the women's suffrage campaign, the anti-lynching movement had its roots in the post-Civil War freedom struggles. Unlike advocates for women's suffrage who achieved success during the Progressive Era, the anti-lynching crusaders never attained their political goal: congressional legislation making lynching a federal offense. Nonetheless, white public opinion eventually turned against the barbarism of lynch law, as white women like Jessie Ames mobilized to stop the carnage through the Association of Southern Women for the Prevention of Lynching, founded in 1930.

The movement to end lynching as an acceptable pastime in the

United States has been studied by a handful of scholars who have looked at the role of white women and at the role of coalitions of whites and blacks, primarily men.[1] No comprehensive study of the role of African-American women in individual or organized efforts to stop lynching has yet been produced. The generation of black women who fought lynching by speaking out against it, by refuting the unfounded justification for it, and by formulating strategies designed to bring lynching to its end deserves examination and analysis.

Official lynching records were first kept in 1882.[2] Although the race riots and mass murders of blacks that had occurred during the Civil War and the postwar years could certainly be defined as lynchings, they were never included in the statistics of the times. During the 1880s and 1890s, mainly journalists at black newspapers reported the atrocities to their readers. Among these were editors such as John Mitchell of the *Richmond Planet,* George Knox of the *Indianapolis Freeman,* Josephine St. Pierre Ruffin of the *Women's Era,* and T. Thomas Fortune of the *New York Age,* as well as columnists like John Edward Bruce and Ida B. Wells. In this predominantly male profession, the goal was to educate and to warn African-Americans to protect themselves. For example, in 1890 Mitchell wrote: "Whenever a Negro is forced to cross the River of Death by a cowardly Bourbon cut-throat, he should strive to the utmost to have that Bourbon accompany him."[3] Similarly, Wells wrote in 1892: "A Winchester rifle should have a place of honor in every Black home and it should be used for that protection which the law refuses to give."[4] Warning African-Americans to protect themselves proved insufficient, as the number of lynchings climbed to nearly two thousand from the mid-1880s and through the 1890s.

Ida B. Wells was the most militant of the anti-lynching journalists, the only one to be run out of a city and lose her printing press for her attacks on lynching and the motivation for it. She was the first to mount an international campaign to educate public opinion in the United States about the true nature of lynch mobs. Frightened by her militancy, several southern-born black ministers and their white benefactors in the North criticized her activism.[5] But many of her fellow journalists supported her, including Bruce, Knox, Fortune, and Frederick Douglass, who was retired but still eminent.

Male black leaders of the times limited their approach to the lynch problem to public outcries. On the other hand, African-American women mounted strategies that included raising funds to publish pamphlets and assist agents like Wells to travel abroad to publicize the horrors of lynch law. Black women also sought support for their campaign from sympathetic whites. Predominantly African-American men's groups of the 1890s, such as the National Afro-American Council, did establish anti-lynching committees, but women were frequently the major activists in these. Wells, for example, was the chair of the council's Anti-Lynching Bureau.[6]

The black women's club movement also began in the early 1890s. Like the white women's clubs of the times, black organizations were concerned with issues such as education for women, moral uplift for the poor, urban reform, and women's suffrage. Unlike white women's groups, black women's clubs focused on issues of unique concern to the women of their race. One of the principle motives for organizing had been to fight against the lynching of blacks, both male and female. Reports about local black organizations such as the Women's Era Club of Boston, the Women's Loyal Union of Brooklyn, and the Chicago Woman's Club, all founded in the early 1890s, indicated that anti-lynching activities were primary. Similarly, the first national African-American women's organization, the National Federation of Afro-American Women, developed anti-lynching strategies.[7]

During the first forty years of the lynching era, the major justification given for lynching was to punish black men for raping white women. Throughout the anti-lynching campaign, African-American women refuted these charges and argued that lynching was motivated by white attempts to intimidate blacks in order to keep them in their social and economic "place." Accusing black men of raping white women was merely a way to frighten white Americans so that mob rule could be justified. Periodic statistical reports indicated that although the overwhelming majority of people lynched were African-American men, lynching victims also included white and black women, black children, and members of other minority groups. African-American women concluded that the barbarous nature of lynch law had epidemic effects, spreading from the South throughout the nation by the early twentieth century, with victims coming from many minority groups.

In refuting the argument that white communities used lynching to protect their women from so-called barbarous black men, African-American women dramatized the fact that black women were often victims of lynch mobs. Using statistics collected by black journalists and investigators like Wells and Walter White of the NAACP, black women's clubs challenged white moral outrage against blacks. The organizations noted that during a forty-five-year period between 1882 and 1927, ninety-two women in the United States had been lynched; seventy-six of them were black. The majority of the cases reported had occurred in the South, but African-American women had been lynched in Nebraska, Missouri, Oklahoma, and Wyoming as well. Even more shocking were reports that, of the eleven black women lynched between 1918 and 1927, three were pregnant.[8]

As early as 1892, Wells and the women in her network challenged the justification of lynching, focusing on African-American women victims. In the preface to her pamphlet *Southern Horrors: Lynch Law in All Its Phases,* Wells acknowledged the African-American women of New York City and Brooklyn who raised the funds necessary to publish their findings. Wells dedicated her work to these women, members of the Woman's Loyal Union, organized and headed by Victoria Earle Matthews, with branches in Brooklyn and Manhattan.[9] Three years later, Wells published *The Red Record: Tabulated Statistics and Alleged Causes of Lynchings in the United States, 1892, 1893, 1894.* Once again, she received financial and moral support from African-American women. Between the two pamphlets, Wells chronicled the lynching of five women in 1892. One of these victims was the fifteen-year-old daughter of a black man in Louisiana. The man was scheduled to be lynched by a white mob because he had killed a white man. Before his execution, he was forced to watch the hanging of his daughter and his teenage son.[10]

The same year, mob violence led to a riot in New Orleans, where, after a group of Italians were massacred, the mob turned on African-Americans. Wells noted: "Even colored women, as has happened many times before, were assaulted and beaten and killed by the brutal hoodlums who thronged the streets." The mob was composed of an estimated 700 whites, who had vowed to teach blacks a lesson. Wells noted that a news article in a New Orleans periodical reported that the mob dragged an old black woman, Hannah Mabry, from her bed in the middle of the night and shot her.[11]

Blacks in New Orleans had not yet recovered from the riots when, in 1893, an African-American man alleged to have killed a white man escaped a lynch mob. When the mob could not find him, the police arrested his mother, three brothers, and two sisters. The brothers were hanged; the mother and the sisters were flogged and run out of town. The same year, Wells reported that six black women were lynched in five different southern states.[12]

In addition to describing the brutality of lynching, Wells articulated the political motivations for mob violence, finding that it was designed to intimidate blacks so that they would "stay in their places." She believed that whites deluded themselves and the world about the true reasons blacks were lynched, asserting that "nobody really believed the lie that colored men really rape white women." If whites did believe this rationalization for lynching, Wells queried, what was their justification for the lynching of women?[13]

Attempts to intimidate African-American women failed. Increased lynchings drove them to resist even more as lynch law began to spread from the South to the North, where larger numbers of educated, articulate black women lived and worked. By 1895, the growing number of black women's clubs had been organized on a national level into the National Federation of Afro-American Women, with Margaret Murray Washington of Tuskegee, Alabama, as president. The following year, the federation merged with another organization to form the National Association of Colored Women, with Mary Church Terrell of the District of Columbia as president. All the clubs, as well as the federation, maintained active anti-lynching committees that reflected the views of Wells and honored her for her dedication to the suppression of lynching.[14]

With Wells taking the lead, other African-American journalists began to report lynchings of women, both black and white, because this approach seemed to make those of both races who read black newspapers recognize the hypocrisy of the lynching justification. By the turn of the century, numerous news items listed female lynching victims, including a white woman in Virginia who was murdered by a lynch mob in 1899 for Mormonism.[15]

Once the NAACP was founded (in 1909) and W.E.B. Du Bois began publishing the official journal, *Crisis*, more reports of lynched women reached the interracial readership. Because the NAACP was supported by white philanthropists, it had the political clout that strictly African-American groups lacked. As a result, NAACP officials could send letters to state officials, like the governor of Oklahoma, and expect answers. The NAACP blamed the state for failing to protect Laura Nelson and her sixteen-year-old son, who were hanged in July 1911 by a lynch mob. Oswald Garrison Villiard, grandson of William Lloyd Garrison and the chair of the Executive Committee, wrote the letter on behalf of the NAACP. African-American women's groups were hopeful, but, by October, Du Bois reported to *Crisis* readers that Oklahoma officials had made no efforts to apprehend the lynchers.[16]

Despite the increased political clout of the NAACP, African-American women's organizations never relied on other groups to carry the weight of the anti-lynching movement. Throughout the early twentieth century, they continued their anti-lynching activities and remained outraged over the lynching of black women. In 1906, Terrell wrote a magazine article aimed at both educated blacks and whites, wherein she indicted lynch mobs for the deaths of black men, women, and children, who were "flayed alive, and burned at the stake, while the murderers not only escape punishment as a rule, but are rarely, if ever, called to account." She argued that, in the South, whites as well as blacks were enslaved by violence and prejudice, which prevented both groups from speaking out against injustices. Terrell believed that the majority of southern whites "acquiesce in the crimes committed by the lynchers"; otherwise, the violence would have long since disappeared. Criticizing the South for its "mental inertia and backwardness,"[17] Terrell reasoned that it was the obligation of the rest of the nation to protect the South from itself. Her words were also directed at the members of the NACW and other African-American women's groups, calling them to action.

Among the black women who subsequently took action were the members of the Federation of Colored Women's Clubs of New Jersey, an umbrella group representing over two thousand African-American clubwomen in the state. At their 1919 convention, leaders were authorized to write President Woodrow Wilson to refute the justification for lynching. The women wrote: "Excuses for lynching colored men and for rioting against them is everywhere made on the grounds that colored men assault white women's honor. As a student of American History you know that the story of assaults white men have made on colored women's honors is written on the faces of our race."[18]

At the NACW convention in 1922, members appointed an anti-lynching delegation of fourteen women to meet with President Warren G. Harding, who had opposed lynching while campaigning for the presidency. Ida Brown, a delegate from New Jersey, spoke for the group and presented the president with lynching statistics, focusing on the eighty-three women who had been lynched in the United States between 1887 and 1922. Brown reminded the president of a speech in which he had recommended that Congress "wipe the stain of barbaric lynching from the banner of a free and orderly representative democracy."[19] The delegation encouraged Harding to continue his attack on lynching.

The rational arguments, historical perspective, and political savvy African-American women leaders presented to the public, usually in the form of magazine and newspaper articles and published pamphlets, reflected a generation of articulate, well-educated, elite working in their own networks, yet cooperating primarily with men, such as the editors of black periodicals, and with interracial organizations, such as the national and local chapters of the NAACP. Educating and reasoning with white Americans had its limitations, however, even during the Progressive Era. As a result, African-American women used other strategies to struggle against lynching.

One of the strategies African-Americans and their white supporters used was political lobbying for a congressional bill to make lynching a federal offense. For the most part, voting African-Americans were Republicans, and their party was the least reluctant to champion a congressional anti-lynching bill. Representative Leonidas C. Dyer, a Republican from Missouri, was the most persistent person in Congress to push for anti-lynching legislation. He first introduced his anti-lynching bill to the House of Representatives in April 1918, and continued to reintroduce it for over three decades.[20] Throughout the period, African-Americans who lobbied and raised money to support anti-lynching lobbying efforts referred to the legislation as the Dyer Bill.

Although the Dyer Bill was first introduced in 1918, the NAACP did not agree to cooperate with Dyer until 1919. By contrast, African-American women were quick to realize the significance of the bill and took steps to endorse it nearly a year before the NAACP did. The Northeastern Federation of Colored Women's Clubs, representing thousands of women from Maine to the District of Columbia, passed a resolution supporting the Dyer Bill at their July 1918 meeting. The language of the resolution included reference to President Wilson's condemnation of lynching and called on Congress to do its part.[21] The following year, the Empire State Federation of Women's Clubs, an organization of African-American women representing over two thousand women in the state of New York, passed a resolution at the annual convention held in Harlem calling for Congress "to enact a Federal law dealing with lynching." In addition, the group donated twenty-five dollars to the NAACP to be used specifically in the anti-lynching campaign.[22]

By 1920, political parties were meeting to select presidential candidates and write platforms. African-American women in the North realized the effect of their votes on the Republican party and urged the convention delegates to write a strong anti-lynching plank into the platform. When the six hundred delegates of the NACW, representing over fifty thousand women, met at Tuskegee Institute in Alabama for the annual meeting, the Republican party platform became a major issue. NACW Vice-President Hallie Q. Brown of Ohio lambasted the Republicans for their unacceptable platform, saying "the platform committee reported not a plank, but a splinter against lynching." Although the NACW received a telegram from presidential candidate Harding praising their work and asking for their support, the convention refused to endorse the Republican or any other party because none had taken a bold enough stand against lynching.[23] Nonetheless, most of the delegates refused to criticize Harding, because he had campaigned vigorously for black women's support and had spoken out against lynching during the campaign. As a result, members of the NACW and affiliates such as the Northeastern Federation of Women's Clubs encouraged their members to support Harding but to keep the matter of lynching before their congressional representatives.[24]

Significantly, the political lobbying came from African-American women living outside the South, for only in these areas were black women able to participate in the political process without fear of white opposition and attempts to keep them from the polls. In several states, especially in the Northeast, African-American women campaigned for candidates through their political organizations. Examples of black women politically pressuring members of Congress to support the Dyer Bill were noted in Rhode Island between 1920 and 1922, and in Delaware in 1922.

Bertha Higgins, the chair of the Julia Ward Howe State Republican Association, led an influential African-American women's club in Rhode Island. The club pressured Representative Clark Burdick and Senator Le Baron Colt to support the Dyer Bill, threatening to withdraw the backing of the association, which was known in the state as having significant influence among blacks. The reality of their strength was revealed by President Harding when he thanked Higgins for the support the association had given his campaign. Higgins made it clear to both legislators that the club would not back their reelection to Congress if they did not support the Dyer Bill. Burdick made clear his support of the bill, but Colt, who obviously had reservations, avoided answering Higgin's telegram and hedged about how he would vote. Presumbly, the women did not support Colt, although there is no extant evidence to prove this.[25]

Similar reports came from Delaware, New Jersey, and Wisconsin, where, in the 1922 election, black voters put their Republican party representatives and senators on notice. In all three states, opponents of the Dyer Bill were defeated. In Delaware, for example, Alice Dunbar led African-American women in the Anti-Layton League, a group of men and women that successfully worked to defeat Congressman Caleb R. Layton, who had opposed the Dyer Bill. The group registered over twelve thousand black voters. Layton was defeated by about seven thousand votes, equal to the number of black votes cast for his Democratic party opponent. Senator

T. Coleman duPont also opposed the Dyer Bill; he was defeated by six hundred key black votes. Where blacks held the balance of power, they used it. Unfortunately, this was only true in areas of the nation where they were able to vote. In the South, where the majority of African-Americans lived, disfranchisement eliminated the majority of black women who had been enfranchised only briefly by the Nineteenth Amendment.[26]

The Dyer Bill was passed in the House of Representatives but failed in the Senate. Hallie Quinn Brown, who by 1923 was president of the NACW, predicted the bill would be revived and urged the women in her network to "labor more arduously."[27] By 1924, Brown was the director of the Colored Women's Republican National Committee. In this position, she used a newsletter to inform Republican women across the nation, including endorsements for political candidates who supported race-related issues. Senator Walter E. Edge, who was running for reelection to the Senate from the state of New Jersey, received a glowing endorsement from the national committee because of his support for the Dyer Bill. Edge was quite aware of the sophisticated political activities of black clubwomen in his state; he spoke to these groups in an effort to receive their endorsement.[28] African-American women were encouraged to support the Coolidge ticket for the presidency, Edge for senator, and any other congressional candidates who favored the Dyer Bill. Unfortunately, the bill failed to pass the Senate in 1925, as it had failed in 1923. In the meantime, African-American women realized that other strategies had to be implemented.

As early a the 1890s, African-American women sought cooperation from white women in attempting to persuade the nation to suppress lynching. White women in the United States resisted, although black women continued attempts to win them over during the early years of the twentieth century. But Ida B. Wells found the strategy especially helpful in Europe. Examples of European cooperation with the anti-lynching movement can be found in the proceedings of the first meeting of the National Federation of Afro-American Women in 1895 in Boston. The delegates resolved that the "convention assembled extend to the Anti-Lynching Committee of Great Britain our thanks for the noble work it has done and is continuing to do to arouse public sentiments against the lynching evil." A special resolution was then sent to Florence Balgarnie of London, the secretary of the British committee.[29]

Other African-American women and their organizations indicted American white women for not taking a stand againt lynching. In 1906, Terrell admonished southern white women for slandering black women and for not working to bring lynching to an end.[30] The 1916 Annual Report of the Women's Convention of the National Baptist Convention included an essay entitled "White and Colored Women Too Far Apart in Practical Sympathy." Among the statements was: "This whole race problem will be quickly and easily solved when white women teach their children around the fireside not to respect white women less, but to respect colored women more. . . . The race problem will never be solved until white and colored women work together for mutual respect and protection."[31]

Just how often these sentiments reached white women is difficult to calculate. The white establishment read black newspapers only to observe the ways African-American leaders advised their following. It is doubtful that white women in the South, who were outside of the male hierarchy in politics and the church, had access to the reports of black groups such as the Baptist Convention.

By the 1920s, white women's organizations were more amenable to interracial cooperation than before. In 1920, the Commission on Inter-Racial Cooperation of the Women's Council of the Methodist Episcopal Church South held a conference of southern white women in Memphis. Because the conference was on race relations, four southern African-American women were invited: Margaret Murray Washington, Mrs. Robert R. Moton, Charlotte Hawkins Brown, and Mrs. George E. Haynes. After the proceedings, the conference issued a statement pledging responsibility to work with black women "for a Christian settlement of the problems that overshadow the homes of both races."[32] One of the issues included in a detailed list of problems was the prevention of lynching.

Gestures like this, though seemingly modest to the more militant African-American women, moved women like Mary B. Talbert of Buffalo into action. As president of the NACW in 1920, she called on the U.S. government to protect the rights of all citizens. In addition, she looked to white Christians to lobby for the end of mob violence. Talbert worked with the NAACP as well as the NACW, struggling for universal suffrage, women's rights, better government, and a host of progressive reforms. As a result of her work, in 1922 she became the first woman to receive the Spingarn Medal from the NAACP, an award given to African-Americans for their efforts in the struggle for freedom.[33]

The same year, Talbert spearheaded the Anti-Lynching Crusade under the auspices of the NAACP. Although the idea for the crusade had come from Helen Curtis, president of the New Jersey Federation of Colored Women's Clubs, Talbert headed the fifteen-woman executive committee with Curtis as the first-vice-president. The committee organized seven hundred African-American women, who acted as state workers across the nation, flooding their communities with literature about the crimes committed by lynchers and appealing to moral and religious believers to condemn the horrors of lynchings. The crusade was planned to begin in November 1922 and to end in January 1923. The goal was to "arouse the conscience of the women of America, both white and Black." Strategies included revealing that eighty-three American women, both black and white, had been lynched. Anti-Lynching Crusade prayers were distributed, which included the statement: "The Land of lynchers cannot long remain in the land of liberty. The nation that fails to destroy lawlessness will be destroyed by it. Save us from this evil fate."[34]

State workers raised thousands of dollars to flood the nation with newspaper ads against lynching and printed prayers warning of societal destruction. Perhaps this was the most significant strategy, for in time it began to have an effect on white women's organizations. For example, the Executive Committee of the National Council of Women, which represented several million American women, resolved unanimously to endorse the Anti-Lynching Crusade.[35]

All the Anti-Lynching Crusaders were African-American women, again from the educated elite throughout the nation; however, their networks included working-class women, especially those affiliated with church organizations and Masonic groups. These middle-class black women obviously interacted with middle-class white women's organizations, perhaps the least difficult to woo to the cause.

It is difficult to determine how grass-roots women's groups participated in the crusade other than in fund-raising. Nonetheless, raising funds to buy ads and to publish and mail prayers required money, and fund-raising remained a significant role for black women in the movement. Most importantly, Talbert, who died of overwork at the age of forty-three shortly after the end of the crusade, had plugged into the strategy needed to stimulate southern white women's interest: moral and religious arguments and rhetoric. By communicating through primarily white newspapers, the crusaders were able to reach the southern women who had not previously received the message.[36]

Several years later, the NAACP's Roy Wilkins described Walter White as the "greatest anti-lynching crusader of the twentieth century."[37] For African-American women who had worked in the movement, this title was debatable. Surely both Wells, who had continued her campaign into the twentieth century, and Talbert could have competed for this title.

Perhaps Wilkins, if he had been asked, would have qualified his statement by calling either Wells or Talbert the greatest "women" crusaders.

This telling oversight demonstrates how men's work and women's work have been perceived in reform movements, which is an important observation when analyzing American culture. The roles of women and the roles of men in the anti-lynching movement were often defined by gender. Men like White were usually paid as investigators or lobbyists, while women usually worked as volunteers. All the Anti-Lynching Crusaders were volunteers. The six women in the thirteen-member NAACP Anti-Lynching Committee were all volunteer African-American women. Wells received funds for her expenses but was never paid for her investigations of lynchings. Nonetheless, volunteers often worked as hard as, if not harder than, paid staff. NAACP officials active in the anti-lynching movement received paid vacations after a long battle, but women's work continued, often until they could work no more. In addition to Talbert, who died in December 1923, Mary E. Evans, the second-vice-president of the Anti-Lynching Crusade Executive Committee, died in 1928. An obituary notice cited the cause of her death as a breakdown following "overwork and strain."[38]

How have African-American women in the anti-lynching movement fallen between the cracks of historical research? Existing scholarship examines the African-American men of the NAACP and the white women of the Association of Southern Women for the Prevention of Lynching but ignores the contributions of black women. As a result, the public concludes that people in the former two groups did all of the work. On the contrary, African-American women were the pioneers, the fundraisers, the strategy initiators, and, in essence, the backbone of the movement, especially in the earlier years. Perhaps they have fallen between the cracks because women's work is often overlooked and undervalued, especially when the workers are not part of the mainstream culture. Public records and accounts are scattered and not always readily available, making these strugglers against injustice invisible. Making invisible African-American women in the anti-lynching campaign visible further illuminates women's roles in the Progressive Era.

Notes

Some of the research for this paper was made possible by a grant from the Faculty Research Committee and Board of Morgan State University Press.

1. See Jacqueline Hall, *Revolt against Chivalry: Jessie Daniel Ames and the Women's*

Campaign against Lynching (New York: Columbia Univ. Press, 1979); Robert L. Zangrando, *The NAACP Crusade against Lynching, 1909-1950* (Philadelphia: Temple Univ. Press, 1980); Ralph Ginzburg, *One Hundred Years of Lynchings* (Baltimore: Black Classics, 1987); and Herbert Shapiro, *White Violence and Black Response: From Reconstruction to Montgomery* (Amherst: Univ. of Massachusetts Press, 1988).

2. See Walter White, *Rope and Faggot: A Biography of Judge Lynch* (New York: Knopf, 1929), 227; and Marcus Garvey Scrapbook, Box B, Marcus Garvey Papers, Fisk University, Nashville.

3. *Richmond Planet,* July 12, 1892.

4. Ida B. Wells, *Southern Horrors: Lynch Law in All Its Phases* (New York: New York Age Print, 1892), reprinted in Ida B. Wells, *On Lynchings* (New York: Arno and the New York Times, 1969), 23.

5. Ida B. Wells, *Crusade for Justice: The Autobiography of Ida B. Wells,* ed. Alfreda M. Duster (Chicago: Univ. of Chicago Press, 1970), 28.

6. Herbert Aptheker, ed., *A Documentary History of the Negro People in the United States* (New York: Citadel, 1968), 2: 792.

7. Wells, *Crusade for Justice,* 120-24.

8. White, *Rope and Faggot,* 20-21, 227.

9. Wells, *Southern Horrors,* preface.

10. See Wells, *Crusade for Justice,* 81; Wells, *Southern Horrors,* 13; Ida B. Wells, *The Red Record: Tabulated Statistics and Alleged Causes of Lynching in the United States, 1892-1894* (Chicago: Donahue and Henneberry, 1895), reprinted in Wells, *On Lynchings,* 20.

11. Ida B. Wells, *Mob Rule in New Orleans* (Chicago: Ida B. Wells-Barnett, 1900), reprinted in Wells, *On Lynchings,* 13, 17.

12. Wells, *Red Record,* 33.

13. Ibid., 11-12.

14. National Federation of Afro-American Women, *The Club Movement, Minutes 1895-1896* (Boston: National Federation of Afro-American Women, 1896), 50.

15. See *Richmond Planet,* Jan. 13, 1900; Aptheker, *A Documentary History* 800-903; *Indianapolis Freeman,* Mar. 26, 1904; *Nashville Globe,* Jan. 10, 1908.

16. "Horizon," *Crisis* 2 (July 1911): 99-100; "Horizon," *Crisis* 2 (Aug. 1911): 153-54; "Horizon," *Crisis* 2 (Oct. 1911): 233.

17. Mary Church Terrell, "A Plea for the White South by a Coloured Woman," *Nineteenth Century* 60 (July 1906): 70-84.

18. *New York Post,* Aug. 7, 1919, Monroe N. Work, Vertical File, Tuskegee University Archives, Tuskegee Institute, Ala. (hereinafter cited as Work Vertical File).

19. Jessie Fauset, "The 13th Biennial of the NACW," *Crisis* 24 (Oct. 1922): 260.

20. Zangrando, *NAACP Crusade,* 43-44.

21. See White, *Rope and Faggot,* introduction; and *Guardian*, Sept. 7, 1918, Work Vertical File.

22. *New York Age,* July 19, 1919.

23. *Tampa Times,* July 15, 1920; *Transcript,* July 17, 1920, Work Vertical File.

24. *Standard Union,* Aug. 9, 1920, Work Vertical File.

25. Letter to Clark Burdick, Nov. 5, 1920; Letter from Charles E. Harding, Feb. 16, 1921; Letter from Clark Burdick, Dec. 14, 1921; Letter to Le Baron Colt, June 10, 1922; Letter from Le Baron Colt, June 10, 1922; all in Bertha Higgins Papers, Rhode Island Black Heritage Society, Providence.

26. "Colored Votes," *Crisis* 25 (Jan. 1923): 117.

27. "Horizon," *Crisis* 25 (Mar. 1923): 211.

28. Colored Women's Department Republican National Committee, *Bulletin*, 1, Oct. 25, 1924, Bertha Higgins Papers.

29. National Federation of Afro-American Women, *Minutes*, 11-12, 28, 50.

30. Terrell, "Plea," 83.

31. National Baptist Convention, *Thirteenth Annual Report of the Executive Board and Corresponding Secretary of the Woman's Convention, 1913* (Nashville: National Baptist Convention, 1913), 31-32.

32. Monroe N. Work, *The Negro Year Book, 1921-22* (Tuskegee: Negro Year Book, 1922), 7-8.

33. *Courier*, Aug. 1, 1920, Work Vertical File; "Horizon," *Crisis* 24 (July 1922): 125.

34. "The Anti-Lynching Crusaders," *Crisis* 24 (Nov. 1922): 8.

35. Ibid.

36. "Mrs. Talbert," *Crisis* 27 (Dec. 1923): 56.

37. White, *Rope and Faggot,* introduction.

38. "NAACP Anti-Lynching Committee," Mary Church Terrell Papers, Box 16, Manuscript Division, Library of Congress, Washington, D.C.; Zangrando, *NAACP Crusade,* 80-81; "Mary Evans Wilson," *Crisis* 35 (July 1928): 229.

11

Harriot Stanton Blatch and the Transformation of Class Relations among Woman Suffragists

ELLEN CAROL DUBOIS

As evidence of women's importance to the Progressive Era accumulates, the need for a new interpretive paradigm grows. One increasingly popular line of analysis traces the evolution of the mid-nineteenth-century "woman's sphere" into a female-centered political culture by the end of the century. This approach allows for coherence and continuity in women's history and frames women's Progressive Era reform activism in terms that arise from women's historical experiences, rather than men's.

As an interpretation of the Progressive Era, the virtues of a separate women's political culture are also its vices. Like many interpretations of women's history that take as their starting point separate spheres, it emphasizes continuity in women's history rather than change. In a similar fashion, the notion of a separate women's political culture assumes difference rather than gives it a history; it appropriates history to the framework of separate spheres rather than the other way around. As such, it tends to keep women's history interpretations separate and misses the opportunity to use them as the basis for more comprehensive interpretations of American history in general.

For both reasons—the inability to account for change and the resistance to general interpretation—separate-spheres interpretations are especially problematic in examining the Progressive Era. No period in American history hints at such profound transformations but is as little understood. The more that is learned of the magnitude and centraility of women's contributions in these years, the more likely it seems that understanding them will provide a basis for the comprehensive analysis of progressivism that has eluded historians until now. On the basis of the career of Progressive Era suffragist Harriot Stanton Blatch, an alternative paradigm for women's history emerges in this period, one that emphasizes the existence of two distinct generations of women progressives, identifies their representative images of womanhood as "mother" and "worker," and uses the shift between them as a way to conceptualize the changes in women's activities in this period as well as to suggest some of the larger transformations of the age.

The first generation of Progressive Era women reformers—the settlement house workers and municipal reformers of the 1890s and early 1900s—saw their reform efforts as public expressions of their place in the family. On the basis of this familial approach, early women progressives made morally loaded distinctions between women's work and men's, between selfless efforts and selfish, between labors of love and paid labor. The characteristic form of their activities was the voluntary association. Born in 1856, Harriot Stanton Blatch was a member of this generation. She was part of the pioneering cohort of women college graduates and by 1900 was an experienced and active public reformer. Like Jane Addams and Florence Kelley, who were her contemporaries, Blatch used images of mothers, children, protection, dependence, and the family in her rhetoric. The familial themes of mother and child are highlighted in Blatch's case because her initial standing in the women's movement came from her matrilineage, the claims she could make to authority because her mother was Elizabeth Cady Stanton.

The second generation of women progressives, born in the 1870s and 1880s, had similar reform goals but expressed them quite differently. If the mother was the symbolic center of the first generation's understanding of womanhood, the woman worker was the emblem of the second. Paid labor, not social mothering, represented their route to women's emancipation, as well as the organizational basis for their reform efforts. What their mothers had done as volunteers they did as paid professionals.

Despite her age, Blatch's suffrage career was more closely associated with these younger women, the suffragettes and career women of progressivism's second generation. While she worked entirely within the voluntary mode herself, she heralded the professional woman worker and the paid reformer. The distinctive emphasis of Blatch's leadership was the woman worker, both wage-earning and professional; Blatch is usually credited with bringing the entire women's suffrage movement to recognize the economic and political significance of working women.

The class relations among women—an emerging theme of women's history scholarship and a particularly important aspect of women's history in the Progressive Era—are much illuminated by this paradigmatic shift in the definition of womanhood in the Progressive Era. Both generations of female Progressives were highly conscious of class relations among women, and in both, the social position of bourgeoise women rested on that of working-class women—and vice versa. Whereas the first generation of progressives constructed women's class relations on the model of the family, in which poor women were as dependent as children on the loving protection of reformer-mothers, the second generation of women progressives tended toward a professional model, with its mutually defining positions of expert and client.

Blatch's career is especially revealing of the changing basis of class relations among women in this shift from woman-as-mother to woman-as-worker. In the Equality League of Self Supporting Women, which Blatch founded and led from 1907 through 1910, both the growing importance of the working woman to women's emancipation and the class relations that ultimately developed between her professional and wage-earning varieties can be identified. In the Equality League's short but significant three-year history, important changes took place in class relations within the women's movement. Wage-earning women finally found their own political voices as suffragists. Yet the history of the Equality League also tells a tale of the reestablishment of bourgeoise leadership among women, albeit on new, more modern grounds. The rise and fall of the Equality League reveals the process by which the professional woman replaced the reform volunteer as the leader of her sex, thus becoming the class-specific embodiment of the power that Blatch and other progressive women claimed for their entire sex.

This shift from "mother" to "worker" as the dominant representation of women's social power during this period can be expanded into a hypothesis about the more basic processes at the heart of progressivism. For male social thinkers and activists as well, the bonds of family were being displaced by the wage relationship, not so much as a form of production—for of course that had happened long before—but at the level of consciousness, in the ways that they understood the relationships that made up their society and sought ways to reform and improve them.

In 1902, Harriot Stanton Blatch returned to the United States after two decades in England. Her mother, Elizabeth Cady Stanton, was dying, and Blatch was ready to take up leadership of the movement her mother had founded and to introduce new ideas and methods. Blatch found existing suffrage organizations conservative and tradition-bound. "The suffrage movement was completely in a rut . . . at the opening of the twentieth century" went her famous description of the suffrage scene as she found it. "It bored its adherents and repelled its opponents. . . . [F]riends, drummed up and harried by the ardent, listlessly heard the same old arguments. Unswerving adherence to the cause was held in high esteem, but alas it was loyalty to a rut run deep and even deeper."[1] After four years, Blatch reached the conclusion that she needed to establish an independent basis for a very different kind of suffrage movement.

In January 1907, therefore, Blatch formed the first new suffrage organization in New York City in over a decade, the Equality League of Self Supporting Women. Its members were working women, according to the *New York Times*, "doctors, lawyers, milliners and shirtmakers." "Any women who earns her own living" could join, boasted Blatch, "from a cook to a mining engineer and we have both of them." What was new and distinctive about the Equality League's suffragism was that it emphasized female self-support: paid work, both as women's social contribution and their route to independence and emancipation. "The suffrage will be won by women who are economically independent," Blatch declared. "The woman who supports herself has a claim upon the state, which legislators are coming to recognize."[2]

Blatch's focus on self-support in the Equality League replaced the nineteenth-century emphasis on domesticity and motherhood as a basis for women's unity. It led her to recognize the importance of working-class women, the vanguard of paid workers for women, and appreciate the leading role they could play in realizing women's unity and giving it political meaning. Her interest in cultivating working-class suffragism grew out of her experience in the New York Women's Trade Union League, which she joined as an "ally" in 1904, soon after it was formed. She initially conceived the Equality League of Self Supporting Women as the political wing of the Trade Union League, from which she recruited members, most notably Leonora O'Reilly and Rose Schneiderman (years before Schneiderman rose to prominence in connection with the Triangle Fire). Several trade unions affiliated directly, so that when speaking before the New York Legislature in 1908, Blatch claimed that the organization representated thousands of wage-earning women who needed the vote to protect their interests, especially in factory and social welfare legislation. Never before had wage-earning women been so numerous or prominent or had their perspective been so central in the suffrage movement.[3]

The feminist case that Blatch made for working women emphasized economic independence, not exploitation. As such, Blatch did not "narrow the claim" of self support "to factory girls" but was equally interested in the small but growing class of "business and professional women." Her innovation in the Equality League was thus to recruit industrial women and to create a cross-class organization that linked wage earners not to clubwomen, whose clients and wards industrial women traditionally were, but to professional workers, on the grounds of their common experience of wage labor. These women professional workers were college-educated—only the second generation of college-educated women in the United States—and often pioneers in their fields. Blatch's own daughter, Nora, the first woman to earn a civil engineering degree in the United States, was working in the New York City Department of Public Works helping to design the water system for greater New York City. These were women workers of a very different sort from the industrial wage earners. They identified deeply with their work and made explicit declarations of their intentions to maintain their professions after marriage. They were also not dependent on their earnings. Most were from financially privileged backgrounds and had inherited money on which they could have lived had they so wished.[4]

To Blatch and other progressive feminists like her, the notion of paid labor for all women held the promise of resolving the differences not only of men versus women (working versus domestic) but of rich versus poor (idle versus industrious). However, for the possibilities of universal work for women to be realized, the dilemma of the working mother had to be solved. Blatch's twentieth-century vision of emancipation, more clearly than her mother's, embraced work and marriage, and both the professional and working-class women of the Equality League shared her belief, which was one of the distinguishing convictions of modern suffragism. Her insistence on the importance of work for all women regardless of marital status was quite similar to that of her friend Charlotte Perkins Gilman. However, whereas Gilman concentrated on the conflict between paid work and homemaking for women, Blatch went further to consider the need to reconcile maternity with paid labor. Unlike many of her generation, she assumed not that mothers should be protected from paid labor but that they should be secured in it. Motherhood thus remained a factor in Blatch's thought but in the context of women's paid labor. As such, from an early date she began to criticize sex-based labor legislation for preserving the dependence of women in the family despite the growing independence of women outside of it.[5]

Blatch herself was not self-supporting, and she ruefully described herself as the only "parasite" in the Equality League. After graduation from Vassar in 1878, she recorded her determination both to find meaningful work and to enjoy sexual passion in marriage. She married an Englishman, which gave her personal and geographical independence from her mother, but she was determined to keep working. She remained a full-time writer, orator, and reformer through the births of two children and the death of one. There was little paid work for women of her type, however, and although she worked, she did not earn. Instead, she was supported by her husband, a wealthy brewer.[6] Paid labor for women outside the working class awaited the next generation. The professional working women of the Equality League were Blatch's daughters—literally in the case of her surviving child Nora and figuratively in the case of other young college graduates active in the organization.

Thus, Blatch had the authority of age over those self-supporters from whom she was not separated by the inequalities of class. Despite its title, the Equality League had only one leader. Young college women who worked, as they put it, "for" Blatch remembered her authoritative, at times dictatorial, manner. She was not alone in this; it was a style she shared with other (to use Rheta Childe Dorr's term) "generalissimos." Even her working relationship with Nora had this character, though mother and daughter seemed to collaborate smoothly and agree politically. Nora's feminism, like Harriot's, emerged in the shadow of her mother's authority, and Nora had to defer her own inclinations toward leadership to those of her mother. Later conflicts between mother and daughter, which were always on personal rather than political terrain and frequently involved money, suggest unacknowledged tension in these years.[7]

Blatch's relationship with her daughter can be taken as paradigmatic for many of the submerged inequalities and conflicts, between classes as well as generations, in the Progressive Era suffrage movement. In a revealing metaphor, Blatch recalled that the Equality League had "mothered radical groups and trade unions," which suggests her own superior (though nurturant) stance, not just to the younger professional women like Nora, but toward the wage-earning women who were the organization's pride.[8] At one level, her limited identification with industrial workers was a relatively simple socioeconomic matter; she was, after all, a wealthy woman. But there was a psychological dimension as well: Why "mother"? Blatch's experience as a daughter helps explain her taste for insurgency and her appreciation for working-class militance, which were crucial in her vision for the Equality League and her commitment to making wage-earning women central to it. But the authority of her own motherhood, and behind that an identification with her mother's authority, underlay other aspects of her feminism, especially the unexamined quality of her leadership and her blindness to power dynamics among women. This conflict with maternal authority, which could be restated as the problem of whether to follow or supersede prior paths of women's power, was a theme throughout the Progressive Era women's movement. The ideology of female unity that Blatch shared with other Progressive Era suffragists assumed sisterhood as the model of female unity, but the patterns of mothers and daughters provide a better framework for the mixture of conflict and cooperation, the covert power dynamics, and the complex class relations between women in these years.[9] The themes of mothers and daughters in this period suggest how Blatch and her entire generation expressed women's distinct needs for power and protection not by integrating them but by splitting them between classes and ranks of women.

The class relations within the Equality League, the role of wage-earning women in it, and its emphasis on the feminist ambition for self-support provided Blatch with the milieu to develop a new style of agitation, more proud and aggressive than anything practiced in the suffrage movement since Elizabeth Stanton's prime. Although the militant posture that Blatch and other American suffrage radicals assumed had indigenous roots, its immediate inspiration was British. Emmeline Pankhurst, founder of the Women's Social and Political Union of England, had been Blatch's close political comrade from her English years. Blatch and Pankhurst had served their political apprenticeship together in the British suffrage movement of the 1880s and the Fabian Society of the 1890s.[10] At about the same time that Blatch returned to the United States, Pankhurst founded the Women's Social and Political Union. Coincidentally, Pankhurst's relationships with her suffrage activist daughters, Christabel and Sylvia, and their conflicting visions for the future of feminism had a profound effect on the history of the WSPU and through it the entire British suffrage movement.

By 1907, the WSPU was shifting from demonstrations to civil disobedience, and its members were just beginning to be arrested for their protests. The developments in Britain were the object of much curiosity in the United States. Blatch had deeper links to England than did any other American suffrage leader, and she introduced into the American movement WSPU-inspired methods, especially tactics that sexually integrated public space, such as open-air meetings and parades. By 1908 the sobriquet "suffragette" had become a word as common in New York as in London.[11]

Although inspired by the British, American suffragettes were different. Not sharing, or forced to share, in the British emphasis on civil disobedience (mass arrests for suffrage activism did not occur in the United States until 1917), American militants focused instead on mastering the principles and enjoying the benefits of publicity. They were pioneers in the political uses of new media technologies such as movies, commercial radio, and telephones, and in the strategic deployment of public opinion. Living in the land of advertising, American suffragettes were convinced that advertising was what their movement needed. The newspapers had long ignored the woman suffrage movement, a practice compounded by orthodox suffragists' acceptance of the Victorian convention that respectable women did not court public attention. The Equality League's emphasis on the importance of paid labor for women of all classes effectively undermined the sexual suspicion that had long surrounded the working woman and underlay this convention. Blatch encouraged open-air meetings and similar devices, in part because of the publicity they generated. She became legendary for her ability to invent stunts that brought newspaper attention, such as sending suffragette "sandwich girls" to Coney Island to advertise a rally. The militant publicity campaign was a rapid success: by 1908 even the sneering *New York Times* was forced to report regularly on the suffrage movement, and Blatch was regularly featured.[12]

The class implications of suffragette tactics were mixed. Like the emphasis on self-support, suffragette tactics looked both to and away from working-class leadership. The suffragette style drew on the militant traditions of the labor movement, and its protest tactics, such as outdoor rallies, were suitable to a constituency with little money. Trade unionists and socialists found the militant platform hospitable to their suffragism, and suffragettes issued propaganda in Yiddish, Italian, and other immigrant languages. Emotionally and symbolically, the core of militance was its challenge to bourgeois standards of femininity. The revolt against "the lady" was signified by the figure who had once defined the limits of womanliness, the woman who worked for a living.

In other ways, however, the ethic of the suffragette obscured class distinctions. Its ultimate goal was not a class movement but a classless one, "a vast army of all classes . . . the largest number of women of all sorts and conditions," united around the common goal of votes for women.[13] The militant focus on femininity ultimately drew suffragettes' attention back to the elite woman, for it was she who was most obligated by womanly convention and who could be most outrageous by flaunting it. The lady, even as an object of attack, was an upper-class construct. In their very desire to redefine femininity, the militants had to stake their claim to it, and it was with respect to the upper-class woman that femininity was ultimately determined.

A similar dynamic characterized the way suffragettes positioned themselves in history. Militants prided themselves in their modernism; they were boldly theatrical. Their greatest hostility was reserved for "old-fashioned methods," usually characterized as "pink parlor teas." The old-time suffragist "plods along in the beaten track," one explained, while the suffragette "is the production of the modern period and is up to date in manner and method."[14] Yet even as militants embraced innovation for its own sake, they wanted precedents for themselves in the past. One New York suffragette group found its ancestor in an aging, titled British woman whom they brought to the United States to endorse their propaganda. Their "pioneer suffragette" was none other than Tennessee Claflin, who with sister Victoria Woodhull had been run out of the United States in the 1870s for premature suffragettism.[15] For Blatch, this relation between the past and the present, the inclination to strike off on her own, to find a new and better way, to be "progressive," and yet to refer to tradition even as she did so, was built into the very sources of her feminism. She appealed to her mother's legacy explicitly as precedent for the suffragettes, and other suffragettes embraced her personal heritage as their own. They appeared at open-air meetings supporting pins with Stanton's likeness.[16] The combination of radicalism and legitimacy that being Stanton's daughter gave Blatch strengthened her claim to leadership at this stage, for the impulse to look backward while moving forward was not just hers but the larger movement's as well.

Signifying this link, Blatch chose to inaugurate the Equality League's first militant campaign, in the spring of 1908, with a meeting organized around her mother's memory, at the place of her mother's birth (and the birth of the suffrage movement itself), Seneca Falls, New York. Blatch invited to Seneca Falls speakers who were literally or figuratively daughters of suffrage "pioneers," representing the future doing honor to the past. As the topic of her speech, Blatch chose her mother's friendships with other women. She portrayed these relationships as harmonious and absolutely unmarred by jealousy. She lingered over Stanton's friendship with Susan B. Anthony, which Blatch described as a perfect match of women of equal wills and complementary intellectual gifts.[17] That this portrait of women's relationships was romanticized, glossing over inequality and buried conflict, was betrayed by the evidence of Blatch's own resentments. She did not ask any of the women Anthony had regarded as her "suffrage daughters" to speak, most likely because several of them (notably Anna Howard

Shaw and Carrie Chapman Catt) were rivals to her own leadership; also, Blatch had already begun to resent the way that the childless Anthony was apotheosized in suffrage history as, in Gertrude Stein's words, "the mother of us all."

As it turned out, the tactical innovations of militant suffragettism triumphed, even as the working-class leadership and self-supporter ideology that had given them birth were superseded. In forming the Equality League, Blatch had created a medium for the revival of suffrage radicalism and the transformation of the New York suffrage movement into a modern politics. Even as Blatch collaborated with working women in the Equality League, however, she began to recruit suffrage activists from the other end of the class spectrum, wealthy and politically influential women whom the newspapers dubbed "society suffragettes." This side of Blatch's leadership connects her not only to the first, innovative stage of the remaking of suffrage class relations in the progressive years but also to the second, reactive phase as well. Blatch grew closer to these wealthy suffragettes at the same time that she determined that her original goals for the suffrage movement—an increase in numbers, in media attention, and in links with the trade union movement—had been met. In late 1910, after almost four years of working through the Equality League, Blatch announced that she was leaving to others the work of base-building and what she called propaganda and was dissolving the Equality League in order to cooperate more closely with these upper-class activists and to concentrate on more narrowly political tasks.

Upper-class women were as new to the suffrage movement, which was relentlessly middle-class throughout the late nineteenth century, as were the wage earners of the Equality League. Indeed, upper-class suffragism is best understood as a direct response to that of working-class women. Because working-class women were demanding the vote for themselves, wealthy women, who had long seen it as their prerogative to speak for the poor, were moved to demand the vote as well. The millionaire suffragist Alva Belmont explained that "women of wealth and social power," having come to understand that women wage earners needed the vote to protect their interests, "soon decide that they want this power for themselves, to protect their own interests and to enforce their own will in many directions."[18] Other historians of suffrage, Sharon Strom for Massachusetts and Steven Buechler for Illinois, have commented on the wealthy women who became active in the movement in this period, and nowhere was this development more pronounced than in New York City.[19]

An extraordinary number of the wealthy women who led the New

York suffrage movement in its final stages, and after that the national movement, were recruited by Blatch. Wealthy and restless, the wives and daughters of rich and powerful men, these women offered unexploited talents and untapped energy that Blatch recognized. The first "queen of society" to become active in the New York suffrage movement was Katherine Mackay, wife of the founder of International Telephone and Telegraph. Blatch, Mackay's suffrage sponsor, appreciated how much Mackay's interest in suffrage was related to her desire for a "broader stage" for her authority and helped Mackay form her own exclusive suffrage organization, the Equal Franchise Society. Many other wealthy women initially came into the movement through this organization, including Alva Belmont, the most flamboyant and ultimately the most powerful of the society suffragettes. Louisine Havemeyer, one of the first American collectors of French impressionist art became, with Blatch's encouragement, a much publicized militant suffragette. "It was Mrs. Blatch who insisted that I could speak; that I must speak; and then saw to it that I did speak," said Havemeyer. "I think I spoke just to please her." Havemeyer raised money for the suffrage movement in New York by exhibiting, for the first time, her personal collection of the paintings of Mary Cassatt. By 1917, she was one of the several hundred women arrested and imprisoned for demonstrations outside the White House.[20] Other upper-class women were Vera Whitehouse, wife of a major investment banker and reputedly the richest suffragist in New York; Eunice Dana Brannan, whose father published the *New York Tribune;* and genteel artist Gertrude Foster Brown. They left similar testimonies about how Blatch had encouraged them to speak in public, march in parades, and find in themselves new skills and a sense of public competence.

These society suffragists were drawn to Blatch because they found the flamboyance and tactical radicalism of the suffragette style that she represented personally compelling, despite its earlier links to working-class activism. If historians like Kathy Peiss and Christine Stansell are correct in suggesting that working-class women were the first to experiment with more modern styles of femininity, suffrage activism may have been one of the ways that wealthy women began to appropriate this new standard of personal freedom. There was something about the claim to power as an individual that the suffragettes made that appealed to these women, who were denied the power of their class by virtue of their gender. The possibility of greater freedom of movement, to go out on their own to parts of the city forbidden to them, was also a special attraction for upper-class women. A chronicler of the suffrage movement recorded that elite women who had initially found militance "not quite ladylike . . . adopted it with enthusiasm, till women . . . who . . . had lived the sheltered life of a petted protected woman would be seen talking freedom for women to huge swelling crowds in the most congested parts of the East Side."[21]

The theme of clothes, the language of fashion, was prominent in accounts of upper-class women's conversion to militant suffragism. The initial enthusiasm for the new activism of society women was not that they made the movement wealthy so much as that they made it fashionable. Most suffragists were thrilled, although one pioneer suffragette, herself a librarian, publicly protested the corrupting effect of this desire to "attract a well dressed crowd."[22] Clothes embodied the complex power relations of upper- and working-class women, both at the level of culture and at the level of production. (In the *New York Times Index,* accounts of the 1909–10 Shirtwaist Strike were listed not under strikes or labor but under fashion, which is how it must have first appeared to the women of New York in 1909.)

Blatch imagined a thriving women's movement, combining the strength and numbers of the working class with the money and influence of the rich. When the Equality League sponsored the American premiere of Elizabeth Robin's suffragette play *Votes for Women,* wage-earning suffragettes filled the audience while society matrons (become patrons) paid large sums to sit in boxes. As one of Blatch's admirers said of her, "She formed a connecting link between the two economic extremes of the suffrage movement . . . joining under one banner the forces of labor and wealth united for the common object of enfranchisement."[23]

However, this image of class harmony was far too romantic and oversimplified. Subtle changes in the class character of the new suffragism were taking place. A careful observer at the *Votes for Women* premiere might have noticed that while the plot centered on the transformative possibilities of political unity between women of different classes, the heroine was a wealthy woman, and her conversion to suffrage activism was the dramatic core. Wealth had a definite impact on the movement. Meetings went inside once there was money to hire halls. Suffrage societies, including the Equality League, began to pay their office workers, enabling wage-earning women to work full-time for suffrage. But, since officers donated their services, only women who did not work for a living led these organizations. Parades went uptown, away from Union Square. Blatch and some of her upper-class converts even tried to hold a street meeting uptown, outside of the exclusive Colony Club; they did their best to assemble a crowd, gave their speeches, and then retired for lunch inside.

Blatch, who had set herself above the younger and working-class women of the Equality League, collaborated on a level of equality with the society suffragettes.[24] There was no mothering here; these were her sisters.

In the midst of this enthusiasm for suffrage's newfound fashionability, the Equality League announced the first American visit of Emmeline Pankhurst. To welcome Pankhurst to New York, Blatch assembled an audience that represented all the classes of suffragism. Hundreds of self-supporters, professional and wage-earning, sat on the platform at Carnegie Hall, while society women, including Mrs. J. Borden Harriman and Mrs. Elbert Gary, paid for boxes, as at the theater. After touring the country, Pankhurst returned to New York to take her farewell. Her overriding message was the glory of a unified womanhood, in which the commonalities of sex obliterated the distinctions of class. Her organizing metaphor was a women's army, a common image in the Progressive Era women's movement. Within her metaphor, the text was women of different classes sharing a common purpose, but the subtext was the structure of rank that organized this fighting womanhood. Pankhurst called for women to "transcend class distinctions"; given the working-class leadership that initially characterized militance both in England and in the U.S., this meant upper-class women displacing working-class women from the front lines. Pankhurst understood this displacement not as an assertion of power but only as wealthy women doing their "duty" to protect working-class women from the abuse of police and politicians. "If there is any distinction of class," she proclaimed, "it is the privileged women, the honored women [who] are doing the hardest and most unpleasant work." There was no way in Pankhurst's maternal, metaphorical imagination—or in Blatch's political one—to speak of inequality or power between women; her language spoke only of duty, harmony, organization, and service.[25]

In the midst of these transformations, an event occurred that seems to have expressed, perhaps even effected, the shift toward upper-class leadership within militant suffragism. That event was the Shirtwaist Strike, the famous uprising of twenty thousand, which preoccupied virtually all activist women in New York City in the winter of 1909-10. Even as Blatch was working to realize a unified suffragism in which society and labor joined hands, and even as Pankhurst evoked the vision of women shoulder-to-shoulder in behalf of the least of their sex, the women industrial workers of New York City declared themselves on general strike, and the suffrage movement, especially its newly prominent upper-class sector, announced its active support. In December 1909, millionaire suffragette Alva Belmont declared that she was putting her considerable resources at the service of the strikers, who had already been out for several weeks. The announcement that she would rent the Hippodrome Theatre for a mass rally in support of the strikers ran side by side with coverage of Pankhurst's departure.[26]

Seen in the context of the revival of the woman suffrage movement that preceded it, the Shirtwaist Strike takes on new meanings. The prominence of working-class women in the suffrage movement in New York contributed to the political confidence of the young garment workers who overrode their union leaders to call a general strike. The vision of a cross-class sisterhood that animated the strike support movement was an import from the suffragism of Blatch, Pankhurst, and others. The strike support movement used tactics—such as mass rallies, auto caravans, even a disciplined women's parade—that had been developed previously by suffrage militants. Even the skillful generation of publicity around the issue of police brutality against strikers was shaped by what American women were learning from the direct action tactics of British suffragettes.

As the strike progressed, power in the support coalition shifted away from the strikers themselves and toward their upper-class allies. As the strike lengthened and pressure for a settlement grew, upper-class leaders of the support movement tried to dictate terms to the strikers. When the strikers objected, the support coalition collapsed, the strike dwindled to a conclusion, and significant numbers of workers returned to their jobs without union protection (one consequence of which was the death of 146 workers by fire at the Triangle Company a year later). Seen from this perspective, the upper-class suffragists who led the support movement, whose political authority was strengthened by the episode, gained at least as much from the collaboration as the strikers, who gained public attention from it. Put another way, the outcome of the strike helped to shift the class dynamic of the suffrage movement away from wage-earning women and toward upper-class leadership.[27] Blatch was caught up in the drama of the strike, but, as conflicts over its conduct intensified, she sided with the wealthy supporters against the strikers. Within the New York Women's Trade Union League, hostility over upper-class women's attempts to control the strike was focused on Ann Morgan (J.P. Morgan's daughter) and veteran woman trade unionist Eva Valesh, who acted as Morgan's proxy. When Morgan and Valesh tried to force the strikers to settle, the Executive Board of the New York Women's Trade Union League (WTUL) voted to censor and remove Valesh from membership. Only Blatch and Frances Kellor voted against the motion. Blatch's choices cost her the crucial trade union support that underlay the Equality League. Ten months later, she was charged by the New York WTUL on behalf of the Bookkeepers, Stenographers, and Accountants Union with obstructing unionization of the Equality League staff. Blatch's response that her office had only one paid worker, who did not wish to join the union, made no difference. From then on, the New York chapter of the WTUL, which had been active in the Equality League since 1907, ceased most of its suffrage activities.[28] By this time, Blatch herself had moved on. At the end of the strike, she and her rich recruits were in Albany, beginning the intensive lobbying effort that would eventually lead to the 1915 New York woman suffrage referendum.

Blatch formalized these developments by announcing in November 1910 that the old Equality League had been dissolved. She would continue her work through a new organization, the Women's Political Union. Within this change in name there were three related references to deeper changes. Most obviously, the title was a reference to the Pankhurst organization, the Women's Social and Political Union. The Women's Political Union's first activity was to sponsor the visit of Sylvia Pankhurst, Emmeline's daughter, and to begin a major fund-raising drive for the British suffragettes. At a somewhat deeper level, the new name signified Blatch's shift, in her words, from "propaganda" to "politics". The new organization would be "an instrumentality keyed exclusively to the political aspect of the suffrage movement." It reflected Blatch's conviction that votes for women could actually be won, and for the next five years her unflinching focus was on legislative and electoral victory. Most deeply, at the level of absence, all references to equality or self-support were gone, and with them all critical attention to the class structures underlying organized womanhood.[29]

No longer dedicated to creating a large organization of wage earners and self-supporters, Blatch established in the Women's Political Union a small cadre structure. Virtually all her collaborators in the WPU were rich and powerful women. In defending her decision to abandon the name and character of the Equality League, Blatch used the language of democracy. The official explanation of the name change was that the new organization "should not carry the idea of discrimination against any class of people." Similarly, Nora Blatch said, "We didn't want the aristocracy, the snobbery if you will, of self support. We wanted to be absolutely democratic, so we decided not to discriminate against the leisure classes."[30] Despite the language of democracy, the reality was quite the opposite. The determined refusal to admit the relevance of class inequities among women ultimately insured the maintenance of those inequities.

Notes

1. Harriot Stanton Blatch and Alma Lutz, *Challenging Years: The Memoirs of Harriot Stanton Blatch* (New York: Putnam's, 1940), 92.

2. *New York Times*, Jan. 3, 1907, 6; *Progress*, June 1907, 1; Harriot Stanton Blatch, "Self Supporting Woman," *Woman's Journal*, Aug. 17, 1907, 129.

3. Nancy Schrom Dye, *As Equals and as Sisters: Feminism, Unionism and the Women's Trade Union League of New York* (Columbia: Univ. of Missouri Press, 1980), 41; *Woman's Journal*, Feb. 29, 1908, 34.

4. *Woman's Journal*, Aug. 17, 1907, 129, and Aug. 3, 1907, 122. Nora S. Barney, "'Spanning Two Centuries': The Autobiography of Nora Stanton Barney," ed. Ellen C. DuBois, *History Workshop* 22 (Fall 1986): 131-52. On the other professional workers, see DuBois, "Working Women, Class Relations and Suffrage Militance: Harriot Stanton Blatch and the New York Woman Suffrage Movement, 1894-1907," *Journal of American History* 74 (June 1987): 50.

5. For Blatch's early ideas about working mothers, see "Specialization of Function in Women," *Gunton's Magazine* 10 (May 1896): 349-56. For her later opposition to sex-based labor legislation, see "The Race Has Two Parents," *Women's Political World*, July 15, 1914, 5.

6. *Woman's Journal*, Nov. 2, 1907, 17. Harriot Eaton Stanton, Diaries, 1879-1881, in the possession of Rhoda Barney Jenkins, Greenwich, Conn., who permitted me to see them. For Blatch's marriage, see Blatch and Lutz, *Challenging Years*, 63-68; this account is full of incidental references to Blatch's ties to her mother, such as her observation that her wedding took place on her mother's sixty-seventh birthday (65).

7. For criticism of Blatch's dictatorial manner, see Laura Ellsworth Seiler, "In the Streets," in Sherna Gluck, ed., *From Parlor to Prison: Five American Suffragists Talk About Their Lives* (New York: Random, 1976), 210. Others, notably her closest aide Caroline Lexow, adored her. Caroline Babcock Furlow, interview with author, Nyack, N.Y., Apr. 1982. Rheta Childe Dorr, *A Woman of Fifty* (New York: Funk and Wagnalls, 1924), 261. Harriot Stanton Blatch to Grace Ellery Channing Stetson, Aug. 27, n.y., Stetson Papers, Schlesinger Library, Cambridge, Mass. Rhoda Barney Jenkins, telephone conversation with author, Oct. 4, 1988.

8. Blatch and Lutz, *Challenging Years*, 121.

9. My interpretation of mother-daughter patterns has been much influenced by Vivian Gornick, "The World of Our Mothers," *New York Times Book Review* 22 November 1987, 1.

10. Blatch and Lutz, *Challenging Years*, 73.

11. Winnifred Harper Cooley, "Suffragists and 'Suffragettes': A Record of Actual Achievement," *World To-Day* 15 (Oct. 1908): 1066-71.

12. Kay Sloan, "Sexual Warfare in the Silent Cinema: Comedies and Melodramas of Woman Suffragism," *American Quarterly* (Fall 1981): 412-37. Mary Tyng, "Self Denial Week," *American Suffragette: Official Organ of the National Progressive Woman Suffrage Union* 1 (Aug. 1909): 3 ("The situation in America is this—all that the cause needs is advertising"). Blatch, "Radical Move in Two Years," unidentified clipping, Nov. 8, 1908, Mrs. Robert Abbe Collection, Manuscript Division, New York Public Library.

13. Blatch to Leonora O'Reilly, Dec. 23, 1911, O'Reilly Correspondence, New York Unversity Library.

14. *American Suffragette* 1 (June 1909): 5.

15. "Our Cook Day," *American Suffragette* 1. (Nov. 1909): 1.

16. *Woman's Journal,* Nov. 14, 1908, 183.

17. *Woman's Journal,* June 6, 1908, 90. "Programme," Anniversary of Seneca Falls Celebration, May 27, 1908, Harriot Stanton Blatch Papers, Manuscript Division, Library of Congress, Washington, D.C.

18. Mrs. Oliver H.P. Belmont, "Woman Suffrage As It Looks Today," *Forum* 43 (Jan. 1910): 268.

19. Steven M. Buechler, *The Transformation of the Woman Suffrage Movement: The Case of Illinois, 1850-1920* (New Brunswick, N.J.: Rutgers Univ. Press, 1986); and Sharon Strom, "Leadership and Tactics in the American Woman Suffrage Movement: A Perspective from Massachusetts," *Journal of American History* 52 (Sept. 1975): 296-315.

20. Blatch and Lutz, *Challenging Years,* 118. Also see Olivia Howard Dunbar, "Mrs. Mackay at Work," *Harper's Bazaar* 44 (April 1910): 240-41. Christopher Lasch, "Alva Belmont," in Edward James, Janet James, and Paul Boyer, eds., *Notable American Women* (Cambridge, Mass.: Harvard Univ. Press, 1971), 1: 126-28. Louisine M. Havemeyer, "The Suffrage Torch: Memories of a Militant," *Scribner's Magazine* 71 (May 1922): 528. See Mabel Potter Daggett, "Suffrage Enters the Drawing Room: Society Has Saluted the Four-Starred Flag and the 'Cause' Enrolls Thousands," *Delineator* 75 (Jan. 1910): 37-38; and Gertrude Foster Brown, *On Account of Sex,* unpublished manuscript, Sophia Smith Collection, Smith College, Northampton, Mass., ch. 4.

21. Kathy Peiss, *Cheap Amusements: Working Women and Leisure in Turn-of-the-Century New York* (Philadelphia: Temple Univ. Press, 1986). Christine Stansell, *City of Women: Sex and Class in New York, 1789-1860* (New York: Knopf, 1986). *New York Sun,* Dec. 9, 1917, unidentified clipping in Abbe Collection, New York Public Library. On the appeal of militance for wealthy women, see Brown, *On Account of Sex,* ch. 6; and Dorr, *Woman of Fifty,* 222.

22. *American Suffragette* 2 (Apr.-May 1910): 20. Inez Haines to Maud Wood Park, Dec. 7, 1910, reel 1, National American Woman Suffrage Association Papers, Manuscript Division, Library of Congress, Washington, D.C. *New York Times,* Mar. 27, 1908, 4. The protesting militant was Maud Malone, who ironically finished her suffrage career as a paid worker for Belmont.

23. *Woman's Journal,* Jan. 16, 1909, 10-11. *New York Times,* Feb. 2, 1909, 6.

24. Elizabeth Robins, *The Convert* (1907; reprint, London: Women's Press Limited, 1980). *New York Times,* May 14, 1909, 5. From the beginning of their suffrage careers, Mackay and Belmont both paid women to do suffrage work for them, as an extension of wealthy women's practice of employing personal secretaries. Helen Rogers Reid, a powerful member of Blatch's circle and eventually publisher of the *New York Tribune,* was private secretary to Mrs. Whitelaw Reid until she met and married Mrs. Reid's son, Ogden.

25. *Woman's Journal,* Oct. 30, 1909, 174-75. For further coverage on Pankhurst's visit, also see *Woman's Journal,* Dec. 11, 1909, 199-202.

26. *New York Times,* Dec. 1, 1909, 6, and Dec. 2, 1909, 3. The initial strikes at the Leiserson and Triangle Companies were called in September. The *New York Times* did not cover the strike until November 5, when the arrest of WTUL president Mary Dreier made page 1. By the next day, however, media attention had faded. Consistent coverage did not begin until December 1, in connection with Belmont's announced intention "to aid the strike," and from then until late January 1910, there were long articles daily.

27. For a full account of the Shirtwaist Strike, see Meredith Tax, *The Rising of the*

Women: Feminist Solidarity and Class Conflict, 1880-1917 (New York: Monthly Review, 1980). My account of class dynamics in the suffrage movement owes much to Tax's work on this period.

28. New York Women's Trade Union League Papers, Executive Board Minutes, Jan. 28, 1910, New York University Library.

29. *Woman's Journal,* Nov. 26, 1910, 219. Caroline Lexow Babcock, "The Women's Political Union: Its Organization, Achievements and Termination," in Isabelle K. Savelle, ed., *Ladies' Lib: How Rockland Women Got the Vote* (Rockland County, N.Y.: Historical Society of Rockland County, 1979), 51.

30. *Women's Political Union Annual Report, 1911-1912,* Harriot Stanton Blatch Collection, Library of Congress, Washington, D.C. *New York Press,* Dec. 29, 1912, clipping in Blatch Collection, Library of Congress, Washington, D.C.

12

Paradigms Gained: Further Readings in the History of Women in the Progressive Era

SUSAN TANK LESSER

Two basic challenges confront the foolhardy reviewer attempting to compile readings in the history of Progressive Era women. First, the selection process is complicated by an exponential rate of increase in this area of scholarship. Second, the imposition of classification generally demanded by such an exercise is defied by a remarkable epistemological volatility within the field. Not only is there an embarrassment of riches, there is also a growing sensitivity to alternative perspectives. In this respect, although gender continues to be a central analytical theme in many studies, its explanatory primacy is modified by considerations of the dynamics of race, ethnicity, and class. The interplay of these elements is at the heart of some of the most provocative and productive studies tackling Progressive Era history. It remains to be seen whether a single paradigm incorporating this conceptual diversity will be successfully identified, or indeed whether it should be, but it is clear that the history of Progressive Era women continues to be enriched both by the expansion in research and by the development of differing perspectives.

The following readings have been selected in response to this multiplicity of voices and viewpoints, introducing and expanding on themes and topics not otherwise addressed or explored in depth elsewhere in this volume. In keeping with the preceding collection of essays, these readings are characterized by a reevaluaton of epistemological and methodological approaches and a broadening of cultural and regional reference points. This supplementary material, most of it recently published, has here been organized into readings clustered around such broad themes as the continuing debate on the nature of knowledge; the contribution of material culture studies; diversity in sexual expression and the structuring of intimate relationships; the interrelationships of family, work, and community; and developments in popular culture and the arts.

Spiking the Canon: Alternative Epistemologies

Epistemological challenges, emerging with increasing frequency from studies of less privileged groups in American society, revive notions of praxis in women's studies and women's history. As well as making important contributions to scholarly discourse, they confront complacent assumptions of sisterhood and social progress.

As Patricia Hill Collins points out in "The Social Construction of Black Feminist Thought," *Signs: Journal of Women in Culture and Society* 14, no. 4 (Summer 1989): 745-73, the way in which knowledge is created and validated has profound political and social implications since it is intrinsic to self-definition and to historical interpretation. Her stress on connectedness and concrete experience, assessed through dialogue and infused with an ethic of caring and personal accountability, is strongly rooted in the African-American historical experience and is distinguished from approaches based on abstraction, individuation, and separation. In the same issue, Elsa Barkley Brown contributes a thoughtful and sometimes lyrical essay on research and pedagogy entitled "African-American Women's Quilting: A Framework for Conceptualizing and Teaching African-American Women's History" (921-29). Building on Bettina Aptheker's concept of "pivoting the center," developed in *Tapestries of Life: Women's Work, Women's Consciousness and the Meaning of Daily Life* (Amherst: Univ. Massachusetts Press, 1989), Brown stresses the need to respect varieties of experience and to share in interpretative authority.

Similarly, Rayna Green's review essay "Native American Women," *Signs: Journal of Women in Culture and Society* 6 (Winter 1980): 248-67, underscores the distortions and omissions caused by the imposition of the Western intellectual tradition on the Native American experience. Both Paula Gunn Allen, in her introduction to *Spider Woman's Granddaughters: Traditional Tales and Contemporary Writing by Native American Women* (Boston: Beacon, 1989), and Gretchen M. Bataille and Kathleen Mullen Sands, eds., *American Indian Women: Telling Their Lives* (Lincoln: Univ. of Nebraska Press, 1984), question the relevance of Western aesthetics in understanding diverse Native American cultures and propose that scholars be sensitive to the distinctive ways in which such realities are expressed.

These assertions are the latest expression of a decidedly iconoclastic impetus in women's history. In her groundbreaking article "The Female

World of Love and Ritual: Relations between Women in Nineteenth-Century America," *Signs: Journal of Women in Culture and Society* 1 (Autumn 1975): 1-29, Carroll Smith-Rosenberg has identified the existence of a vibrant and supportive culture enjoyed by white middle-class women, which helps to counter the stereotype of the isolated and passive Victorian female. In light of this study, the close female friendships and the gender-related justification of many Progressive Era reform initiatives become more comprehensible. Paula Baker extended this analysis in her review of middle-class women's political role in American life, "The Domestication of Politics: Women and American Political Society, 1780-1920," *American Historical Review* 89 (June 1984): 620-47. Both studies are structured within a separate spheres framework, positing the existence of public and private arenas ordering American social and political life.

As an explanatory model, the concept of separate spheres has gained some ground within the field of women's history, particularly in late nineteenth-century and early twentieth-century studies, in which it acts as a tidy metaphor for complex processes of change. This is perhaps understandable since the prescriptive literature advocating gender-role ideals was so forceful and so prevalent and its theoretical dichotomies are so seductive in their easy visualization. One particularly ambitious example is Carl Degler's *At Odds: Women and the Family in America from the Revolution to the Present* (Oxford: Oxford Univ. Press, 1980), a sweeping account of women's domestic experiences and public forays. Another example, presenting some interesting material on the impact of women and gender-role ideology on the formation of social policy, is Sheila Rothman, *Woman's Proper Place: A History of Changing Ideals and Practices, 1870 to the Present* (New York: Basic, 1978). An important historiographical assessment of separate spheres theory and a consideration of many of its implications can be found in Linda Kerber, "Separate Spheres, Female Worlds, Woman's Place: The Rhetoric of Women's History," *Journal of American History* 75 (June 1988): 9-39.

A separate spheres rationale suggests the moral underpinning of the domestic and professional lives of many privileged, mostly white, middle-class women, although the sincerity and extent of their acquiescence is often unclear. However, many scholars are becoming increasingly wary of a "New Englandization" tendency in women's history and are raising a number of questions concerning the relevance of race, ethnicity, class, and regionalism to this model. A discussion of the impact of broader power relations on gender formation may be found in Ellen DuBois et al., "Politics and Culture in Women's History: A Symposium," *Feminist Studies* 6, no. 1

(Spring 1980): 26-64. In her study *Give Us Bread But Give Us Roses: Working Women's Consciousness in the United States, 1890 to the First World War* (Boston: Routledge & Kegan Paul, 1983), Sarah Eisenstein has investigated the connection between changing conditions in work, family relationships, and gender-role attitudes of mainly Jewish and Italian working-class immigrant women. Susan Armitage has called for a rethinking of western history that is sensitive to racial and class diversity as well as to the specific conditions of the region, in "Through Women's Eyes: A New View of the West," in Susan Armitage and Elizabeth Jameson, eds., *The Women's West* (Norman: Univ. of Oklahoma Press, 1987), 9-18. Elizabeth Jameson develops this further in "Toward a Multicultural History of Women in the Western United States," *Signs: Journal of Women in Culture and Society* 13, no 4 (Summer 1988): 761-91. In an earlier study, "Race, Sex, and Region: Black Women in the American West, 1850-1920," *Pacific Historical Review* 49, no. 2 (May 1980): 285-313, Lawrence B. de Graaf compares the experiences of African-American and white women, concluding that race was the prime determinant of African-American women's lives. Another regional study, Sarah Deutsch's *No Separate Refuge: Culture, Class, and Gender on an Anglo-Hispanic Frontier in the American Southwest, 1880-1940* (New York: Oxford Univ. Press, 1987), challenges the gender stereotyping of Hispanic women, emphasizing cultural conflicts and mediations as well as the shifting intersections of gender, ethnicity, and class in various localities.

Drawing the Line: Space and Image in Material Culture

In recent years, material culture studies have been establishing a foothold within the academy. Artifacts and images, spatial relationships and designs, have become the subjects of a growing body of scholarship. Thomas J. Schlereth's edited collection of wide-ranging essays, *Material Culture Studies in America* (Nashville, Tenn.: AASLH, 1982), serves as an important introduction to this discipline. Basing their work on the premise that material constructs are invested with social meanings whose interpretation may help to illuminate the social construction of gender, various scholars are making use of innovative techniques derived from material culture and are applying them to aspects of Progressive Era history. The following readings focus primarily on the use and design of space and the creation of gender-related imagery in this period.

Estelle Freedman, "Separatism as Strategy: Female Institution Building and American Feminism, 1870-1930," *Feminist Studies* 5 (Fall 1979):

512-29, asserts the importance of an autonomous space within which women's culture and women's activism could flourish. Karen Blair's essay "The Limits of Sisterhood: The Woman's Building in Seattle, 1908-1912," *Frontiers* 8 (Spring 1985): 45-52, traces the efforts of a community of clubwomen to strengthen their networking and to promote their reform agenda through the construction of a Woman's Building for the 1909 Alaska-Yukon-Pacific Exposition. Hazel V. Carby, *Reconstructing Womanhood: The Emergence of the Afro-American Woman Novelist* (New York: Oxford Univ. Press, 1987), introduces her call for a new feminist critical practice with an account of the discriminatory dealings of the 1893 Exposition's Board of Lady Managers and their role in the perpetuation of dominant sexual and racial ideologies within this public form.

The settlement movement constituted another arena in which women carved out a physical space for themselves. Kathryn Kish Sklar, "Hull House in the 1890s: A Community of Women Reformers," *Signs: Journal of Women in Culture and Society* 10 (Summer 1985): 658-77, describes how this independent base provided accommodation and familial support for single women reformers and also furnished opportunities for innovative reform programs. Helen Lefkowitz Horowitz has produced two extremely interesting material culture studies focusing on the development of two female-dominated institutions during this period. Her investigation of the expansion of both Hull House and of a number of women's colleges pays close attention to the evolution of their architectural layout and design and links it to the values and priorities of their founders. The former study is entitled "Hull House as Women's Space," *Chicago History* 12, no. 4 (Winter 1983-84): 40-55; the latter is *Alma Mater: Design and Experience in the Women's Colleges from Their Nineteenth-Century Beginnings to the 1930s* (New York: Knopf, 1984).

A concern with the social and political implications of the design and use of space is at the center of Dolores Hayden's *The Grand Domestic Revolution: A History of Feminist Designs for American Homes, Neighborhoods, and Cities* (Cambridge, Mass.: MIT, 1981). She identifies a distinctive material feminist tradition in a number of Progressive Era women's contention that women's social and political powerlessness could best be improved by the creation of new living patterns, made possible by redesigned homes and cities. Although her focus is primarily on well-educated middle-class women, Hayden also includes some interesting material on the working-class activist Mary Kenney O'Sullivan, who initiated a boarding house for single working-class women, providing decent and affordable living arrangements imbued with the values of labor activism and class solidarity.

A comparable concern inspired Nannie Helen Burroughs to establish the National Training School in Washington, D.C., which provided shelter and education for black migrant women and girls. Her work has been examined by Evelyn Brooks Barnett's "Nannie Helen Burroughs and the Education of Black Women," in Sharon Harley and Rosalyn Terborg-Penn, eds., *The Afro-American Woman: Struggles and Images* (Port Washington, N.Y.: Kennikat, 1978): 97-108. Although not explicitly a material culture study, it does suggest the importance of this structure and its infusion with the principles of "Bible, bath, and broom" to aid the advancement of the race.

Home design and furnishings have been popular material culture subjects. Gwendolyn Wright, *Moralism and the Model Home: Domestic Architecture and Cultural Conflict in Chicago, 1873-1913* (Chicago: Univ. of Chicago Press, 1980), examines the links between important shifts in home designs and broader social transformations. The rise of the home economics movement, with its emphasis on the scientific improvement of domestic design and practice, is a unifying theme in much of this work. See, for example, Glenna Matthews, *"Just a Housewife": The Rise and Fall of Domesticity in America* (New York: Oxford Univ. Press, 1987); Ruth Schwartz Cowan, "The Industrial Revolution in the Home: Household Technology and Social Change in the Twentieth Century," in Schlereth, *Material Culture Studies,* 222-35; and Kimberley W. Carrell, "The Industrial Design Comes to the Home: Kitchen Design Reform and Middle Class Women," *Journal of American Culture* 2, no. 3 (Fall 1979): 488-99. Susan Strasser's *Never Done: A History of American Housework* (New York: Pantheon, 1982) reviews the impact of technological change on household chores, its conclusions deftly summed up in its aphoristic title. Harvey Green's *The Light of the Home: An Intimate View of the Lives of Women in Victorian America* (New York: Pantheon, 1983), with illustrations from the Margaret Woodbury Strong Museum, offers a closer look at a wide range of domestic artifacts. Laura Schapiro provides an entertaining and insightful review of the rise of scientific cooking, shaped by the principles of the domestic science movement, in *Perfection Salad: Women and Cooking at the Turn of the Century* (New York: Farrar, Straus, Giroux, 1986).

Domestic science courses were soon established in public schools and settlements, where they played an important role in Americanization programs. Cynthia Neverdon-Morton, *Afro-American Women of the South and the Advancement of the Race, 1895-1925* (Knoxville: Univ. of Tennessee Press, 1989), has uncovered many similar programs among the black settlements, schools, and women's clubs in the small towns and rural districts of the South, where domestic science courses were used as a means of racial uplift. Such programs were not necessarily absorbed by their subjects without resistance or modification. Lizabeth A. Cohen, "Embellishing a Life of Labor: An Interpretation of the Material Culture of Working-Class Homes, 1885-1915," in Schlereth, *Material Culture Studies,* 289-305, describes the decoration and furnishing of tenement homes in New York and concludes that immigrant families created an identifiable working-class style, using both ethnically distinct objects and the mass-produced items of an industrial economy.

Material culture studies have also produced some interesting perspectives on female images and representations, grounding graphic and symbolic analyses in their historical context and offering important insights into the social construction of gender. A comprehensive treatment of popular female types, their creators, and their audience may be found in Martha Banta, *Imaging American Women: Idea and Ideals in Cultural History* (New York: Columbia Univ. Press, 1987). She looks in depth at the emergence of "New Woman" graphics, identifying this type as a subset of the "American Girl" motif, which was itself a product of a growing anxiety to define what being American should mean in a society fearing increasing fragmentation. Carroll Smith-Rosenberg, "The New Woman as Androgyne: Social Disorder and Gender Crisis, 1870-1936," in *Disorderly Conduct: Visions of Gender in Victorian America* (New York: Oxford Univ. Press, 1986), 245-96, explores the metaphors and symbols shaping this phenomenon, arguing that it constituted a serious, though failed, attempt to turn gender relations on its head. A darker view of the representation of female types in this era in both Europe and America is offered by Bram Dijkstra, *Idols of Perversity: Fantasies of Feminine Evil in Fin-de-Siecle Culture* (New York: Oxford Univ. Press, 1986). The manipulation of images to fit preconceived notions of womanhood and racial identity is the subject of Patricia Albers and William James, "Illusion and Illumination: Visual Images of American Indian Women in the West," in Armitage and Jameson, *Women's West,* 35-50. The cultural impact of the movies and the creation of powerful new role models that glamorously transformed women's daily lives is addressed by Mary P. Ryan, "The Projection of a New Womanhood: The Movie Moderns in the 1920s," in Jean E. Friedman and

William J. Shade, eds., *Our American Sisters: Women in American Life and Thought* (Lexington, Mass.: D.C. Heath, 1982), 500-518.

Lois Banner's *American Beauty* (New York: Knopf, 1983) is a useful overview of shifts in beauty and fashion and their relationship to broader social and cultural transformations. Sexual distinctions in dress are the subject of Jo B. Paoletti, "Clothing and Gender in America: Children's Fashions, 1880-1920," *Signs: Journal of Women in Culture and Society* 13, no. 1 (Autumn 1987): 136-43. Although she raises more questions than she answers, she effectively contrasts an increasingly androgynous tendency in women's clothing with a marked conservatism in male fashions and growing gender divisions in children's wear. An interesting case study in dress reform and its energetic advocates at the 1893 World's Columbian Exposition is provided by Jeanne Madeline Weimann, "Fashion and the Fair," *Chicago History* 12 (Fall 1983): 48-56. Two other studies look at ways in which activist women themselves both took advantage of and challenged expectations about women's role in the American polity. Developing a striking iconography derived from idealized images of both domestic and mythical womanhood and adapting the aggressive tactics of the British suffragettes to local needs, they revived the American suffrage scene. Sharon Hartman Strom's "Leadership and Tactics in the American Woman Suffrage Movement: A New Perspective from Massachusetts," *Journal of American History* 62 (Sept. 1975): 296-315, is an important case study in this new suffrage phase, while Alice Sheppard's "Political and Social Consciousness in the Woman Suffrage Cartoons of Lou Rogers and Nina Allender," *Studies in American Humor* 4 (Fall 1985): 39-50, looks at the cartoons that conveyed a pointed political message in suffrage publications.

Close Encounters: Sexuality and Intimate Relationships

Despite the methodological difficulties implicit in such research, the formation of intimate relationships and questions of sexual choice are receiving an increasing amount of scholarly attention. A comprehensive study, sensitive to issues of race and class as well as gender, has been provided by John D'Emilio and Estelle Freedman in *Intimate Matters: A History of Sexuality in America* (New York: Harper & Row, 1988). Ellen K. Rothman, *Hands and Hearts: A History of Courtship in America* (New York: Basic, 1984), examines the courtship patterns of mostly privileged white couples since the colonial period. Sondra R. Herman, "Loving Courtship or the Marriage Market? The Ideal and Its Critics, 1871-1911," in Friedman and Shade, *Our American Sisters,* 329-47, investigates the links between sexual standards, the economic dependence of women, and marital choices. Candace Falk's *Love, Anarchy, and Emma Goldman* (New York: Holt Rhinehart & Winston, 1984) permits a closer view of the political and physical passions that shaped the intimate relationships in this activist woman's life.

Lillian Faderman, *Surpassing the Love of Men: Romantic Friendship and Love between Women from the Renaissance to the Present* (New York: Morrow, 1981), confirms the existence of a vital homosocial world during the Progressive Era. The great majority of female partnerships currently identified are from the literary and social reform scenes, often the most easily documented, given the educational levels and the letter-writing habits of those involved. These relationships provided emotional and practical support, enabling women to feel a sense of family while at the same time freeing them from many familial constraints. See, for example, Leila J. Rupp, "'Imagine My Surprise': Women's Relationships in Historical Perspective," *Frontiers* 5, no. 3 (1981): 61-70; Blanche Wiesen Cook, "Female Support Networks and Political Activism: Lillian Wald, Crystal Eastman, and Emma Goldman," in Nancy F. Cott and Elizabeth H. Pleck, eds., *A Heritage of Her Own: Toward a New Social History of American Women* (New York: Simon and Schuster, 1979), 412-44; and Judith Schwartz, "Yellow Clover: Katherine Lee Bates and Katherine Coman," *Frontiers* 4, no. 1 (1979): 59-67.

An aspect of sexuality most consistently addressed with respect to working-class women, other than prostitution which more appropriately belongs alongside considerations of work, is that of birth control. Linda Gordon, *Woman's Body, Woman's Right: A Social History of Birth Control in America* (New York: Grossman, 1976), looks at its varied proponents and opponents and traces judicial and social policy responses. In her review of western women's daily lives, "Women as Workers, Women as Civilizers: True Womanhood in the American West," in Armitage and Jameson, *Women's West,* 145-64, Jameson describes the sharing of illicit birth-control techniques among communities of women.

The growing readiness of the Progressive Era state to intervene in family relationships through legislation, agencies, and social work professionals is addressed in a number of contexts. For example, Susan Lehrer looks at the protective labor law debates in *Origins of Protective Labor Legislation for Women, 1905-1925* (Albany: State Univ. of New York Press, 1987). The question of family violence has been examined by both

Elizabeth Pleck in *The Making of American Social Policy against Family Violence from Colonial Times to the Present* (New York: Oxford Univ. Press, 1987), and by Linda Gordon in *Heroes of Their Own Lives: The Politics and History of Family Violence* (New York: Viking, 1988). A case study examining competing adoption philosophies is offered by Paula F. Pfeffer, "Homeless Children, Childless Homes," *Chicago History* 16, no. 1 (spring 1987): 51-65.

Shifting Boundaries: Family, Community, and Work

A general introduction to demographic change, family relationships, and domestic value systems, in the context of broader structural shifts and legislative responses, may be found in Steven Mintz and Susan Kellogg, *Domestic Revolutions: A Social History of American Family Life* (New York: Free Press, 1988). Women's working experience was shaped by educational opportunity, industrial growth, a rapidly expanding service economy and consumer culture, and entrenched gender, racial, ethnic, and class prejudices. Alice Kessler-Harris looks closely at the exigencies of economic survival for working-class women and their families in *Out to Work: A History of Wage-Earning Women in the United States* (New York: Oxford Univ. Press, 1982). Jacqueline Jones, in her research into the domestic and working lives of rural and urban African-American women, *Labor of Love, Labor of Sorrow: Black Women, Work, and the Family, from Slavery to the Present* (New York: Vintage, 1986), describes a level of geographic mobility and aspirations for a better life comparable to that of the many foreign immigrants flooding into cities during the same period. Family disruption was a typical feature of life for working women from many different backgrounds during these years.

Increasing educational opportunities and their social repercussions are the subject of Barbara Solomon's *In the Company of Educated Women: A History of Women and Higher Education in America* (New Haven, Conn.: Yale Univ. Press, 1985). She investigates the remarkable expansion in women's educational institutions but also recognizes disparities in admissions policies and availability of resources. Paula Giddings, *In Search of Sisterhood: Delta Sigma Theta and the Challenge of the Black Sorority Movement* (New York: Morrow, 1988), considers these educated women's strong commitment both to the liberal arts and to the social and economic welfare of all African-Americans in a racist and sexist society.

The development of a consumer culture and a growing service sector opened up new working opportunities. See, for example, Susan Porter

Benson, *Counter Cultures: Saleswomen, Managers, and Customers in American Department Stores, 1890-1940* (Urbana: Univ. of Illinois Press, 1986). Margery W. Davies explores the growth of clerical work in *Woman's Place Is at the Typewriter: Office Work and Office Workers, 1870-1930* (Philadelphia: Temple Univ. Press, 1983). Medicine and the sciences attracted a growing number of educated women. Barbara Melosh has looked at the interplay of gender and class and the undermining of women's professional aspirations in her history of nursing, *"The Physician's Hand": Work Culture and Conflict in American Nursing* (Philadelphia: Temple Univ. Press, 1982). Darlene Clark Hine's "'They Shall Mount up with Wings as Eagles': Historical Images of Black Nurses, 1890-1950," in Anne Hudson Jones, ed., *Images of Nurses: Perspectives from History, Art, and Literature* (Philadelphia: Univ. of Pennsylvania Press, 1988), 177-96, recounts examples of the widespread practical and symbolic denigration that confronted black nurses. Margaret W. Rossiter, *Women Scientists in America: Struggles and Strategies to 1940* (Baltimore: Johns Hopkins Univ. Press, 1982), profiles a number of women scientists and analyzes the barriers facing them within the male preserve of the sciences. The establishment of the social sciences within academe opened up faculty and research opportunities for various women. In *Beyond Separate Spheres: Intellectual Roots of Modern Feminism* (New Haven, Conn.: Yale Univ. Press, 1982), Rosalind Rosenberg considers the professional careers of these women and their scientific challenges to gender-role theories.

A number of immigration histories have investigated cultural variations in family relationships, domestic arrangements, and work experiences. Elizabeth Ewen's research into the lives of New York's Jewish and Italian women may be found in *Immigrant Women in the Land of Dollars: Life and Culture on the Lower East Side, 1890-1925* (New York: Monthly Review, 1985). Mario T. Garcia's study of the domestic labor and wage-earning work of immigrant Mexican women is entitled "The Chicana in American History: The Mexican Women of El Paso, 1880-1920: A Case Study," *Pacific Historical Review* 49 (May 1980): 315-37. In his sweeping account of Japanese and Chinese immigration, *Asian America: Chinese and Japanese in the United States since 1850* (Seattle: Univ. of Washington Press, 1988), Roger Daniels describes the series of exclusionary laws and restrictive policies that were intended to curtail Asian immigration and markedly affected family structure and working opportunities. Two studies by Judy Yung, "'A Bowful of Tears': Chinese Women Immigrants on Angel Island," *Frontiers* 2, no. 2 (1977): 52-55, and *Chinese Women of America: A Pictorial History* (Seattle, Univ. of Washington Press for the Chinese

Cultural Foundation of San Francisco, 1986), focus on Chinese women's experiences. The Japanese perspective has been addressed by Yuji Ichioka, "Amerika Nadeshiko: Japanese Immigrant Women in the United States, 1900-1924," *Pacific Historical Review* 49, no. 2 (1980): 339-57. Evelyn Nakano Glenn has looked at Japanese women domestic servants in "The Dialectics of Wage Work: Japanese-American Women and Domestic Service, 1905-1940," *Feminist Studies* 6 (1980): 432-71; and *Issei, Nisei, War Bride: Three Generations of Japanese American Women in Domestic Service* (Philadelphia: Temple Univ. Pres, 1986).

There is some interesting scholarship that looks at women whose primary status was neither mother nor wife, a social marginality that held a precarious balance between personal autonomy and economic vulnerability. Arlene Scadron's edited collection of essays, *On Their Own: Widows and Widowhood in the American Southwest, 1848-1939* (Urbana: Univ. of Illinois Press, 1988), takes a regional and cross-cultural approach in the investigation of widows' emotional and economic survival strategies. The essays range from studies of Native American societies in which there appears to have been a comparative lack of social and economic penalties, as in Sarah M. Nelson, "Widowhood and Autonomy in the Native-American Southwest," 22-41, to more uncertain situations of white urban women, as in Joyce D. Goodfriend, "The Struggle for Survival: Widows in Denver, 1880-1912," 166-94. An interesting perspective on single working women's pursuit of meaningful domestic experiences in an impersonal, sometimes hostile city may be found in Joanne J. Meyerowitz, *Women Adrift: Independent Wage Earners in Chicago, 1880-1930* (Chicago: Univ. of Chicago Press, 1988). Her account of the growth of cooperative housing, apartments shared by single women, indicates a search for domestic support systems outside the confinement of the family.

Prostitutes may have been repudiated by respectable society, but they were nonetheless an integral part of the Progressive Era scene. Prostitution's economic and ideological dimenisions have been explored by Ruth Rosen in *The Lost Sisterhood: Prostitution in America, 1900-1918* (Baltimore: Johns Hopkins Univ. Press, 1982). Mary Murphy, "The Private Lives of Public Women: Prostitution in Butte, Montana, 1878-1917," in Armitage and Jameson, *Women's West,* 193-205, examines prostitutes' status and social interactions in a western mining town. The social and economic history of Chinese prostitution and its role in perpetuating patriarchal aspects of the Chinese family and servicing an expatriate male workforce are central themes in Lucie Cheng Hirata, "Free Indentured,

Enslaved: Chinese Prostitutes in Nineteenth Century America," *Signs: Journal of Women in Culture and Society* 5, no. 1 (Autumn 1979): 3-29.

Popular Culture and the Arts

Expositions showcased many aspects of contemporary culture and provide the historian with insights into popular themes. Jeanne Madeline Weimann's *The Fair Women* (Chicago: Academy Chicago, 1981) is an exhaustive account of the creation of the Woman's Building at the 1893 World's Columbian Exposition. The Women's Building showcased the activities and achievements of many women, although it tended to reflect the cultural preferences of an elite group.

Adherents of the arts and crafts movement were among the numerous women artists exhibiting in the Woman's Building. The arts and crafts movement not only offered a fresh design sensibility but also incorporated a moral aesthetic and political values into daily life. Wendy Kaplan's edited collection of essays, *"The Art That Is Life": The Arts and Crafts Movement in America, 1875-1920* (Boston: Little, Brown, 1987), explores various aspects of the movement. Also of interest are Anthea Callen, *Women Artists of the Arts and Crafts Movement, 1870-1914* (New York: Pantheon, 1979); and Eileen Boris, *Art and Labor: Ruskin, Morris and the Craftsman Ideal in America* (Philadelphia: Temple Univ. Press, 1986).

The development of modernism, its literary expressions, and the unresolved debate around the "woman question" have been analyzed by Sandra M. Gilbert and Susan Gubar in *No Man's Land: The Place of the Woman Writer in the Twentieth Century* Vol. 1: *The War of the Words* (New Haven, Conn.: Yale Univ. Press, 1988). In "Culture and Radical Politics: Yiddish Women Writers, 1890-1940," *American Jewish History* 70 (Sept. 1980): 68-90, Norma Fain Pratt looks at the lives and works of Jewish immigrant women writers and considers how their experience of gender and class distinctions in the Jewish community shaped their work. Paula Gunn Allen's edited collection of Native American women's storytelling and writing, *Spider Woman's Granddaughters,* conveys the importance of this art form in the expression and reinforcement of tribal philosophy and social principles. Helen Carby's *Reconstructing Womanhood* and Mary Helen Washington's *Invented Lives: Narratives of Black Women, 1860-1960* (Garden City, N.Y.: Doubleday, 1987) offer critical studies of the influences of racism and sexism on African-American women writers.

Kathy Peiss has looked at different modes of entertainment enjoyed by working women and reformers' efforts to divert women into more "respectable" recreation in *Cheap Amusements: Working Women and Leisure in Turn-of-the-Century New York* (Philadelphia: Temple Univ. Press, 1986). Women's recreational use of city parks has been investigated by Galen Cranz, "Women in Urban Parks," in Catherine R. Stimpson et al., eds., *Women and the American City* (Chicago: Univ. of Chicago Press, 1981): 76-92. In another essay in that collection, Elizabeth Ewen assesses the appeal of movies in "City Lights: Immigrant Women and the Rise of the Movies," 42-62. Movies were not only a source of entertainment, they played an important role in acculturation, impressing their audience with easily assimilated lessons in American social mores. Linda Dahl has looked at some early female jazz and blues performers in *Stormy Weather: The Music and Lives of a Century of Jazzwomen* (New York: Pantheon, 1984).

Truth and Consequences

An inclusive history of the role of women in the Progressive Era has yet to be attempted, and an extraordinary range of empirical work still needs to be done. Furthermore, there is no agreement concerning the analytical tools to be used in research and there is a continuing debate as to whether a single theoretical model is possible or even desirable. However, this apparent fragmentation is perhaps a prelude to an expanding universe of thought: at very least, it encourages a sensitivity to alternative experiences; at its best, it suggests that the relationship between theory and practice is both intimate and fluid, and it encompasses the exploration of relationships between disparate perspectives. The cultivation of a diligent humility in the face of this task, and a recognition that perhaps the most honest history is often compiled of "partial truths"—as Jacqueline Dowd Hall speculated in her address to the First Southern Conference on Women's History, *Signs* 14, no. 4 (Summer 1989): 902-11—are possibly the most important, and the most challenging, prerequisites.

Contributors

Eileen Boris is associate professor of history at Howard University. She is the author of *Art and Labor: Ruskin, Morris, and the Craftsman Ideal in America* and coeditor of *Homework: Historical and Contemporary Perspectives on Paid Labor at Home.* Boris is working on a book called *In Defense of Motherhood: The Politics of Industrial Homework in the United States, 1880s-1980s.*

Ardis Cameron, assistant professor of New England Studies at the University of Southern Maine, is completing a work called *Radicals of the Worst Sort: The Laboring Women of Lawrence, Massachusetts, 1860-1912.* Her current work-in-progress is entitled "I Never Dreamed of Such a Fate: Rural Women Down East, 1880-1920."

Ellen Carol DuBois, professor of history at UCLA, wrote *Feminism and Suffrage: The Emergence of an Independent Women's Movement in America 1849–1869* and coauthored *Unequal Sisters: A Multicultural Reader in U.S. Women's History.* Her next book will be *Generation of Power: Harriot Stanton Blatch and the Winning of Woman Suffrage.*

Nancy S. Dye is dean of the faculty and professor of history at Vassar College. She is the author of *As Equals and as Sistes: Feminism, the Labor Movement and the Women's Trade Union League of New York* and of numerous articles and reviews on U.S. women's history.

Noralee Frankel is assistant director on women and minorities with the American Historical Association. She is completing a work called *The Emancipation of African-American Women in Mississippi during the Civil War and Reconstruction.*

Sharon Harley is associate professor of African-American Studies at the University of Maryland, College Park. She is coeditor of *The Afro-American Woman: Struggles and Images* and *Women in Africa and the African Diaspora.*

Nancy A. Hewitt is associate professor of history at the University of South Florida. She is the author of *Women's Activism and Social Change: Rochester, New York, 1822-1872* and *Women, Families and Communities: Readings in American History.* Currently, Hewitt is working on *Material and Moral Terrains: Anglo, Black, and Latin Women in the Formation of a New South Community, 1885-1945.*

Alice Kessler-Harris is professor of history and director of Women's Studies at Rutgers University. She is the author of *Out to Work: A History of Wage-Earning Women in the United States* and *A Woman's Wage: Historical Meanings and Social Consequences.*

Molly Ladd-Taylor is assistant professor of history at Carleton College. She edited *Raising a Baby the Government Way: Mothers' Letters to the Children's Bureau, 1915-1932.* She is currently completing a book called *Mother-Work: Women, Child Welfare and the State, 1890-1930.*

Susan Tank Lesser is an independent scholar whose areas of interest include women's history and political culture. She is currently working on a manuscript for the Twayne series, *American Women in the Twentieth Century,* dealing with the years 1900-1920.

Jacqueline A. Rouse is Landmarks Associate Professor of African-American History at the American University. She is the author of *Lugenia Burns Hope, Black Southern Reformer* and coeditor of *Women in the Civil Rights Movement, 1941-1965: Trailblazers and Torchbearers.*

Barbara Sicherman is William R. Kenan, Jr., Professor of American Institutions and Values at Trinity College. She is the coeditor of *Notable American Women: The Modern Period* and the author of *Alice Hamilton: A Life in Letters.* Her current project is titled *Gender and the Culture of Reading in Late-Victorian America.*

Rosalyn Terborg-Penn is professor of history and coordinator of graduate programs in history at Morgan State University. She is coeditor of *The Afro-American Woman: Struggles and Images* and *Women in Africa and the African Diaspora.* She is associate editor of *Black Women in America: An Historical Encyclopedia.*

Index